MIAMI:

"On and on they came, the clean, the well-bred, the extraordinarily prosperous, and, for the most astonishing part, the entirely proper. Yes, in San Francisco in '64, they had been able to be insane for a little while, but now they were subdued, now they were modest, now they were looking for a leader to bring America back to them, their lost America. . . . The Wasp had come to take power."

CHICAGO:

"Children, and youths, and middle-aged men were being pounded and gassed and beaten, hunted and driven by teams of policemen who had exploded out of their restraints like the bursting of a boil. . . . It was as if war had finally begun, as if the gods of history had come together before the television cameras of the world and the eyes of the campaign workers and the delegates' wives and half the principals at the convention . . . as if the Democratic Party had broken in two before the eyes of the nation."

Other Norman Mailer Titles
in SIGNET Editions

☐ **THE ARMIES OF THE NIGHT** (#W5722—$1.50)

☐ **EXISTENTIAL ERRANDS** (#E5422—$1.75)

☐ **THE NAKED AND THE DEAD** (#E6052—$1.75)

☐ **OF A FIRE ON THE MOON** (#E4765—$1.75)

☐ **THE PRISONER OF SEX** (#Y4822—$1.25)

Miami and the Siege of Chicago

An Informal History of the Republican and Democratic Conventions of 1968

by Norman Mailer

A SIGNET BOOK from
NEW AMERICAN LIBRARY
TIMES MIRROR

SIGNET TRADEMARK REG. U.S. PAT. OFF. AND FOREIGN COUNTRIES
REGISTERED TRADEMARK—MARCA REGISTRADA
HECHO EN CHICAGO, U.S.A.

SIGNET, SIGNET CLASSICS, MENTOR, PLUME AND MERIDIAN BOOKS
are published by The New American Library, Inc.,
1301 Avenue of the Americas, New York, New York 10019

FIRST SIGNET PRINTING, OCTOBER, 1968

8 9 10 11 12 13 14 15 16

PRINTED IN THE UNITED STATES OF AMERICA

To my Father

CONTENTS

I
Nixon in
Miami

Miami Beach, August 3–9

They snipped the ribbon in 1915, they popped the cork, Miami Beach was born. A modest burg they called a city, nine-tenths jungle. An island. It ran along a coastal barrier the other side of Biscayne Bay from young Miami—in 1868 when Henry Lum, a California 'forty-niner, first glimpsed the island from a schooner, you may be certain it was jungle, cocoanut palms on the sand, mangrove swamp and palmetto thicket ten feet off the beach. But by 1915, they were working the vein. John S. Collins, a New Jersey nurseryman (after whom Collins Avenue is kindly named) brought in bean fields and avocado groves; a gent named Fisher, Carl G., a Hoosier—he invented Prestolite, a millionaire—bought up acres from Collins, brought in a work-load of machinery, men, even two elephants, and jungle was cleared, swamps were filled, small residential islands were made out of baybottom mud, dredged, then relocated, somewhat larger natural islands adjacent to the barrier island found themselves improved, streets were paved, sidewalks put in with other amenities—by 1968, one hundred years after Lum first glommed the beach, large areas of the original coastal strip were covered over altogether with macadam, white condominium, white luxury hotel and white stucco flea-bag. Over hundreds, then thousands of acres, white sidewalks, streets and white buildings covered the earth where the jungle had been. Is it so dissimilar from covering your poor pubic hair with adhesive tape for fifty years? The vegetal memories of that excised jungle haunted Miami Beach in a steam-pot of miasmas. Ghosts of expunged flora, the never-born groaning in vegetative chancery beneath the asphalt came up with a tropical curse, an equatorial leaden wet sweat of air which rose from the earth itself, rose right up through the baked asphalt and into the heated air which entered the lungs like a hand slipping into a rubber glove.

The temperature was not that insane. It hung around 87 day after day, at night it went down to 82, back to the same 87 in the A.M.—the claims of the News Bureau for Miami Beach promised that in 1967 temperature exceeded 90° only four times. (Which the Island of Manhattan could never begin to say.) But of course Miami Beach did not have to go that high, for its humidity was up to 87 as well —it was, on any and every day of the Republican Convention of 1968, one of the hottest cities in the world. The reporter was no expert on tropical heats—he had had, he would admit, the island of Luzon for a summer in World War II; and basic training in the pine woods of Fort Bragg, North Carolina, in August; he had put in a week at Las Vegas during July—temperatures to 110; he had crossed the Mojave Desert once by day; he was familiar with the New York subway in the rush hour on the hottest day of the year. These were awesome immersions—one did not have to hit the Congo to know what it was like in a hothouse in hell—but that 87° in Miami Beach day after day held up in competition against other sulphuric encounters. Traveling for five miles up the broken-down, forever in-a-state-of-alteration and repair of Collins Avenue, crawling through 5 P.M. Miami Beach traffic in the pure miserable fortune of catching an old taxi without air conditioning, dressed in shirt and tie and jacket—formal and implicitly demanded uniform of political journalists—the sensation of breathing, then living, was not unlike being obliged to make love to a 300-pound woman who has decided to get on top. Got it? You could not dominate a thing. That uprooted jungle had to be screaming beneath.

Of course it could have been the air conditioning: natural climate transmogrified by technological climate. They say that in Miami Beach the air conditioning is pushed to that icy point where women may wear fur coats over their diamonds in the tropics. For ten miles, from the Diplomat to the Di Lido, above Hallandale Beach Boulevard down to Lincoln Mall, all the white refrigerators stood, piles of white refrigerators six and eight and twelve stories

high, twenty stories high, shaped like sugar cubes and
ice-cube trays on edge, like mosques and palaces, shaped
like matched white luggage and portable radios, stereos,
plastic compacts and plastic rings, Moorish castles shaped
like waffle irons, shaped like the baffle plates on white
plastic electric heaters, and cylinders like Waring blend-
ers, buildings looking like giant op art and pop art
paintings, and sweet wedding cakes, cottons of kitsch
and piles of dirty cotton stucco, yes, for ten miles the
hotels for the delegates stood on the beach side of Collins
Avenue: the Eden Roc and the Fontainebleau (Press
Headquarters), the Di Lido and the De Lano, the Ivanhoe,
Deauville, Sherry Frontenac and the Monte Carlo, the
Cadillac, Caribbean and the Balmoral, the Lucerne, Hilton
Plaza, Doral Beach, the Sorrento, Marco Polo, Casablanca,
and Atlantis, the Hilyard Manor, Sans Souci, Algiers,
Carillon, Seville, the Gaylord, the Shore Club, the Nautilus,
Montmartre, and the Promenade, the Bal Harbour on North
Bay Causeway, and the Twelve Caesars, the Regency and
the Americana, the Diplomat, Versailles, Coronado, Sover-
eign, the Waldman (dig!), the Beau Rivage, the Crown
Hotel, even Holiday Inn, all oases for technological man.
Deep air conditioning down to 68°, ice-palaces to chill the
fevered brain—when the air conditioning worked. And
their furnishings were monumentally materialistic. Not all
of them: the cheaper downtown hotels like the Di Lido and
the Nautilus were bare and mean with vinyl coverings on
the sofas and the glare of plastic off the rugs and tables and
tiles, inexpensive hotel colors of pale brown and buff and
dingy cream, sodden gray, but the diadems like the Fontainebleau and the Eden Roc, the Doral Beach, the Hilton
Plaza (Headquarters for Nixon), the Deauville (Hq for
Reagan) or the Americana—Rockefeller and the New York
State delegation's own ground—were lavish with interlock-
ings, curves, vaults and runs of furnishings as intertwined
as serpents in the roots of a mangrove tree. All the rivers
of the very worst taste twisted down to the delta of each
lobby in each grand Miami Beach hotel—rare was the
central room which did not look like the lobby of a movie
palace, imitation of late-Renaissance imitations of Greek
and Roman statues, imitations of baroque and rococo and
brothel Victorian and Art Nouveau and Bauhaus with gold
grapes and cornucopias welded to the modern bronze

tubing of the chair, golden moldings which ran like ivy from room to room, chandeliers complex as the armature of dynamos, and curvilinear steps in the shape of amoebas and palettes, cocktail lounge bars in deep rose or maroon with spun-sugar white tubes of plaster decor to twist around the ceiling. There was every color of iridescence, rainbows of vulgarity, aureoles of gorgeous taste, opium den of a middle-class dollar, materialistic as meat, sweat, and the cigar. It is said that people born under Taurus and Capricorn are the most materialistic of us all. Take a sample of the residents in the census of Miami B.—does Taurus predominate more than one-twelfth of its share? It must, or astrology is done, for the Republicans, Grand Old Party with a philosophy rather than a program, had chosen what must certainly be the materialistic capital of the world for their convention. Las Vegas might offer competition, but Las Vegas was materialism in the service of electricity— fortunes could be lost in the spark of the dice. Miami was materialism baking in the sun, then stepping back to air-conditioned caverns where ice could nestle in the fur. It was the first of a hundred curiosities—that in a year when the Republic hovered on the edge of revolution, nihilism, and lines of police on file to the horizon, visions of future Vietnams in our own cities upon us, the party of conservatism and principle, of corporate wealth and personal frugality, the party of cleanliness, hygiene, and balanced budget, should have set itself down on a sultan's strip.

That was the first of a hundred curiosities, but there were mysteries as well. The reporter had moved through the convention quietly, as anonymously as possible, wan, depressed, troubled. Something profoundly unclassifiable was going on among the Republicans and he did not know if it was conceivably good or a concealment of something bad—which was the first time a major social phenomenon like a convention had confused him so. He had covered others. The Democratic Convention in 1960 in Los Angeles which nominated John F. Kennedy, and the Republican in San Francisco in 1964 which installed Barry Goldwater, had encouraged some of his very best writing. He had felt a gift for comprehending those conventions. But the Republican assembly in Miami Beach in 1968 was a different affair—one could not tell if nothing much was going on, or to the contrary, nothing much was going on near the surface but everything was shifting down below. So dialogue with other journalists merely depressed him—the complaints were unanimous that this was the dullest convention anyone could remember. Complaints took his mind away from the slow brooding infusion he desired in the enigmas of conservatism and/or Republicanism, and any hope of perspective on the problem beyond. The country was in a throe, a species of eschatological heave. The novelist John Updike was not necessarily one of his favorite authors, but after the assassination of Robert F. Kennedy, it was Updike who had made the remark that God might have withdrawn His blessing from America. It was a thought which could not be forgotten for it gave insight to the perspectives of the Devil and his political pincers: Left-wing demons, white and Black, working to inflame the conservative heart of America, while Right-wing devils exacerbated Blacks and drove the mind of the New Left and liberal middle class into prides of hopeless position. And the country roaring like a bull in its wounds, coughing like a sick lung in the smog, turning over in sleep at the sound of motorcycles, shivering at its need for new phalanxes of order. Where were the new phalanxes one could trust? The reporter had seen the faces of too many police to balm his dreams with the sleep they promised. Even the drinks tasted bad in Miami in the fever and the chill.

2

His first afternoon in Miami Beach was spent by the reporter in Convention Hall. He stepped up on the speaker's podium to see how it might feel, nosed into the jerrybuilt back room back of the podium where speakers would wait, and Press be excluded, once the convention was begun. A room unmatched for dreariness. Dull green daybeds and sofas, a nondescript powder-blue rug, open studding and therefore open wall-board color, brown and tan leatherette chairs, a dreary cloth throw on a table. Every quiet color clashed with every other quiet color—it was the sort of room which could have served for the bridge players in an old folks' summer camp in some flat and inland state. In this room, while preparing to orate, would wait some of the more ambitious men in America, and some of the more famous; looking at their manuscripts might be John Wayne, Barry Goldwater, John Lindsay, Thomas E. Dewey, Ronald Reagan, Governor Rockefeller, George Romney, Richard Nixon himself—not to mention Billy Graham—they would pass through the splendors of this profoundly American anteroom. Examination completed, the reporter abruptly decided he would actually go out to the airport to greet the arrival of a baby elephant which was arriving on a Delta cargo plane as a gift to Richard Nixon from the people of Anaheim, California. That seemed an appropriate way to open coverage of the convention.

3

Unless one knows him well, or has done a sizable work of preparation, it is next to useless to interview a politician. He has a mind which is accustomed to political questions. By the time he decides to run for President, he may have answered a million. Or at least this is true if he has been in politics for twenty years and has replied to an average of one hundred-fifty such queries a day, no uncharacteristic amount. To surprise a skillful politician with a question is then approximately equal in difficulty to hitting a professional boxer with a barroom hook. One cannot therefore tell a great deal from interviews with a candidate. His teeth are bound to be white, his manner mild and pleasant, his presence attractive, and his ability to slide off the question and return with an answer is as implicit in the work of his jaws as the ability to bite a piece of meat. Interviewing a candidate is about as intimate as catching him on television. Therefore it is sometimes easier to pick up the truth of his campaign by studying the outriggers of his activity. Therefore the reporter went to cover the elephant.

It was, as expected, a modest story in a quiet corner of International Airport in Miami. Not more than ten reporters and a dozen photographers showed up. And a band, and a quorum of Nixonettes wearing blue dresses and white straw hats with a legend "NIXON'S THE ONE." A publicity puff was handed around which informed the Press that the beast was named Ana (for Anaheim, California) and was 52″ high, 2½ years old, weighed 1,266 lbs. and had been given to Nixon by the happy citizens of the town—Ana!

Ana came in on a Lockheed 100, a hippo of a four-motor plane with four-bladed propellers. The cargo door was in the rear, and as the musicians, Don Goldie and his Dixieland Band, white musicians from the Hilton-Miami—accordion, tuba, trombone, snares, clarinet, banjo, and trumpet—began to play, and the six Nixonettes began to strut (they looked to be high school juniors) and the plane to unload, so the black cloud on the horizon moved over, and began its drop, black tropical rain so intense even photographers had to take shelter, and a dozen, then another dozen of musicians, Nixonettes, cameramen, photographers, and animal handlers piled into a small 6 x 8 Hertz trailer later to be used for the elephant. In the steam of the interior, the day took on surreal and elegant proportions —two dozen amateurs and professionals on call for one baby elephant (said to be arriving in her tutu) were equal across the board to the logic of one political convention; by the time the rain stopped five minutes later and the elephant crate was unloaded, hoisted on a fork lift off the carrier, brought near the trailer and opened, everyone gave a cheer to Ana who came out nervously from her crate, but with a definite sense of style. She took a quick look at the still photographers surrounding her, and the larger movie cameras to which certain humans were obviously connected, stepped on the still-wet steaming runway, threw a droll red-eye at her handler, dropped a small turd to X the spot of her liberation from the crate (and as a marker in case she wanted later to retrace her steps) then did a good Republican handstand, trunk curved as graciously as a pinkie off a teacup. To which the media corps responded with approval, Nixonettes squealing, Don Goldie Band playing Dixieland, still cameras clicking, movie cameras ticking within the gears of their clockwork, Dade County police grinning as they stood to one side (four men—all armed). Then Ana from Anaheim walked on her hind legs. To much approval. She curtsied, bowed, turned in a circle, obviously pleased with herself, then stretched out her trunk in the general area of everybody's midsection. "Hey, chum, watch your peanuts," a man called out.

It went on for a period, the Nixonettes having their pictures taken, one girl who was not a high school junior but most likely a professional model taking care to see she was in the picture often, and all the girls kept trying to put a straw Nixon hat on Ana, but the hat kept falling off. After ten minutes, the handlers tried to coax Ana into the Hertz trailer, but she was not about to, not yet, so they walked her around a hangar, brought her back, then slipped her 1200-lb. bulk into the box with a bit of elephant handler's legerdemain. The arrival was over.

It had been pleasant; in truth, more pleasant than the reporter had expected. It had not been tense, not even with the four armed cops. The air had been better than one might have thought. So it was a warning to one's perspective and proportion: the Nixon forces and the Nixon people were going to be in command of small subtleties he had not anticipated. It was his first clue to the notion that there was a new Nixon. He could have read a dozen articles which said the same thing and paid no mind, for the men who wrote them were experts and so were wrong in their predictions as often as they were right. Experts he would disregard—so far as he was able—but Ana had been happy doing her handstand: that was an unexpected fact he would have to absorb into the first freshets of his brooding. Of course the reporter had once decided (using similar methods) that Barry Goldwater could win the 1964 election. This, at least, was the method at its extreme. Still, a happy elephant spoke of luck for Nixon, or at the least, agreeable management down the line.

4

Rockefeller came in at Opa Locka Airport next day, and again it rained. The skies over Miami were at their best when rain was near, for cumulus clouds piled high on themselves, making towers, pyramids, turrets, and heavenly Miami Beach hotels two miles up in the air while dark horizontal tides of oncoming tropical storm washed through the sky, crossed the sun, gave gildings of gold and black to the towers of cumulus.

The schedule for arrival was Rockefeller on Saturday, Reagan later that evening, and Nixon on Monday. They were all of course coming in on charter flights, and the Rockefeller plane, an American Airlines 727 jet which had carried the candidate 65,000 miles into forty-five states during the campaign, was landing, for security reasons, at the Coast Guard Airport, Opa Locka, out to the west of Miami, almost in red-neck country, the town of Opa Locka still another sad sweet real estate failure of Southern Florida for it had been built to recapitulate a piece of North Africa. Residential streets with names like Ali Baba Avenue, Sesame Street, Sharazad Boulevard, Arabia Avenue, Sultan Avenue, Caliph Street, and Salim Street wound around the center of Opa Locka in complicated ovals and ellipses all planned thirty-plus or forty years ago by a real estate genius, now a town all but deserted in the afternoon sun with the storm coming on, just occasional palmettoes and the crumbling white stucco center where a small old hotel and bar stood like the molderings of a Foreign Legion fort, holding the crossroads before the Coast Guard pushed onto the airport.

Perhaps a hundred or a hundred-fifty newsmen, TV cameras, and still photographers were out at the main hangar with the Press bus, way out in the quiet empty reaches of the all but deserted airdrome, and overhead, light planes and helicopters patrolled the near sky, and four or five police cars were parked in uneasy relation to the crowd. The reporter had to show no identification to enter the gate, and needed none now; a potential assassin, tipped to Rockefeller's entrance at Opa Locka, could have packed a piece to within a yard of him—of course, afterward, he could never have escaped. If he managed to shoot past the twenty-odd cops in the direct vicinity, the helicopters would have followed his car all the way to Miami, maybe nailed him on Arthur Godfrey Causeway from the sky. Like pieces of flesh fragmented from the explosion of a grenade, echoes of the horror of Kennedy's assassination were thus everywhere: helicopters riding overhead like roller coasters, state troopers with magnums on their hip and crash helmets, squad cars, motorcycles, yet no real security, just powers of retaliation. It forced one to cherish major politicians—no matter how colorless, they all had hints of charisma now that they were obviously more vulnerable to sudden death than bullfighters, and so they were surrounded with a suggestion of the awe peasants reserve for the visit of the bishop—some rushed to touch them, others looked ready to drop to their knees. Thus, at least, for Rockefeller and the Press. He was surrounded almost immediately after he came down the landing ramp, and never left alone, surrounded by Press and cameramen five deep, the photographers by long practice holding their cameras and even their movie cameras up over their heads, aiming down by skillful guess, so that from a distance one could always tell exactly where the candidate was situated, for a semicircle of cameras crooned in from above like bulbs of seaweed breaking surface at high tide, or were they more like praying mantises on the heads of tall grass?—a bazaar of metaphor was obviously offered.

Rocky had come off the plane with his entourage and his wife. She was surprisingly attractive, with a marvelous high color which made her vastly better-looking than her photographs, and Rocky looked like much less than his photographs, gray beyond gray in the flesh, gray as New York City pavements, gray as an old con—the sun could not have touched him in a month or else all the fighting blood of the heart was somewhere deep inside the brain, working through the anxiety-ridden calculations with which he must have come to Miami, for Nixon with his six-hundred-plus votes now almost secure was a handful or a score or at best not fifty votes from the first ballot nomination. Anxiety had to be stirred by every omen: the weather, the first unfamiliar face to greet you off the plane, the sudden flight of a bird, the warmth of the policeman's salutation, or the enthusiasm of the Press corps.

But if it were for that, he was elected already. Rockefeller was obviously the near-unanimous choice of the Press, and above all, the television—a mating of high chemical potentials existed between the media and the man as if they had been each conceived for the other. Except for his complexion, Rocky had an all but perfect face for President, virile, friendly, rough-hewn, of the common man, yet uncommon—Spencer Tracy's younger brother gone into politics. He had only one flaw—an odd and unpleasant mouth, a catfish mouth, wide, unnaturally wide with very thin lips. In the center of the mouth there seemed almost another mouth which did the speaking, somewhat thicker lips which pursed, opened, deliberated—all the while the slit-thin corners of the mouth seemed off on their own, not really moving with the center. So he gave the impression of a man to whom expert instruction had disclosed what he might be expected to say—therefore only the middle of the mouth would be on call.

The rain which had begun to come down and then providentially stopped, was coming on again. So he was able to slip out of the tight ring of interviewers locked about him after answering fifty more of the million political questions he would reply to in his life, and now the press bus and the private cars were off in a race across Miami to the 72nd Street public beach in Miami Beach maybe ten miles away where a big rally was scheduled. The helicopters rode lead and flank cowhand overhead, the cavalcade sped from Opa Locka; not thirty minutes later, band playing, cymbals smashing, Rocky walked a half-block through a crowd on 72nd Street and Collins Avenue, accepting the mob, walking through them to partial deliriums of excitement, a crazy mob for politicking, dressed in bathing suits, bikinis, bathrobes, surfers' trunks, paper dresses, terry cloth shirts, they jammed the pavement in bare feet, sandals, clod-hoppers, bathers screaming, calling out, falling in line around the free Pepsi-Cola wagon, good-natured but never super-excited—the rally was on the edge of the beach after all, and a leaden milky-green sea was pounding an erratic, nervous foam of surf onto the water's-edge of the beach not fifty yards away.

As Rocky moved forward in his brown-gray business suit, murmurs went up everywhere—"There goes the next President of the United States." But the crowd was somehow not huge enough to amplify this sentiment—they looked more like tourists than Republicans—all those votes he would get some day if ever he would capture the nomination. And as he moved forward through the crowd, shaking hands, saying "Hiya, hiya," big grin on his face at the shouts of, "We want Rocky," so also at that instant a tall skinny Negro maybe thirty years old leaped in front to shake hands and with the other hand looking for a souvenir, he flipped Rocky's purple handkerchief out of his breast pocket. But Rockefeller showed true Republican blood. A look of consternation for one stricken gap of an instant— *was this an attempt?*—until seeing the handkerchief in the man's hand, the situation was recovered: Rocky strode forward, pulled the handkerchief back, gave an admonishing look, as if to say, "Come on, fellow!" and immediately had some cardboard sunglasses pilfered from the same breast pocket by a heated happy hysterical lady tourist with whom he could not wrestle. Kerchief recovered, sunglasses offered up in tribute, he made the speaker's stand—the flat bed of a truck—and the meeting began. *The New York Times* was to report 3,000 people there, perhaps it was half; they cheered everything he said, those who could hear him. The acoustics varied from punko to atrocious, and the reporter circling the crowd heard one plain buxom girl with long brown hair—hippie hints of trinket and dungarees, girl formed out of the very mold of Rockefeller supporters— turn nonetheless sadly to her friend and say, "I can't hear a thing—bye bye." Next step, a sixty-year-old blonde in a bikini with half of a good figure left (breast and buttocks) the flesh around her navel unhappily equal to the flesh around her neck, wearing orange plastic bracelets, gold charm necklace, rings, rhinestone sunglasses, wedgies, painted toes, red hot momma kisser lips, a transistor radio giving rock, and she—whatever she was hearing—out to yell, "Rocky, we want Rocky," beating out the rhythm on one of her two consorts, the one younger than herself; the older, a husband? had a cigar, a paunch, and that benign cool which speaks of holding property in Flatbush in Brooklyn, and putting up with a live-wire wife.

But indeed it must have been reminiscent to Rocky of campaigning on beaches in Brooklyn and Queens, not Coney Island so much as Brighton or Manhattan Beach or Jacob Riis Park: the crowd had the same propinquity, same

raucous cheery wise hard middle-class New York smarts—
take the measure of everything and still give your cheer
because you are there, Murray. Even the smells were the
same—orgiastic onions in red hot dog and knish grease,
dirty yellow sand—Rocky had to recognize it all, for when
he introduced Claude Kirk, "the young alive Governor of
Florida" (sole vote for him in the Florida delegation) a
smattering of applause came up, a spattering of comment,
and one or two spit-spraying lip blats—it was obvious the
crowd didn't know Kirk from a Mafia dance-contest winner. So Rocky shifted gears. "It's a thrill for us from New
York to be here, in Florida," he said, "and half of you must
be here from New York." The laugh told him he was right.
A delicate gloom began to come in equal to the first ten-
drils of mist over a full moon; God would know what his
advisers had been telling him about the possible power of
this open street rally on the 72nd Street beach—with luck
and a mass turnout massive enough to break all records in
category, he could be on his way—a people's candidate
must ride a tidal wave. This was not even a bona fide
breaker. Half of his audience was from New York. Well,
he was no weak campaigner. He kept it going, hitting the
hard spots, "The Republican Party must become again a
national party, the voice of the poor and the oppressed."
Great cheers for the size of the crowd. "The Republican
Party cannot afford parochialism any longer." Smaller
cheer, slight confusion in his audience. "Parochialism" had
vague connotations of Roman Catholic schools. Rocky had
a good voice, man-to-man voice, Tracy, Bogart, hints of
Gable. When the very rich desert their patrician holdings
on the larynx (invariably because they have gone into politics) and would come over as regular grips, mill-hands and
populists, they lean dependably into the imitation of movie
stars they have loved. One could psych a big bet that Spencer Tracy was Rocky's own Number One and would be on
the ticket as Vice President if the election were held in
heaven. It was an honest voice, sincere, masculine, vibrant,
reedy, slightly hoarse, full of honest range-rider muscle,
with injections from the honest throatiness of New York. It
was a near-perfect voice for a campaigner; it was just a
question of whether it was entirely his own or had gravi-
tated to its function, much as the center of his mouth had
concentrated itself away from the corners of his lips.

"And while we're on it," said Rocky, powers of transition not notably his true preserve, "Senator McCarthy deserves a vote of commendation for getting the eighteen-year-olds back into politics again," (was this the Rockefeller who had once tried to shove fallout shelters into every suburban back yard?) "and when I'm President, I want to pass a bill letting the eighteen-year-olds vote." Big cheers for this. The kids were out—everybody was enjoying Rocky —and those with him on the flatbed truck. Kirk, Rocky's brother, and several former Republican National Committee Chairmen, came in on the noise machine. In the background, Miami Mummers wearing pink and orange and yellow and white and sky-blue satin outfits with net wings and white feathers, Miami Beach angels playing triangles and glockenspiels piped up tinklings and cracklings of sweet sound. Oompah went the oompah drum. "I offer," said Rocky, "a choice. It is . . . victory in November . . . victory for four years." He held up both hands in V for Victory signs.

"Eight years," shouted someone from the crowd.

"I won't quibble," said Rocky with a grin. But then, defeat licking at the center of this projected huge turnout which was finally not half huge enough, he added drily, "The gentleman who just spoke must be from New York."

The rally ended, and a black sky mopped out the sun for ten minutes, hid the cumulus. Rain came in tropical force, water trying to work through that asphalt, reach the jungle beneath. Everyone scattered, those who were dressed not quite in time. The rain hit with a squall. And the luminaries on the flatbed truck went off with Rocky—Leonard Hall, Bill Miller, and Meade Alcorn. It may be worthwhile to take a look at them.

5

The former Republican National Committee Chairmen who were committed to Rockefeller and had been out at Opa Locka were on display earlier in a press conference in the French Room of the Fontainebleau.

A yellow drape hung behind a long table covered in kelly green. On the walls were wall paintings of pink ribbons and pink trumpets in heraldic hearts ten feet high; dirty blue drapes contested dingy wallpaper. A small piece of plaster was off the ceiling in a corner. It was not a room equal to the talent present.

Meade Alcorn first, his presentation hard, driving, full of Wasp authority—his voice had a ring, "I like to articulate it in terms of the greater electibility of Governor Rockefeller"—he had answered in response to a question whether he thought Richard Nixon, if nominated, might lose the election. By all agreement one of the few superb professionals in the Republican party, Alcorn had a friendly freckled face and sandy hair, black horn-rims, a jaw which could probably crack a lobster claw in one bite, his voice drilled its authority. He was the kind of man who could look you in the eye while turning down your bid for a mortgage. "We don't name the ballot where Rockefeller is going to take it. Could be the fourth, the fifth. Wendell Willkie took it on the sixth. We expect a convention not unlike the one in 1940." He hadn't been National Committee Chairman for nothing; whatever political stand he might be obliged to support came out with the crackling conviction of personal truth.

Then Senator Hugh Scott of Pennsylvania was on. Scott had modest but impeccable aplomb as he explained that since only 12 per cent of the delegates had been in San Francisco in 1964, he did not expect bitterness from old Goldwater followers to hurt Rockefeller's chances now. A fine character actor had been lost when Hugh Scott went to politics—he could have played the spectrum from butler to count.

Leonard Hall, heavy, imperturbable, was there with figures—he counted 535 for Nixon, 350 for Rockefeller. He was a man noted for relative accuracy, but was probably structuring his figures today. He gave the impression of an extraordinarily intelligent man, in appearance not unlike Jack E. Leonard doing a straight turn, as if all of Jack E. Leonard's hyper-acute intelligence had gone into the formidable bastions of Squaresville. "My goodness," said Hall at one point, "Rockefeller means the difference for thirty or forty Republican Congressmen between getting elected . . . and being in trouble." He was not about to say Nixon would certainly make them go down. "These Congressmen are human beings. They want to win." But picture Jack E. Leonard talking like that. Some part of conviction was lacking. When Hall said "My goodness" he looked too much like the director of the most impressive funeral establishment in the nation, the kind of man who certainly couldn't think much of you if, my goodness, you wouldn't spring ten thousand smackeroonies for a casket.

There had also been Bill Miller, the man who had run for Vice President on Barry Goldwater's ticket in '64. Now he was supporting Rockefeller. When asked if he and Goldwater were still friends, he said, "I've promised to go along with Governor Rockefeller, and he has said that if he is not nominated, he will support the convention's choice. Goldwater has said he will work for anybody the convention nominates. So sooner or later, Barry and I will be together again." Miller had the big head, big nose, and little hunched shoulders which are reminiscent of an ex-jockey. He had become popular with the Press during the last Presidential campaign. Becoming convinced somewhere en route that Barry's cause was hopeless, he had spent his time on the Vice Presidential campaign plane drinking bourbon and playing cards; when the plane came to a stop, he would get out, give his airport speech to the airport rally—usually a small crowd at a small airport—get back in the plane again, his card hand still warm, and pick up the play. Now he was wending his way through trick questions, emphasizing his long continuing relations with Rockefeller, whom he had supported for election four times while Rockefeller indeed had supported him seven times, so no curiosity that he was back of Rocky now. Miller talked in a barking voice full of snap. Where it had once been disagreeable in a formal speech, it was not unattractive here. Maybe all that bourbon and bridge had mellowed him since '64—he no longer looked like the nastiest yap in town.

To the contrary, he now had all the political oils. He was for Rockefeller because Rockefeller solved problems through action. "You name a problem, and in New York we've got it." So he went on to cite the Governor's fine record in highways and air pollution and conservation. It was hard to know just what he was talking about. Every year the traffic in New York was worse, and the air less possible to breathe, the Hudson River more polluted. It gave a hint of the extra-terrestrial dimension where Rockefeller and his advisers must live. Plans, large projects, huge campaigns, government fundings, mass participation in government, successful prosecution of air pollution, comprehensive surveys of traffic control, people's candidate, public opinion polls—the feather of doubt would whisper that Rockefeller was better suited for the Democrats than the Republicans. There were nuts and bolts and small tools necessary for unscrewing a Republican delegate from a first attachment to a second, and Rockefeller might have nothing smaller to employ than a bulldozer. But on to the Nixon camp.

6

The Orpheum Room in the Hilton Plaza where Herb Klein, Director of Press Relations for Nixon, held his conferences, looked like a public room for small gatherings which had been converted to a surgical theater. The approach was along a red corridor with red carpet, red ceiling, red velvet flock on the walls, and mirrors in gold frames, but the Orpheum Room had gold flock on a cream base in ivy figured wallpaper with heavy gold molding on the ceiling, and a gold and tan figured rug. Two huge glass chandeliers with about 800 prisms in each completed allegiance to the eighteenth century. The twentieth century was a foot away from the chandeliers in the form of a big square aluminum baffle plate flush in the ceiling for air

conditioning. The chairs for Press were the ubiquitous
brown leatherette sprinkled with gold dust.

The podium was a structure covered with formica processed to look like walnut grain. Behind it hung a shrine-
like photograph of Richard Nixon, exhibiting the kind of
colors one saw on Jack Kennedy photographs after his
assassination; also on pictures of Manolete, Franklin
Delano Roosevelt, Abraham Lincoln.

Klein was a slim neat man with a high forehead, a
pleasant demeanor—men in public relations are not noted
for disagreeable dispositions—and a smile which would
have delivered the simile of a cat licking cream if no
previous investor of the simile had yet existed. He was
claiming 700 votes for Nixon on the first ballot. Since
Leonard Hall had insisted not two hours before that his
most careful estimates put Nixon at 535, it was obvious—
both men revealing no shiver of incertitude—that one of
them was a liar.

Since Nixon would not be arriving until Monday, he had
little news to offer before introducing Governor John Volpe
of Massachusetts, a Republican of Italian extraction who
had come into prosperous political life by way of the con-
struction business. Volpe was a self-made man, and looked
not unlike a small version of Rockefeller. He was no great
orator as he read his prepared speech which declared him
all-out for Nixon, indeed he seemed to hire no great speech
writers either. "Americans see in Mr. Nixon a leader who
can unite this country in an effort that will preserve and
enhance our position in the world, while simultaneously
providing the needed inspiration and new thoughts required in the next four years." Sock it to 'em, Volpe! His
strength was in other places. In concrete. All the while,
standing behind him, Herb Klein smiled his happy tabby-
cat smile. They made a good pair standing side by side.
When he smiled, Herb Klein's narrow eyes became slits.
Just after Volpe smiled, his narrow mouth became a slit.
It was a modest conference without much news and nothing was disturbed. Afterward came a fashion show: outfits
were shown for the Nixon dancers, and the Nixonaires—
airline stewardesses based in Miami who were willing or
eager to work for Nixon in their spare time. A bevy of
good-looking chicks with sharp noses and tight mouths
modelled the stuff. They were carefully balanced between

blondes—Women for Nixon—wearing sleeveless blue A-
line cotton dresses, and several brunettes—Nixonaires—in
orange leatherette vests, white miniskirts, and black and
white leatherette jockey caps.

By the next day, when Nixon's daughters arrived, it was
obvious that such notion of balance—blondes to share
stage with brunettes—had been calculated for many an
aspect of his campaign. There were, for instance, two
complete bands in the lobby of the Hilton Plaza to celebrate the arrival of his daughters, and one band was white,
the other Black. Yet if not for the mezzanine which was
inlaid, it will be recollected, with red velvet flock for the
walls and red fleur-de-lis for the rugs, the Hilton Plaza
could have been converted to a hospital. Even with entertainment, the lobby was relatively bare and colorless. Com-
pared to the Fontainebleau and the Americana it was
ascetic. Hints of some future American empire and some
future American sterility were in the seed of the architect's
conception.

It was filled now of course with the two bands and the
Nixon Dancers and Nixonaires and TV cameras and
crowds and Nixon workers and a man dressed like Uncle
Sam on ten-foot stilts who bore a curious but undeniable
resemblance to Senator Eugene McCarthy. The Nixon
daughters had come in to pleasant cheers, cries of pleasure
from those who could see them in the crowd, the beating
of the two bands, and they had passed through the crowd
and into the lobby, both lovely looking girls. The older
(who looked younger) was Tricia, gentle, bemused, a
misty look to her face, but incontestably a beauty with
very blonde hair. She had an extraordinary complexion—
one would be forced to describe it with the terminology of
the Victorian novel, alabaster and ivory could vie for
prominence with peaches and cream. The other daughter,
Julia, brown-haired, apple-cheeked, snub-nosed, was
healthy, genial, a perfect soubrette for a family comedy on
television. She was as American as Corporate Bakeries
apple pie. And now engaged to David Eisenhower, grandson of Old Ike. It was an engagement which had caused
much bitter chortling and a predictable tightening of the
collective mouth when word came to liberal circles. There
seemed at the time no limit to Richard Nixon's iniquity.
But in fact daughter Julia was a nice-looking girl, and

Ike's grandson who looked to be not yet twenty had a pleasant face, more than a hint of innocence in it, not only small-town but near to yokel, redeemed by the friendliest of simple smiles. An ambitious high school dramatics teacher might have picked him to play Billy Budd.

The arrival of the girls and covert scrutiny of them by the reporter had produced one incontestable back-slapping turn-of-the-century guffaw: a man who could produce daughters like that could not be all bad. The remote possibility of some reappraisal of Richard Nixon was now forced to enter the works. It was, of course, remote, but the reporter was determined to be fair to all, and the notion was incontestably there. Nothing in his prior view of Nixon had ever prepared him to conceive of a man with two lovely girls. (Since the reporter had four fine daughters of his own, he was not inclined to look on such matters as accident.) And indeed later that night, the voice (agreeably well-brought-up but not remarkable) of one of Nixon's daughters was heard for a fragment of dialogue on radio. No, she was saying, their father had never spanked them. It was indicated that Mother had been the disciplinarian. "But then," the girl's voice went on, simple clarity, even honest devotion in the tone, "we never wanted to displease him. We wanted to be good." The reporter had not heard a girl make a remark like that about her father since his own mother had spoken in such fashion thirty-odd years ago.

Of course the remote contingency of reappraising Nixon had been kept comfortably remote by the nature of the entertainment provided in the lobby of the Hilton Plaza after the daughters had made their entrance and well-regulated escape to some private suite upstairs. The Nixon Dancers were now entertaining the crowd. Thirty-six adolescent girls all seemingly between five feet, four inches and five feet, six inches came out to dance various sorts of cheerleader-type dances. Impossible to define the steps more neatly, it was some sort of cross between television entertainment at half-time and working on a farm team for the Rockettes. Later the girls made an exit in file, in profile, and a clear count was there to be made in noses. Six of the thirty-six had aquiline curves, six were straight-nosed, and the other twenty-four had turned-up buttons at the tip.

Now heard was the white band. There were sixteen of them, about as good, and about as simple, as a good high school marching band. The Black band was something else, Eureka Brass Band by name, right out of Beale Street sixty years ago, ten Negroes in black pants, white shirts and white yachting caps with black visors did a Dixieland strut up and around the floor, led by their master, a tall disdainful wizardly old warlock, a big Black in a big black tuxedo, black felt Homburg on his head, medals and green sashes and Nixon buttons all over him. He was no ad for anybody but the most arcane Black Power, he was an old prince of a witch doctor—insult him at your peril—but the other ten musicians with their trumpets and snares and assorted brass would prove no pull for Nixon on TV with any Black votes watching, for they were old and meek, naught but elderly Black Southern musicians, a veritable Ganges of Uncle Toms. They had disappeared with Tom Swift and Little Lord Fauntleroy.

7

That evening at the Fontainebleau, on the night before the convention was to begin, the Republicans had their Grand Gala, no Press admitted, and the reporter by a piece of luck was nearly the first to get in. The affair was well-policed, in fact strict in its security, for some of the most important Republican notables would be there, but strolling through the large crowd in the lobby the reporter discovered himself by accident in the immediate wake of Governor Reagan's passage along a channel of security officers through the mob to the doors of the Gala. It was assumed by the people who gave way to the Governor that the reporter must be one of the plainclothesmen assigned to His Excellency's rear, and with a frown here, judicious tightening of his mouth there, look of concern for the Governor's welfare squeezed onto his map, offering a security officer's look superior to the absence of any ticket, he went right in through the ticket-takers, having found time in that passage to observe Governor Reagan and his Lady, who were formally dressed to the hilt of the occasion, now smiling, now shaking hands, eager, tense, bird-like, genial, not quite habituated to eminence, seeking to make brisk but not rude progress through the crowd, and obviously uneasy in the crowd (like most political figures) since a night in June in Los Angeles. It was an expected observation, but Mr. and Mrs. Reagan looked very much like an actor and actress playing Governor and Wife. Still Reagan held himself sort of uneasily about the middle, as if his solar plexus were fragile, and a clout would leave him like a fish on the floor.

Once inside the ballroom, however, the reporter discovered that the Governor had been among the first guests to enter. His own position was therefore not comfortable. Since there were no other guests among whom to mix (nothing but two hundred and forty empty tables with settings for two thousand people, all still to come in) and no cover to conceal him but small potted trees with oranges attached by green wire, since Security might be furious to the point of cop-mania catching him thus early, there was no choice but to take up a stand twenty feet from the door, his legs at parade rest, his arms clasped behind, while he scrutinized the entrance of everybody who came in. Any security officer studying him might therefore be forced to conclude that he belonged to *other* Security. Suffice it, he was not approached in his position near the entrance, and for the next thirty minutes looked at some thousand Republicans coming through the gate, the other thousand entering out of view by an adjacent door.

It was not a crowd totally representative of the power of the Republican Party. Some poor delegates may have been there as guests, and a few other delegates might have chosen to give their annual contribution of $1,000 for husband and wife here ($500 a plate) rather than to some other evening of fund raising for the party, indeed an air of sobriety and quiet dress was on many of the Republicans who entered. There were women who looked like librarians and schoolteachers, there were middle-aged men who looked like they might be out for their one night of the year. The Eastern Establishment was of course present in degree, and powers from the South, West, Midwest, but it was not a gang one could hold up in comparative glitter to an opening at the Met. No, rather, it was modesty which hung over these well-bred subscribers to the Gala.

Still, exceptions noted, they were obviously in large part composed of a thousand of the wealthiest Republicans in the land, the corporate and social power of America was here in legions of interconnection he could not even begin to trace. Of necessity, a measure of his own ignorance came over him, for among those thousand, except for candidates, politicians and faces in the news, there were not ten people he recognized. Yet here they were, the economic power of America (so far as economic power was still private, not public) the family power (so far as position in society was still a passion to average and ambitious Americans) the military power (to the extent that important sword-rattlers and/or patriots were among the company, as well as cadres of corporations not unmarried to the Pentagon) yes, even the spiritual power of America (just so far as Puritanism, Calvinism, conservatism and golf still gave the Wasp an American faith more intense than the faith of cosmopolitans, one-worlders, trade-unionists, Black militants, New Leftists, acid-heads, tribunes of the gay, families of Mafia, political machinists, fixers, swingers, Democratic lobbyists, members of the Grange, and government workers, not to include the *Weltanschauung* of every partisan in every minority group). No, so far as there was an American faith, a belief, a mystique that America was more than the sum of its constituencies, its trillions of dollars and billions of acres, its constellation of factories, empyrean of communications, mountain transcendant of finance, and heroic of sport, transports of medicine, hygiene, and church, so long as belief persisted that America, finally more than all this, was the world's ultimate reserve of rectitude, final garden of the Lord, so far as this mystique could survive in every American family of Christian substance, so then were the people entering this Gala willy-nilly the leaders of this faith, never articulated by any of them except in the most absurd and taste-curdling jargons of patriotism mixed with religion, but the faith existed in those crossroads between the psyche and the heart where love, hate, the cognition of grace, the all but lost sense of the root, and adoration of America congregate for some.

Their own value was in this faith, the workings of their seed from one generation into the next, their link to the sense of what might be life-force was in the faith. Yes, primitive life was there, and ancestral life, health concealed in their own flesh from towns occupied and once well-settled, from farms which prospered, and frontiers they had—through ancestors—dared to pass. They believed in America as they believed in God—they could not really ever expect that America might collapse and God yet survive, no, they had even gone so far as to think that America was the savior of the world, food and medicine by one hand, sword in the other, highest of high faith in a nation which would bow the knee before no problem since God's own strength was in the die. It was a faith which had flared so high in San Francisco in 1964 that staid old Republicans had come near to frothing while they danced in the aisle, there to nominate Barry, there to nominate Barry. But their hero had gone down to a catastrophe of defeat, blind in politics, impolite in tactics, a sorehead, a fool, a disaster. And if his policies had prevailed to some degree, to the degree of escalating the war in Vietnam, so had that policy depressed some part of America's optimism to the bottom of the decade, for the country had learned an almost unendurable lesson—its history in Asia was next to done, and there was not any real desire to hold armies on that land; worse, the country had begun to wear away inside, and the specter of Vietnam in every American city would haunt the suburb, the terror of a dollar cut loose from every standard of economic anchor was in the news, and some of the best of the youth were mad demented dogs with teeth in the flesh of the deepest Republican faith.

They were a chastened collocation these days. The high fire of hard Republican faith was more modest now, the vision of America had diminished. The claims on Empire had met limits. But it was nonetheless uncommon, yes bizarre, for the reporter to stand like an agent of their security as these leaders of the last American faith came through to the Gala, for, repeat: they were in the main not impressive, no, not by the hard eye of New York. Most of them were ill-proportioned in some part of their physique. Half must have been, of course, men and women over fifty and their bodies reflected the pull of their character. The dowager's hump was common, and many a man had a flaccid paunch, but the collective tension was rather in the shoulders, in the girdling of the shoulders against anticipated lashings on the back, in the thrust forward of the neck, in the maintenance of the muscles of the mouth forever locked in readiness to bite the tough meat of resistance, in a posture forward from the hip since the small of the back was dependably stiff, loins and mind cut away from each other by some abyss between navel and hip.

More than half of the men wore eyeglasses, young with old—the reporter made his count, close as a professional basketball game, and gave up by the time his score was up to Glasses 87, No Glasses 83. You could not picture a Gala Republican who was not clean-shaven by eight A.M. Coming to power, they could only conceive of trying to clean up every situation in sight. And so many of the women seemed victims of the higher hygiene. Even a large part of the young seemed to have faces whose cheeks had been injected with Novocain.

Yet he felt himself unaccountably filled with a mild sorrow. He did not detest these people, he did not feel so superior as to pity them, it was rather he felt a sad sorrowful respect. In their immaculate cleanliness, in the somewhat antiseptic odors of their astringent toilet water and perfume, in the abnegation of their walks, in the heavy sturdy moves so many demonstrated of bodies in life's harness, there was the muted tragedy of the Wasp—they were not on earth to enjoy or even perhaps to love so very much, they were here to serve, and serve they had in public functions and public charities (while recipients of their charity might vomit in rage and laugh in scorn), served on opera committees, and served in long hours of duty at the piano, served as the sentinel in concert halls and the pews on the aisle in church, at the desk in schools, had served for culture, served for finance, served for salvation, served for America—and so much of America did not wish them to serve any longer, and so many of them doubted themselves, doubted that the force of their faith could illumine their path in these new modern horrorhead times. On and on, they came through the door, the clean, the well-bred, the extraordinarily prosperous, and for the most astonishing part, the almost entirely proper. Yes, in San Francisco in '64 they had been able to be insane for a little while, but now they were subdued, now they were modest, now they were looking for a leader to bring America back to them, their lost America, Jesusland.

"Nelson Rockefeller is out of his mind if he thinks he can take the nomination away from Richard Nixon," the reporter said suddenly to himself. It was the first certitude the convention had given.

8

Still, Rockefeller was trying. He had been mounting a massive offensive for weeks. In speeches which came most often as prepared announcements for television and in full-page advertisements in newspapers all over the country, he had been saturating America with Rockefeller philosophy, paying for it with Rockefeller money, the rhetoric in the style of that Madison Avenue Eminent, Emmet Hughes.

On Vietnam: The country must never again "find itself with a commitment looking for a justification. . . . The war has been conducted without a coherent strategy or program for peace." Of course he had been until recently a hawk with the hawks—like Nixon, he was now a dove of a hawk, a dove of a hawk like all the Republicans but Reagan.

The ads had come with text in 20-point type, 30-point type, larger. "We must assure to all Americans two basic rights: the right to learn and the right to work." (The right to learn would come in mega-universities with lectures pulled in on television and study halls with plastic bucket seats—the right to work? or was it the right to take pride in one's work?)

On Cities: ". . . . the confidence that we can rebuild

our great cities—making slums of old despair into centers of new hope. . . ."

Or: "I see . . . the welfare concept . . . as a floor below which nobody will be allowed to fall, but with no ceiling to prevent anyone from rising as high as he wants to rise."

It was the best of potency-rhetoric for the thriving liberal center of America where most of the action was, building contracts, federal money for super-highways, youth programs for the slums, *wars* against poverty, bigotry, violence, and hate. (But how did one go to war with hate? "On your knees, mother-fucker!" said the saint.)

Yes, Rockefeller had only to win the nomination and it might take an act of God to keep him from the Presidency. He was the dream candidate for all Democratic voters—they could repudiate Johnson and Humphrey and still have the New Deal, the Fair Deal, Stevenson, Eleanor Roosevelt, Kennedy, Bobby Kennedy, Gene McCarthy, and Folk Rock with Rocky. He would get three-quarters of the Democrats' votes. Of course he would get only one-fourth of the Republicans' votes (the rest would go to Humphrey or Wallace or stay at home) but he would be in, he could unite the country right down that liberal center which had given birth to a Great Society, a war in Vietnam, and a permanent state of police alert in the cities in the summer.

He was like a general who had mounted the most massive offensive of a massive war but had neglected to observe that the enemy was not on his route, and the line of march led into a swamp. Rockefeller took out ads, pushed television, worked with hip musicians and groovy bands (Cannonball Adderley, Lionel Hampton) got out the young at every rally (the adolescents too young to vote) hob-nobbed with governors and senators, made the phone calls, hit the high pressure valve (Bill Miller and Meade Alcorn and Leonard Hall and Thruston Morton called in old debts from old friends) hit the hustings in his plane. "Hiya fellow,"—did everything but enter the campaign at the right time, fight it out in the primaries, or design his attack for the mollification of Republican fears. He did everything but exercise choice in serving up the best political greens and liver juice for the rehabilitation of Republican pride. In secret he may have detested the Average Republican—it

was no secret that same Republican hated him: they had
never forgiven each other for his divorce and his remar-
riage. A man married for thirty-two years should have
known all marital misery by then—to smash such a scene
spoke to the average Republican of massive instability, no
fear of God, an obvious hankering for the orgiastic fats of
the liberal center, and no saving secret gifts of hypocrisy
—this latter being indispensable, reasons the conservative
mind, to prudence and protection in government.

Besides, the sort of passion for a late-entering candidate
which can lead a delegate to make a last-minute switch in
his choice must have roots in hysteria, and thereby be near
to that incandescent condition of the soul when love and/or
physical attraction is felt for three or four people at
once. Hysteria is not in high demand among Republicans.
Their lives have been geared to keep *ménage-à-trois* at a
minimum. If love is then sometimes also at a minimum,
well, that's all right. Misers can feel vertiginous titillation
if they are worked upon for years to give up their coin,
their kiss, their delegate's vote. And Nixon had worked on
them for many months and just some of those years, you
bet! The miser giving up his gift once is the happiest of
men—being asked to switch his choice again is the invitation to hysteria—it can only end by sending him to the nut
house, the poorhouse, or a school for the whirling dervish.

What Rockefeller needed was delegate votes, not millions of Americans sending good thoughts. There were
dreams of repeating Wendell Willkie's sixth ballot in 1940,
but those were scandalous military dreams, for Republicans then hated Roosevelt to such distraction they would
have nominated any man who had a chance against him,
whereas in 1968 their loyalty was to the philosophy of the
party— to Republicanism!

Rocky had spent and would spend, it was said, ten million bucks to get the nomination. (One journalist remarked
that he would have done better to buy delegates: at $25,000
a delegate, he could have had four hundred.) On Sunday
afternoon, there was an opportunity to see how the money
was spent. Some rich men are famous for penury—it was
Rocky's own grandfather after all who used to pass out the
thin dime. But generosity to a rich man is like hysteria to a
miser: once entertain it, and there's no way to stop—the
bitch is in the house. Having engaged the habit of spend-

ing, where was Rocky to quit? After the television came
the rallies and the chartered planes; now in Miami, the
rented river boats on Island Creek for delegates who wanted
an afternoon of booze on an inland waterway yacht; or the
parties. Rocky threw open the Americana for a Sunday reception and supper for the New York delegation. On Monday
from 5:00 to 7:00 P.M., after Nixon's arrival, he gave a
giant reception for all delegates, alternates and Republican
leadership. The party jammed the Continental Room and
the Grand Ballroom of the Americana, and the numbers
could not be counted; 5,000 could have gone through,
6,000, the *Times* estimated 8,000 guests and a cost of
$50,000. Half of Miami Beach may have passed through
for the free meal and the drinks. On the tables (eight bars,
sixteen buffet tables) thousands of glasses were ready with
ice cubes; so, too were ready shrimp and cocktail sauce,
potted meat balls, turkeys, hams, goulash, aspic, éclairs,
pigs in blankets, chicken liver, *pâté de volailles,* vats of
caviar (black), ladyfingers, jelly rings, celebration cakes—
where were the crepes suzette? What wonders of the American gut. On the bandstand in each room, a band; in the
Continental Room, dark as a night club (indeed a night
club on any other night) Lionel Hampton was vibrating a
beat right into the rich middle octave of a young Black
singer giving up *soul* for Rocky. "We want Rocky," went
the chant. *Sock . . . sock . . .* went the beat, driving,
lightly hypnotic, something reminiscent in the tempo of
shots on the rim of the snare when the drummer backs the
stripper's bumps. But Rocky wasn't coming out now, he
was somewhere else, so members of his family, his older
children and wives of his older children and sister and
Helen Hayes and Billy Daniels were out on the stage with
Hampton and the happy young Black singer snapping his
fingers and the happy Black girl singer full of soul and zap
and breasts!

Everybody was eating, drinking—young Rockefeller
family up there on happiness beat, arms locked, prancing,
natives of Miami Beach on the floor cheering it up, America ready to truck its happiness right out on One World
Highway One.

And here and there a delegate, or a delegate's family
from Ohio or Colorado or Illinois, delegate's badge on the
lapel, mixed look of curiosity, wonder, and pleasure in the

eye: "If the man wants to throw his money around like that, well, we're not here to stop him!" And the pleasure in the eye is reserved for the thought of telling the home folks about the swinishness, sottishness, and *waste* expenditure of the occasion. "They were spilling half the drinks they were in such a hurry to serve them up."

And in the corridor between the Caribbean Room and the Ballroom a jam of guests. The line would not move. Trapped in the rush hour again. In the first world war, Marshal Haig used to send a million men over the top in a frontal attack. One hundred yards would be gained, one hundred thousand casualties would be the price. It was possible Nelson Rockefeller was the Marshal Haig of presidential hopefuls. Rich men should not surround themselves with other rich men if they want to win a war.

9

Nixon had come in earlier that day. A modestly large crowd, perhaps six hundred at the entrance to the Miami Hilton, two bands playing "Nixon's the One," and the Nixonettes and the Nixonaires, good clean blonde and brown-haired Christian faces, same two Negresses, a cluster of 2,000 balloons going up in the air, flings of color, thin dots of color, and Nixon himself finally in partial view at the center of the semicircle of cameras held overhead. Just a glimpse: he has a sunburn—his forehead is bright pink. Then he has made it into the hotel, pushed from behind, hands in hand-shakes from the front, hair recognizable—it is curlier than most and combed in roller coaster waves, not unreminiscent of the head of hair on Gore Vidal. (But where was Nixon's Breckinridge?)

The crowd had been enthusiastic without real hurly-burly or hint of pandemonium. More in a state of respectful enthusiasm, and the hot patriotic cupidity to get near the man who is probably going to be the next American

President. The office, not the man, is moving them. And
Nixon passes through them with the odd stick-like motions
which are so much a characteristic of his presence. He is
like an actor with good voice and hordes of potential, but
the despair of his dramatic coach (again it is High School).
"Dick, you just got to learn how to move." There is something almost touching in the way he does it, as if sensitive
flesh winces at the way he must expose his lack of heart for
being warm and really winning in crowds, and yet he is all
heart to perform his task, as if the total unstinting exercise
of the will must finally deliver every last grace, yes, he is
like a missionary handing out Bibles among the Urdu.
Christ, they are filthy fellows, but deserving of the *touch*.
No, it is not so much that he is a bad actor (for Nixon in
a street crowd is *radiant* with emotion to reach across the
prison pen of his own artificial moves and deadly reputation and show that he is sincere) it is rather that he grew
up in the worst set of schools for actors in the world—
white gloves and church usher, debating team, Young Republicanism, captive of Ike's forensic style—as an actor,
Nixon thinks his work is to signify. So if he wants to show
someone that he likes them, he must smile; if he wishes to
show disapproval of Communism, he frowns; America
must be strong, out goes his chest. Prisoner of old habit or
unwitting of a new kind of move, he has not come remotely
near any modern moves, he would not be ready to see that
the young love McCarthy because he plays forever against
his line. "If I'm nominated, I can't see how I'd possibly fail
to win," says McCarthy in a gloomy modest mild little
voice, then his eyes twinkle at the myriad of consequences
to follow: raps in the newspaper about his arrogance, the
sheer delicious zaniness of any man making any claim
about his candidacy—yes, many people love McCarthy
because his wan wit is telling them, "We straddle ultimates:
spitballs and eternals."

Nixon has never learned this. He is in for the straight
sell. No wonder he foundered on "America can't stand
pat."

But the reporter is obsessed with him. He has never
written anything nice about Nixon. Over the years he has
saved some of his sharpest comments for him, he has disliked him intimately ever since his Checkers speech in 1952
—the kind of man who was ready to plough sentimentality

in such a bog was the kind of man who would press any button to manipulate the masses—and there was large fear in those days of buttons which might ignite atomic wars. Nixon's presence on television had inspired emotions close to nausea. There had been a gap between the man who spoke and the man who lived behind the speaker which offered every clue of schizophrenia in the American public if they failed to recognize the void within the presentation. Worse. There was unity only in the way the complacency of the voice matched the complacency of the ideas. It was as if Richard Nixon were proving that a man who had never spent an instant inquiring whether family, state, church, and flag were ever wrong could go on in secure steps, denuded of risk, from office to office until he was President.

In 1962 the reporter had given a small celebration for the collapse of Nixon after his defeat in the election for Governor of California. To the Press: "Well, gentlemen," the defeated man had said, "you won't have Nixon to kick any more." It had seemed the absolute end of a career. Self-pity in public was as irreversible as suicide. In 1964, Nixon had stood about in the wings while Barry was nominated. Now, in 1968, he was on the edge of becoming the nominee. It was obvious something was wrong with the reporter's picture. In his previous conception of Richard Nixon's character there had been no room for a comeback. Either the man had changed or one had failed to recognize some part of his character from the beginning. So there was interest, even impatience to hear him speak.

He was not having a press conference, however, on the day of his arrival. That would wait until the next morning at 8:15. Then, he would face the Press.

10

The room filled slowly. By the time Nixon began, it was apparent that 500 seats had been an excessive estimate.

Perhaps half of them were filled, certainly no more than two-thirds. It was nonetheless a large press conference. Nixon came in wearing a quiet blue-gray suit, white shirt, black and blue close-figured tie, black shoes, and no hand-kerchief for the breast pocket. He stepped up on the dais diffidently, not certain whether applause would be coming or not. There was none. He stood there, looked quietly and warily at the audience, and then said that he was ready for questions.

This would be his sole press conference before the nomination. He was of course famous for his lack of sparkling good relation with the Press, he had in fact kept his publicity to a functional minimum these past few months. The work of collecting delegates had been done over the last four years, particularly over the last two. Their allegiance had been confirmed the last six months in his primary victories. He had no longer anything much to gain from good interviews, not at least until his nomination was secured; he had everything to lose from a bad interview. A delegate who was slipping could slide further because of an ill-chosen remark.

To the extent that the Press was not Republican, and certainly more than half, privately, were not, he would have few friends and more than a few determined enemies. Even among the Republicans he could expect a better share of the Press to go to Rockefeller. Even worse, for the mood of this conference, he did not, in comparison with other political candidates, have many reporters who were his personal friends. He was not reputed to smoke or drink so he did not have drinking buddies as Johnson once had, and Goldwater, and Bill Miller, and Humphrey; no brothel legends attached to him, and no outsize admiration to accompany them; no, the Press was a necessary tool to him, a tool he had been obliged to employ for more than twenty years but he could not pretend to be comfortable in his use of the tool, and the tool (since it was composed of men) resented its employment.

Probably Nixon had agreed to this conference only to avoid the excess of bad feeling which no meeting with the Press would be likely to cause. Still, this was an operation where his best hope was to minimize the loss. So he had taken the wise step of scheduling the conference at 8:15 in the morning, a time when his worst enemies, presumably

the heavy drinkers, free lovers, and free spenders on the
Reagan Right and Far Left of the press corps, would
probably be asleep in bed or here asleep on their feet.

Nonetheless his posture on the stage, hands to his side
or clasped before him, gave him the attentive guarded look
of an old ball player—like Rabbit Maranville, let us say,
or even an old con up before Parole Board. There was
something in his carefully shaven face—the dark jowls
already showing the first overtones of thin gloomy blue at
this early hour—some worry which gave promise of never
leaving him, some hint of inner debate about his value before eternity which spoke of precisely the sort of improvement that comes upon a man when he shifts in appearance
from looking like an undertaker's assistant to looking like
an old con seriously determined to go respectable. The Old
Nixon, which is to say the young Nixon, used to look, on
clasping his hands in front of him, like a church usher (of
the variety who would twist a boy's ear after removing him
from church). The older Nixon before the Press now—the
new Nixon—had finally acquired some of the dignity of the
old athlete and the old con—he had taken punishment,
that was on his face now, he knew the detailed schedule
of pain in a real loss, there was an attentiveness in his eyes
which gave offer of some knowledge of the abyss, even the
kind of gentleness which ex-drunkards attain after years in
AA. As he answered questions, fielding them with the sure
modest moves of an old shortstop who hits few homers but
supports the team on his fielding (what sorrow in the faces
of such middle-aged shortstops!) so now his modesty was
not without real dignity. Where in Eisenhower days his
attempts at modesty had been as offensive as a rich boy's
arrogance, for he had been so transparently contemptuous
of the ability of his audience to *witness* him, now the
modesty was the product of a man who, at worst, had grown
from a bad actor to a surprisingly good actor, or from an
unpleasant self-made man—outrageously rewarded with
luck—to a man who had risen and fallen and been able to
rise again, and so conceivably had learned something about
patience and the compassion of others.

When the reporter was younger, he might have said,
"Nixon did not rise again; they raised him; if a new Nixon
did not exist, they would have had to invent him." But the
reporter was older now—presumably he knew more about

the limits of the ruling class for inventing what they needed; he had learned how little talent or patience they had. Yes, at a certain point they might have decided, some of them at any rate, to dress Richard Nixon for the part again, but no one but Nixon had been able to get himself up from the political deathbed to which his failure in California had consigned him. He was here, then, answering questions in a voice which was probably closer to his own than it had ever been.

And some of the answers were not so bad. Much was Old Nixon, extraordinarily adroit at working both sides of a question so that both halves of his audience might be afterward convinced he was one of them. ("While homosexuality is a perversion punishable by law, and an intolerable offense to a law-abiding community, it is life-giving to many of those who are in need of it," he might have said if ever he had addressed a combined meeting of the Policemen's Benevolent Association and the Mattachine Society.) So he worked into the problem of Vietnam by starting at A and also by starting at Z which he called a "two-pronged approach." He was for a negotiated settlement, he was for maintaining military strength because that would be the only way to "reach negotiated settlement of the war on an honorable basis." Later he was to talk of negotiations with "the next superpower, Communist China." He spoke patiently, with clarity, gently, not badly but for an unfortunate half-smile pasted to his face. The question would come, and he would back-hand it with his glove or trap it; like all politicians he had a considered answer for every question, but he gave structure to his answers, even a certain relish for their dialectical complexity. Where once he had pretended to think in sentimentalities and slogans, now he held the question up, worked over it, deployed it, amplified it, corrected its tendency, offered an aside (usually an attempt to be humorous) revealed its contradiction, and then declared a statement. With it all, a sensitivity almost palpable to the reservations of the Press about his character, his motive, and his good intention. He still had no natural touch with them, his half-smile while he listened was unhappy, for it had nowhere to go but into a full smile and his full smile was as false as false teeth, a pure exercise of will. You could all but see the signal pass from his brain to his jaw. "SMILE," said the signal, and so he flashed teeth in a painful kind of joyous grimace which spoke of some shrinkage in the liver, or the gut, which he would have to repair afterward by other medicine than good-fellowship. (By winning the Presidency, perhaps.) He had always had the ability to violate his own nature absolutely if that happened to be necessary to his will—there had never been anyone in American life so resolutely phony as Richard Nixon, nor anyone so transcendentally successful by such means—small wonder half the electorate had regarded him for years as equal to a disease. But he was less phony now, *that was the miracle*, he had moved from a position of total ambition and total alienation from his own person (at the time of Checkers, the dog speech) to a place now where he was halfway conciliated with his own self. As he spoke, he kept going in and out of focus, true one instant, phony the next, then quietly correcting the false step.

Question from the Press: *You emphasized the change in the country and abroad. Has this led you to change your thinking in any shape or form specifically?*

Answer: *It certainly has.* (But he was too eager. Old Nixon was always ready to please with good straight American boyhood enthusiasm. So he tacked back, his voice throttled down.) *As the facts change, any intelligent man* (firm but self-deprecatory, he is including the Press with himself) *does change his approaches to the problems.* (Now sharp awareness of the next Press attitude.) *It does not mean that he is an opportunist.* (Now modestly, reasonably.) *It means only that he is a pragmatist, a realist, applying principles to the new situations.* (Now he will deploy some of the resources of his answer.) *For example . . . in preparing the acceptance speech I hope to give next Thursday, I was reading over my acceptance speech in 1960, and I thought then it was, frankly, quite a good speech. But I realize how irrelevant much of what I said in 1960 in foreign affairs was to the problems of today.* (The admission was startling. The Old Nixon was never wrong. Now, he exploited the shift in a move to his political left, pure New Nixon.) *Then the Communist world was a monolithic world. Today it is a split world, schizophrenic, with . . . great diversity . . . in Eastern Europe* (a wholesome admission for anyone who had labored in John Foster Dulles' world.) *. . . after an era of confrontation . . . we now enter an era of negotiations with the Soviet Union.*

While he was never in trouble with the questions, grow-ing surer and surer of himself as he went on, the tension still persisted between his actual presence as a man not al-together alien to the abyss of a real problem, and the polit-ical practitioner of his youth, that snake-oil salesman who was never back of any idea he sold, but always off to the side where he might observe its effect on the sucker. The New Nixon groped and searched for the common touch he had once been able to slip into the old folks with the ease of an incubus on a spinster. Now he tried to use slang, put quotes around it with a touching, almost pathetic, reminder of Nice-Nellyism, the inhibition of the good clean church upbringing of his youth insisting on exhibiting itself, as if he were saying with a YMCA slick snicker, "After we break into slang, there's always the danger of the party getting *rough*." It was that fatal prissiness which must have driven him years ago into all the militaristic muscle-bending witch-hunting foam-rubber virilities of the young Senator and the young Vice President. So, now he talked self-consciously of how the members of his staff, counting delegates, were "playing what we call 'the strong game.' " SMILE said his brain. FLASH went the teeth. But his voice seemed to give away that, whatever they called it, they probably didn't call it "the strong game," or if they did, *he* didn't. So he framed little phrases. Like "a leg-up." Or "my intuition, my 'gut feelings,' so to speak." Deferential air followed by SMILE —FLASH. Was it possible that one of the secrets of Old Nixon was that his psyche had been trapped in rock-forma-tions, nay, geological strata of Sunday school inhibitions? Was it even possible that he was a good man, not a bad man, a good man who had been trapped by an early milieu whose habits had left him with such innocence about three-quarters of the world's experience that he had become an absolute monster of opportunism about the quarter he com-prehended all too well? Listening to Nixon now, studying his new modesty, it was impossible to tell whether he was a serious man on the path of returning to his own true seri-ousness, out to unite the nation again as he promised with every remark: "Reconciliation of the races is a primary objective of the United States," or whether the young devil had reconstituted himself into a more consummate devil, Old Scratch as a modern Abe Lincoln of modesty.

Question from the Press: *A little less than six years ago,*

*after your defeat for the Governorship of California, you
announced at the ensuing press conference that that was
going to be your last news conference. Could you recall for
us this morning two or three of the most important points
in your own thinking which made you reverse that statement and now reach for political office on the highest level?*

Answer: *Had there not been the division of the Republican Party in 1964 and had there not been the vacuum of
leadership that was created by that division and by that
defeat, I would not be here today. . . . I believe that my
travels around the country and the world in this period of
contemplation and this period of withdrawal from the political scene* (some dark light of happiness now in his eye, as
if withdrawal and contemplation had given him the first
deep pleasures, or perhaps the first real religious pleasures of
his life) *in which I have had a chance to observe not only the
United States but the world, has led me to the conclusion
that returning to the arena was something that I should do*
(said almost as if he had heard a voice in some visitation of
the night)—*not that I consider myself to be an indispensable man.* (Said agreeably in a relaxed tone as if he had
thought indeed to the bottom of this and had found the
relaxation of knowing he was not indispensable, an absurd
vanity if one stares at Nixon from without, but he had been
Vice President before he was forty, and so had had to see
himself early, perhaps much too early, as a man of destiny.
Now, reservation underlined, he could continue.) *But
something that I should do* (go for the Presidency) *because this is the time I think when the man and the
moment in history come together.* (An extraordinary admission for a Republican, with their Protestant detestation
of philosophical deeps or any personification of history.
With one remark, Nixon had walked into the oceans of
Marx, Spengler, Heidegger, and Tolstoy; and Dostoevski
and Kierkegaard were in the wings. Yes, Richard Nixon's
mind had entered the torture chambers of the modern
consciousness!)

*I have always felt that a man cannot seek the Presidency
and get it simply because he wants it. I think that he can
seek the Presidency and obtain it only when the Presidency
requires what he may have to offer* (the Presidency was
then a mystical seat, mystical as the choice of a woman's
womb) *and I have had the feeling* (comfortably pleasant

and modest again—no phony Nixon here) *and it may be a presumptuous feeling, that because of the vacuum of leadership in the Republican Party, because of the need for leadership particularly qualified in foreign affairs, because I have known not only the country, but the world as a result of my travels, that now time* (historical-time—the very beast of the mystic!) *requires that I re-enter the arena.* (Then he brought out some humor. It was not great humor, but for Nixon it was curious and not indelicate.) *And incidentally, I have been very willing to do so.* (Re-enter the arena.) *I am not being drafted. I want to make that very clear. I am very willing to do so. There has never been a draft in Miami in August anyway.* (Nice laughter from the Press—he has won them by a degree. Now he is on to finish the point.) . . . *I believe that if my judgment—and my intuition, my "gut feelings" so to speak, about America and American political tradition—is right, this is the year that I will win.*

The speech had come in the middle of the conference and he kept fielding questions afterward, never wholly at ease, never caught in trouble, mild, firm, reasonable, highly disciplined—it was possible he was one of the most disciplined men in America. After it was over, he walked down the aisle, and interviewers gathered around him, although not in great number. The reporter stood within two feet of Nixon at one point but had not really a question to ask which could be answered abruptly. "What, sir, would you say is the state of your familiarity with the works of Edmund Burke?" No, it was more to get a sense of the candidate's presence, and it was a modest presence, no more formidable before the immediate Press in its physical aura than a floorwalker in a department store, which is what Old Nixon had often been called, or worse—Assistant Mortician. It was probable that bodies did not appeal to him in inordinate measure, and a sense of the shyness of the man also appeared—shy after all these years!—but Nixon must have been habituated to loneliness after all those agonies in the circus skin of Tricky Dick. Had he really improved? The reporter caught himself hoping that Nixon had. If his physical presence inspired here no great joy nor even distrust, it gave the sense of a man still entrenched in toils of isolation, as if only the office of the Presidency could be equal (in the specific density of its importance) to the labyrinthine delivery of the natural man to himself. Then and only then might he know the strength of his own hand and his own moral desire. It might even be a measure of the not-entirely dead promise of America if a man as opportunistic as the early Nixon could grow in reach and comprehension and stature to become a leader. For, if that were possible in these bad years, then all was still possible, and the country not stripped of its blessing. New and marvelously complex improvement of a devil, or angel-in-chrysalis, or both––good and evil now at war in the man, Nixon was at least, beneath the near to hermetic boredom of his old presence, the most interesting figure at the convention, or at least so the reporter had decided by the end of the press conference that Tuesday in the morning. Complexities upon this vision were to follow.

11

The next press conference to be noted was in the French Room of the Fontainebleau for 11:00 A.M. The Reverend Ralph D. Abernathy, former assistant to the Reverend Martin Luther King, Jr., and leader of the Poor People's March after King had been assassinated, was scheduled to read a statement and answer questions. While the assembly was nowhere near so large as Nixon's, close to a hundred reporters must nonetheless have appeared, a considerable number of Negroes among them, and then proceeded to wait. Abernathy had not shown up. About fifteen minutes past the hour, another Negro came to the podium and said that the Reverend was on his way, and could be expected in a few minutes.

The gossip was livelier. "We had to look for him in five hotels," said a Black reporter to some other members of the Press, and there was a mental picture of the leader waking heavily, the woes of race, tension, unfulfilled commitment, skipped promises, and the need for militant effort in the day ahead all staring down into whatever kind of peace had been reached the night before in the stretch before sleep.

Still it was unduly irritating to have to wait at a press conference, and as the minutes went by and annoyance mounted, the reporter became aware after a while of a curious emotion in himself, for he had not ever felt it consciously before—it was a simple emotion and very unpleasant to him—he was getting tired of Negroes and their rights. It was a miserable recognition, and on many a count, for if he felt even a hint this way, then what immeasurable tides of rage must be loose in America itself? Perhaps it was the atmosphere of the Republican convention itself, this congregation of the clean, the brisk, the orderly, the efficient. A reporter who must attempt to do his job, he had perhaps committed himself too completely to the atmosphere as if better to comprehend the subterranean character of what he saw on the surface, but in any event having passed through such curious pilgrimage—able to look at Richard Nixon with eyes free of hatred!—it was almost as if he resented the presence of Abernathy now (or the missing Abernathy) as if the discomfort of his Black absence made him suddenly contemplate the rotting tooth and ulcerated gum of the white patient. What an obsession was the Negro to the average white American by now. Every time that American turned in his thoughts to the sweetest object of contemplation in his mind's small town bower, nothing less than America the Beautiful herself—that angel of security at the end of every alley—then *there* was the face of an accusing rioting Black right in the middle of the dream—smack in the center of the alley—and the obsession was hung on the hook of how to divide the guilt, how much to the white man, how much to the dark? The guiltiest man alive would work around the clock if he could only assign proportions to his guilt; but not to know if one was partially innocent or very guilty had to establish an order of paralysis. Since obsessions dragoon our energy by endless repetitive contemplations of guilt we can neither measure nor forget, political power of the most frightening sort was obviously waiting for the first demagogue who would smash the obsession and free the white man of his guilt. Torrents of energy would be loosed, yes, those same torrents which Hitler had freed in the Germans when he exploded their ten-year obsession with whether they had lost the war through betrayal or through material weakness. Through betrayal, Hitler had told them: Germans were actually strong and good. The consequences would never be counted.

Now if suburban America was not waiting for Georgie Wallace, it might still be waiting for Super-Wallace. The thought persisted, the ugly thought persisted that despite all legitimate claims, all burning claims, all searing claims, despite the fundamental claim that America's wealth, whiteness, and hygiene had been refined out of the most powerful molecules stolen from the sweat of the Black man, still the stew of the Black revolution had brought the worst to surface with the best, and if the Black did not police his own house, he would be destroyed and some of the best of the white men with him, and here—here was the sleeping festering hair of his outrage now that Abernathy was scandalously late in this sweaty room, over-heated by the hot TV camera lights, the waiting bodies, yes, the secret sleeping hair of this anti-Black fury in himself was that he no longer knew what the Black wanted—was the Black man there to save mankind from the cancerous depredations of his own white civilization, or was the Black so steeped in his curse that he looked forward to the destruction of the bread itself? Or worst of all, and like an advance reconnaissance scout of the armies of the most quintessential bigotry, one soldier from that alien army flung himself over the last entrenchment, stood up to die, and posed the question: "How do you know the Black man is not Ham, son of Evil? How do you really know?" and the soldier exploded a defense works in the reporter's brain, and bitterness toward Negroes flowed forth like the blood of the blown-up dead: over the last ten years if he had had fifty friendships with Negroes sufficiently true to engage a part of his heart, then was it ten or even five of those fifty which had turned out well? Aware of his own egocentricity, his ability to justify his own actions through many a strait gate, still it seemed to him that for the most part, putting color to the side—if indeed that were ever permissible—the fault, man to man, had been his less often, that he had looked through the catechism of every liberal excuse, had adopted the blame, been ready to give blessing and forgive, and had succeeded merely in deadening the generosity of his heart. Or was he stingier than he dreamed, more lacking in the true if exorbitant demand for compassion without measure, was the Black liberty to exploit the white man without measure, which he had claimed for the Black so often, "If I were a Negro, I'd exploit everything in sight," was this Black liberty he had so freely offered finally too offensive for him to support? He was weary to the bone of listening to Black cries of Black superiority in sex, Black superiority in beauty, Black superiority in war . . . the claims were all too often uttered by Negroes who were not very black themselves. And yet dread and the woe of some small end came over him at the thought itself —it was possible the reporter had influenced as many Black writers as any other white writer in America, and to turn now . . . But he was so heartily sick of listening to the tyranny of soul music, so bored with Negroes triumphantly late for appointments, so depressed with Black inhumanity to Black in Biafra, so weary of being sounded in the subway by Black eyes, so despairing of the smell of booze and pot and used-up hope in blood-shot eyes of Negroes bombed at noon, so envious finally of that liberty to abdicate from the long year-end decade-drowning yokes of work and responsibility that he must have become in some secret part of his flesh a closet Republican—how else account for his inner, "Yeah man, yeah, go!" when fat and flatulent old Republicans got up in Convention Hall to deliver platitudes on the need to return to individual human effort. Yes, he was furious at Abernathy for making him wait these crucial minutes while the secret stuff of his brain was disclosed to his mind.

Abernathy came in about forty minutes late, several other Negroes with him, his press secretary, Bernard Lee, wearing a tan suede collarless jacket, sullen and composed behind an evil-looking pair of dark sunglasses, possessor of hostility which seemed to say, "I got the right, man, to look at you from behind these shades, but you deserve no chance, man, to look at me."

Abernathy was of different stuff, deep, dreamy, sly, bemused—one could not detect if he were profoundly melancholy, or abominably hung over. He spoke in a measured slow basso, slow almost beyond measure, operatic in a

echoes, but everything he said sounded like *recitatif* for he
seemed to read his statement with more attention for the
music of the language than the significance of the words.
"If the Republican Party can afford this lavish convention,
and the Administration can spend billions of dollars in a
disastrous war, and America can subsidize unproductive
farms and prosperous industries, surely we can meet the
modest demands of the Poor People's Campaign," he read,
and the logic was powerful, the demands well nailed to the
mast, but his voice lingered on "lavish" as if he were in-
trigued with the relation of sounds to palpable luxuries he
had known and glimpsed, "disastrous" appealed to him for
its sibilants as though he were watching some scythe of
wind across a field, so "subsidize" was a run of the voice
up and down three steps, and "unproductive" hung like the
echo of a stalactite. He was a man from Mars absolutely
fascinated with the resonance of earthly sound.

He had begun by apologizing to the Press for being late,
and had said this in so deep and gracious a voice that pools
of irritability were swabbed up immediately, but then he
trod over this first good move immediately by saying, "Of
course, I understand much of the convention is running
behind schedule." The one indisputable virtue of the convention hitherto had been the promptitude of each event
—how casual and complacent, how irresponsibly attracted
to massacre! that he must issue the one accusation all
courts would find unjustified.

But the reporter was soon caught up in trying to form
an opinion of Abernathy. He was no equal, it was unhappily true to see, of Martin Luther King. The reporter had
met that eminent just once: King in a living room had a
sweet attentive gravity which endeared him to most, for he
listened carefully, and was responsive when he spoke. He
had the presence of a man who would deal with complexity
by absorbing its mood, and so solve its contradiction by
living with it, an abstract way of saying that he comprehended issues by the people who embodied them, and so
gave off a sense of social comfort with his attendance in a
room. Abernathy had no such comfort. A plump, badgered,
perhaps bewildered man, full of obvious prides and scars
and wounds, one could not tell if he were in part charlatan,
mountebank, or merely elevated to monumental responsibility too early. But his presence gave small comfort be-

cause he was never in focus. One did not know if he were strong or weak, powerfully vibrant and containing himself, or drenched in basso profundos of gloom. "Poor people," he intoned, with his disembodied presentation, "no longer will be unseen, unheard, and unrepresented. We are here to dramatize the *plight* of poor people . . ."—his voice went off on a flight of reverberation along the hard "i" of plight. Later, he asked for "control by all people of their own local communities and their own personal destinies," incontestable as a democratic demand, but no fire in the voice, no power to stir, more an intimation of gloom in the caverns of his enriched tone as if he must push upon a wagon which would never mount his hill, so he went off again on "communities"—the hard "u" concealed certain new mysteries of the larynx—and relations to re*mune*ration. He ended by saying, "Part of our Mule Train will be here on Miami Beach in front of this hotel and Convention Hall to dramatize *poverty*"—he stated the word as if it were the name of a small town—"in this beautiful city of luxury."

In the questioning, he was better. Asked if he considered Ronald Reagan a friend of the Blacks, Abernathy smiled slowly and said with ministerial bonhomie, "Well, he may have *some* friends. . . ." Queried about the failure of the Poor People's March on Washington, he offered a stern defense, spoke of how every campaign of the Southern Christian Leadership Conference had been described as a failure, an obvious cuff at those who had once described King's work as failure, and then for a moment he rose above the dull unhappy scandals of Resurrection City, the mess, the breakdowns of sanitation, the hoodlumism, and the accusations by his own that some had lived in hotels while they had been squalid in tents, and spoke of what had been gained, funds pried loose from the government "to the tune of some many millions," he said in his musical voice, and named the figure, more than 200 million, and the fact of the continuation of the Poor People's Campaign, and the sense came again of the painful drudgery of the day to day, the mulish demands of the operation, the gloom of vast responsibility and tools and aids and lieutenants he could count on even less than himself, and the reporter, as though washed in bowls of his own bile, was contrite a degree and went off to have lunch when the conference was done, a little weary of confronting the mystery of his own good or ill motive.

Of course, having lunch, the reporter, to his professional shame, had not the wit to go looking for it, so here is a quotation from Thomas A. Johnson of *The New York Times* concerning the immediate aftermath of Abernathy's appearance:

> When the news conference ended about 12:30 P.M., 65 members of the Poor People's Campaign, dressed in straw hats and blue work shirts, entered the lobby of the Fontainebleau Hotel.
>
> With raised fists, they greeted Mr. Abernathy with shouts of "Soul Power! Soul Power!"
>
> Convention delegates, few of whom are Negroes, crowded around. In the background, two white girls dressed in red and blue tights, paraded through the hall singing "When Ronnie Reagan comes marching in," to the tune of "When the saints come marching in."
>
> The Negro demonstrators would not be interrupted, however.
>
> Thirteen-year-old James Metcalf of Marks, Miss., wearing an army jungle fatigue jacket that came down to his knees led the group in a chant.
>
> "I may be black," he shouted.
>
> "But I am somebody," the demonstrators responded.
>
> "I may be poor."
>
> "But I am somebody."
>
> "I may be hungry."
>
> "But I am somebody."

It was a confrontation the reporter should not have missed. Were the Reagan girls livid or triumphant? Were the Negro demonstrators dignified or raucous or self-satisfied? It was a good story but the *Times* was not ready to encourage its reporters in the thought that there is no history without nuance.

12

After lunch, in a belated attempt to catch up with the Governor of California and the direction of his campaign, the reporter had gone up to one of the top floors of the Deauville where Mrs. Reagan was scheduled to have a conference at 2:30 P.M., indeed the listing in the National Committee News had stated that the Press was requested to be present by 2:15, but embarrassment prevailed in the high headquarters of the Deauville, for Mrs. Regan was not there and could not be found: the word given out was that she had not been informed. The inevitable deduction was that no one in his headquarters had read the Schedule for the day, and the Press was disassembled with apologies by an attractive corn-fed blonde young lady possessing a piggie of a turned-up nose and the delicate beginning of a double chin. Her slimness of figure suggested all disciplines of diet. The young lady had been sufficiently attractive for the Press to forgive much, but a few of the more European journalists were forced to wonder if the most proficient of performances had been presented here by representatives of the man who cried out, "What is obviously needed is not *more* government, but better government. . . ."

At any rate it was time to catch up with Nixon again. It was not that Nixon's activities attracted the reporter's hoarded passion, it was more that there was little else which puzzled him. If he had been more of a reporter (or less of one) he would have known that the Reagan forces were pushing an all-out attack to pry, convert, cozen, and steal Southern delegates from Nixon, and that the Nixon forces were responding with a counter-offensive which would yet implicate their choice of Vice President, but the reporter worked like a General who was far from the front —if he could not hear the sound of cannon, he assumed the battle was never high. Nothing could have convinced him on this particular intolerably humid afternoon that Nixon's forces were in difficulty, and perhaps he was right, perhaps the lack of any echo of such strife in the lobbies of the Deauville or the Hilton was true sign of the issue, and the long shadows of history would repeat that the verdict was never in doubt.

The reporter was off at any rate to witness the reception for delegates in the same American Scene of the Hilton where Nixon had had his press conference early that morning, and if one was interested in the science of comparative political receptions, the beginning of all such study was here. As many as eight thousand people had ganged through the aisles and banquet rooms and exits of the Americana when Rockefeller had had his party, and that, it may be remembered, was a bash where the glamour was thrown at a man with the cole slaw, and the bottom of every glass the bartender handled was wet, the caviar on the buffet table crawled along the cloth and plopped to the floor. Here in the comparative stateliness of the Hilton— only God could save this mark!—not twenty-two hours later, the Nixon forces were showing how a reception for Republican delegates should be run. If a thousand men and women were waiting outside, jammed in the lobby and the approaches to the stairs, and if the resultant theater-line, six and eight people thick, inched up the stairs at a discouraging slow rate, there was consolation at the top for they were let through a narrow door, two by two, and there advanced behind a cord which ran around a third of the circular curve of the room to move forward at last onto a small dais where Mr. and Mrs. Nixon were receiving, there to be greeted individually by each of them with particular attention, and on from that eminence to the center of the room where a bar was ready to give a drink and food to be picked up from a buffet table, turkey, ham, a conventional buffet, a string orchestra.

Perhaps two thousand people went through in the hours from three to six, probably it was less, for Nixon spent five or ten or fifteen seconds with each delegate or couple who passed by. Perhaps the invitations had been restricted to those delegates who would vote for him or leaned toward his candidacy. No matter how, there were not too many to handle, just the largest number consonant with the problem which was: how to convert a mass of delegates and wives and children back to that sense of importance with which they had left their hometown.

Nixon knew how to do it. Here was Nixon at his very best. He had not spent those eight years in harness, highest flunky in the land, aide-de-camp to a five-star General, now President, who had been given such service in his

NATO days that no new servant could ever please him, yes, Nixon had not put in his apprenticeship as spiritual butler to the Number One representative of the High Beloved here on earth, without learning how to handle a Republican line of delegates by ones and twos.

This was no line like the wealthy Republicans at the Gala, this was more a pilgrimage of minor delegates, sometimes not even known so well in their own small city, a parade of wives and children and men who owned hardware stories or were druggists, or first teller in the bank, proprietor of a haberdashery or principal of a small town high school, local lawyer, retired doctor, a widow on tidy income, her minister and fellow-delegate, minor executives from minor corporations, men who owned their farms, an occasional rotund state party hack with a rubbery look, editor of a small-town paper, professor from Baptist teachers' college, high school librarian, young political aspirant, young salesman—the stable and the established, the middle-aged and the old, a sprinkling of the young, the small towns and the quiet respectable cities of the Midwest and the Far West and the border states were out to pay their homage to their own true candidate, the representative of their conservative orderly heart, and it was obvious they adored him in a quiet way too deep for applause, it was obvious the Nixons had their following after all in these middle-class neatly-dressed people moving forward in circumscribed steps, constrained, not cognizant of their bodies, decent respectables who also had spent their life in service and now wanted to have a moment near the man who had all of their vote, and so could arouse their happiness, for the happiness of the Wasp was in his moment of veneration, and they had veneration for Nixon, heir of Old Ike—center of happy memory and better days—they venerated Nixon for his service to Eisenhower, and his comeback now—it was his comeback which had made him a hero in their eyes, for America is the land which worships the Great Comeback, and so he was Tricky Dick to them no more, but the finest gentleman in the land; they were proud to say hello.

The Nixons talked to each one in turn. The candidate was first on the receiving line and then his wife, each taking the arm or shaking the hand of the delegate before them and saying a few words, sometimes peering at the name

on the delegate's badge, more often recognizing the face
from some all-but-forgotten banquet or fund-raiser in Platte,
or Akron, or Evansville, Chillicothe, or Iowa City; in Columbia, South Carolina, and Columbia, Mo.; in Boulder
or Fort Collins; in Fayetteville, Arkansas, Fayetteville,
North Carolina; in Harrisburg and Keene and Spokane and
Fort Lauderdale and Raleigh and Butte—yes, Nixon had
travelled the creeping vine of small-town Republicanism,
he had won delegates over these last two years by ones and
twos, votes pulled in by the expenditure of a half hour here,
an hour there, in conversations which must have wandered
so far as the burial specifications of Aunt Matty in her
will, and the story of the family stock, he had worked
among the despised nuts and bolts of the delegates' hearts,
and it showed up here in the skill and the pleasure with
which he greeted each separate delegate, the separate
moves of his hands upon them, for some he touched by
the elbow, others patted on the back, some he waved on to
his wife with a personal word, never repeating the sequence,
fresh for each new delegate. He still did not move with any
happiness in his body, the gestures still came in such injunctions from the head as: "Grab this old boy by the elbow,"
but he was obviously happy here, it was one of the things
in the world which he could do best, he could be gracious
with his own people, and Pat Nixon backed him up, con-
centrating on the wives and children, also skillful, the tense
forbidding face of her youth (where rectitude, ambition,
and lack of charity had been etched like the grimace of an
addict into every line of the ferocious clenched bite of her
jaw) had eased now somewhat; she was almost attractive,
as if the rigid muscle of the American woman's mind at its
worst had relaxed—she looked near to mellow: as a husband and wife they had taken the long road back together,
somewhere in the abyss she must have forgiven him for
"America can't stand pat."

And the reporter had an insight that perhaps it was possible the Nixons had grown up last of all. Young ambitious
couple, electrified by sudden eminence, and for eight years
slave to eminence, false in every move—for how could any
young couple so extravagantly advanced ever feel true to
themselves (or even perhaps cognizant that there might
be a psychic condition one could term *the true*) how was
one ever to acquire such a knowledge when one's life was

served as a creature of policies, a servant of great men and empty men, a victim of the very power one's ambition had provided. Nixon had entered American life as half a man, but his position had been so high, the power of the half man had been so enormous that he could never begin to recognize until he fell, that he was incomplete. Nor Mrs. Nixon.

As the string orchestra near them played away—five violins (four male musicians and a lady) plus one guitar, one accordion, one bass—as this elderly band continued to pick out the kind of sweet popular string music which is usually background for movie scenes in inexpensive Brighton hotels where elderly retired India colonels brood through dinner, as the afternoon and the orchestra continued and the slow procession of the delegates, so a sense came at last to the reporter of how Nixon must see his mission. There was a modesty among these delegates today, they were the center of the nation, but they were chastened in their pride—these same doctors and small-town lawyers, or men not so unlike them, had had their manic dreams of restoring order to America with the injunction and the lash just four years ago. Then the nation had lived in their mind like the sure strong son of their loins, and they had been ready to take the fight anywhere, to Vietnam, to China, into the Black ghettoes, they had been all for showing the world and some minorities in America where the real grapes of wrath were stored. But the last four years had exploded a few of their secret policies, and they were bewildered now. No matter what excuse was given that there might have been better ways to wage the war, the Wasp had built his nest with statistics, and the figures on the Vietnam war were badly wrong. How could the nation fail to win when its strength was as five to one, unless God had decided that America was not just?—righteousness had taken a cruel crack on the bridge of its marble brow. Much else was wrong, the youth, the Negro, the dollar, the air pollution and river pollution, the pornography, the streets—the Wasps were now a chastened crew. It was probable the Presidency would soon be theirs again, but the nation was profoundly divided, nightmares loomed—for the first time in their existence, the Wasps were modest about power. They were not certain they would know what to do with it.

What a vision must exist then now in Nixon, what a

dream to save the land. Yes, the reporter would offer him this charity—the man had become sincere. All evidence spoke for that. How could there be, after all, a greater passion in a man like Nixon, so universally half-despised, than to show the center of history itself that he was not without greatness. What a dream for such a man! To cleanse the gangrenous wounds of a great power, to restore sanity to the psychopathic fevers of the day, to deny the excessive demand, and nourish the real need, to bring a balance to the war of claims, weed the garden of tradition, and show a fine nose for what was splendid in the new, serve as the great educator who might introduce each warring half of the nation to the other, and bring back the faith of other nations to a great nation in adventurous harmony with itself —yes, the dream could be magnificent enough for any world leader; if the reporter did not think that Nixon, poor Nixon, was very likely to flesh such a dream, still he did not know that the attempt should be denied. It was possible, even likely, even necessary, that the Wasp must enter the center of our history again. They had been a damned minority for too long, a huge indigestible boulder in the voluminous ruminating government gut of every cow-like Democratic administration, an insane Republican minority with vast powers of negation and control, a minority who ran the economy, and half the finances of the world, and all too much of the internal affairs of four or five continents, and the Pentagon, and the technology of the land, and most of the secret police, and nearly every policeman in every small town, and yet finally they did not run the land, they did not comprehend it, the country was loose from them, ahead of them, the life style of the country kept denying their effort, the lives of the best Americans kept accelerating out of their reach. They were the most powerful force in America, and yet they were a psychic island. If they did not find a bridge, they could only grow more insane each year, like a rich nobleman in an empty castle chasing elves and ogres with his stick. They had every power but the one they needed—which was to attach their philosophy to history: the druggist and the president of the steel corporation must finally learn if they were both pushing on the same wheel. Denied the center of political power, the corporation and the small town had remained ideologically married for decades; only by wielding the power could they discover which concepts in conservative philosophy were viable, and what parts were mad. One could predict: their budgeting would prove insane, their righteousness would prove insane, their love for order and clear-thinking would be twisted through many a wry neck, the intellectual foundations of their anti-Communism would split into its separate parts. And the small-town faith in small free enterprise would run smash into the corporate juggernauts of technology land; their love of polite culture would collide with the mad aesthetics of the new America; their livid passion for military superiority would smash its nose on the impossibility of having such superiority without more government spending; their love of nature would have to take up arms against the despoiling foe, themselves, their own greed, their own big business. Yes, perhaps the Wasp had to come to power in order that he grow up, in order that he take the old primitive root of his life-giving philosophy—which required every man to go through battles, if the world would live, and every woman to bear a child—yes, take that root off the high attic shelf of some Prudie Parsley of a witch-ancestor, and plant it in the smashed glass and burned brick of the twentieth century's junkyard: see from that what might grow in the arbors of modern anomaly. Of course, Republicans might yet prove frightening, and were much, if not three-quarters, to blame for every ill in sight, they did not deserve the Presidency, never, and yet if democracy was the free and fair play of human forces then perhaps the Wasp must now hold the game in his direction for a time. The Left was not ready, the Left was years away from a vision sufficiently complex to give life to the land, the Left had not yet learned to talk across the rugged individualism of the more rugged in America, the Left was still too full of kicks and pot and the freakings of sodium amytol and orgy, the howls of electronics and LSD. The Left could also find room to grow up. If the Left had to live through a species of political exile for four or eight or twelve good years, it might even be right. They might be forced to study what was alive in the conservative dream. For certain the world could not be saved by technology or government or genetics, and much of the Left had that still to learn.

So the reporter stood in the center of the American Scene—how the little dramas of America, like birds, seemed

to find themselves always in the right nest—and realized
he was going through no more than the rearrangement of
some intellectual luggage (which indeed every good citizen
might be supposed to perform) during these worthy operations of the democratic soul when getting ready to vote.

13

The force of his proposition, however, was there to taunt
him early the following day, so early as two in the morning.
He had begun to drink that evening for the first time in
several days. He did not like to drink too much when he
was working, but the Wednesday session, nominating day,
would not begin until five in the afternoon tomorrow, and
it would be a long night, seven or nine or ten hours long,
and at the end, Nixon all nominated, he did not believe
that would be cause sufficient for him to celebrate—besides,
it might be too late. Besides, he wanted to drink. Equal to
the high contrast a stain can give to a microscope slide, was
the clarity his dear booze sometimes offered a revery, and
he had the luck to finish downing his drinks at Joe the
Bartender's in the Hilton Plaza, a large and this night rollick-
ing cellar bar where the Nixon people came to celebrate.
The kids were out, the Young Republicans and the YAF
(the Youth for American Freedom), a table or two of
Southern delegates, even a table of Rockefeller Republicans
he knew, so it was not the political make-up of the audience so much as the mood, a mood he could have found
as easily in a dozen bars he knew in New York on almost
any night, and a thousand there must have been in America, a thousand at least, maybe ten thousand. It was at first
no more than a loud raucousness of the kind one could
hear in many a bar with college drinkers, or skiers, or surfers, intricate interlocked songs with nonsense syllables and
barnyard howls—Old Macdonald is perhaps the first of
these songs—but the songs were more sophisticated, varia-

tions with fraternity house riffs, and jouncing repetitions, which could twist you off the beat. The band had three singers, girls in electric blue and electric green and electric pink dresses, not miniskirts so much as little girl dresses, girls a cross between cheerleaders, swingers, and Nixon-ettes—that hard healthy look in the blank and handsome face which spoke of action each night and low tolerance for being bored—they sang with a cornucopia of old-fashioned cutes, hands on hips, dipping at the knees, old-fashioned break into two bars of tap dance, more they could not fake, arms around each other's waist in four bars of can-can, they did solos, made faces, stuck their hips akimbo, and a virtuoso on the trombone played loud gut-bucket backings, cluckings and cryings, trombone imitating unrest in the barnyard, neighings and bleatings in the air-conditioned cool, the trombonist big and fat with a huge black sack of a shirt on which was the legend TUBA 24, and there was a tuba player as well, also virtuoso, top hat in tricolor, Uncle Sam with black coat, black pants. Two banjos in black shirts, red and blue striped pants, were there to whang away, one of the girls played a drum, a red drum, there was a rooty-toot to the barnyard, and rebel yells from the crowd all next to broken eggs and splats, some stew of loutishness, red-eyed beer drinkers pig-faced in the dark, and the hump on the back of their neck begins to grow fat, beef on beef, pig on pig, primeval stirrings, secret glee, fun and games are mounting and vomit washed in blood, it was oom-pah, oom-pah and upsy daisy weight lifters dancing, merry and raw, beer hall, beer hall, bleat of a cow, snort of a pig, oomps went the tuba and yes, the boar of old Europe was not dead, the shade had come to America, America it was.

There was slyness in the air, and patience, confidence of the win—a mood was building which could rise to a wave: if there was nihilism on the Left, there were dreams of extermination on the Right. Technology land had pushed cancer into every pore, so now the cure for cancer was dismemberment of order, all gouging of justice. There would be talk of new order before too long.

Nixon might have his dream to unify the land, but he would yet have to stare, face to face, into the power of his own Right Wing, soon to rise on the wave of these beer-hall bleats, the worst of the Wasp, all bull in his muscles, all murder in his neck—would Nixon have the stance to meet them? Or would he fall captive to the madmen in the pits of his own party, those madmen absent from Miami, those madmen concealed this week? The convention had been peaceful, too peaceful by far.

At large on the ocean, would people yet pray for Nixon and wish him strength as once they had wished strength to old Hindenburg and Dollfuss and Schuschnigg and Von Papen? Oom-pah went the tuba, starts! went the horn. Blood and shit might soon be flying like the red and brown of a *verboten* flag. It had had black in it as well. For death perhaps. Areas of white for purity. They would talk yet of purity. They always did. And shave the shorn. God give strength to Richard Nixon, and a nose for the real news. Oom-pah went the tuba, *farts* went the horn.

14

On Wednesday night Alabama ceded to California, and Reagan was first to be in nomination. Ivy Baker Priest made the speech, Ivy Baker Priest Stevens was her name now, a handsome woman who had been Treasurer of the United States in Eisenhower's cabinet, and then an assistant to Reagan. She had a dual personality. She was a wretched speaker with the parched nasal mean stingy acid driving tones of a typical Republican lady speaker: "A man who will confront the radicals on our campuses and the looters on our streets and say, 'The laws will be obeyed.' " It was a relief when her nasalities began to drive up the hill and one knew the mention of Reagan's name was near. "A man to match our mountains and our plains, a man steeped in the glorious traditions of the past, a man with a vision of the unlimited possibilities of a new era. Yes, Destiny has found the man." A minute later she was done, and a fairly large demonstration went to work. It was to prove milder and less impressive than the Rockefeller and Nixon break-outs, but it was at least notable for a sight of the opposite side of the lady's personality. She now looked confident, enthusiastic, round, sexy, warm, and gloriously vital, the best blond housemother you could ever see, waving the fraternity boys around the bend as they sang "Dixie" and "California, Here I Come," clapping her hands in absolute delight at signs like "I'm gone on Ron," as if that were absolutely the most attractive thing she'd ever seen, then jazzed it like a cheerleader beating her palms and smiling, smiling at the sight of each new but familiar crew-cut face who had gotten up to whoop and toot it through the aisles for Ronnie. There were five cages of balloons overhead, and Reagan got one of them, the balloons came down in a fast cascade —each one blessed with a drop of water within so as to tend to plummet rather than tend to float—and they came down almost as fast as foam rubber pillows and were detonated with lighted cigarettes and stomping feet thus immediately that a string of firecrackers could have gone off.

When that was done, a monumental sense of tedium overtook the night. Hickel of Alaska and Winthrop Rockefeller of Arkansas were put in as favorite sons, the latter with two seconding speeches and an eight-minute demonstration—he was conceivably giving nothing to his brother —Romney used all of forty minutes, Nelson Rockefeller's band boosting his demonstration as Romney troops were later to boost Rockefeller's. Senator Carlson of Kansas was named as favorite son, then Hiram Fong of Hawaii. It was after nine before Governor Shafer of Pennsylvania stood up to put Nelson Rockefeller on the lists. More than two and a half hours had elapsed between the end of Reagan's presentation and the beginning of Rocky's. Reporters had left the convention hall, and were huddled backstage in places like the Railroad Lounge where free sandwiches and beer were available, and everybody was concerned with the most attractive proposition of the night—that if they were all to go to their hotels, check out, and catch a plane, they could be at their homes before nominations were done and balloting had begun. They could watch it on television, which was the real gloom of the occasion. The convention had demonstrated that no reporter could keep up any longer with the event unless checking in periodically with the tube; the politicians, themselves, rushed forward to TV men, and shouldered note-pads aside. During this lull, therefore, one bitter reporter, a big heavy Southern boy with horn-rimmed glasses, delivered the remark of the evening. Sipping beer and glumly munching his sandwich (which held an inch of paper-dry turkey) he said, "Yessir, the only thing which could liven up this convention is if Ike was to croak to-night." So the respect journalists had been obliged to pay over the years could be tolerated now only by the flensing knives of the club.

Shafer put Rockefeller in ". . . because he is in tune. The people, young and old, rich and poor, Black and white, have responded to him. He has never lost an election. . . . Ladies and gentlemen, we should nominate Nelson Rocke-feller because he is the Republican who can most surely win. . . ." It was an inept speech—Rocky's name was men-tioned seven times before the signal was given to the dele-gates, and tension was dissipated. It didn't matter. Everyone knew that Rockefeller would have an enormous demon-stration and that it would not matter. The day when dem-onstrations could turn a convention were gone. The demonstrators knew they would be chided in newspaper editorials the following day, and therefore were sheepish in the very middle of their stomping and their jigging. Soon they would hold conventions in TV studios.

Then came Spiro Agnew for Nixon. If he had not been selected for Vice President next day, his speech would have gone unnoticed and unremarked—"It is my privilege to place in nomination for the office of President of the United States the one man whom history has so clearly thrust forward, the one whom all America will recognize as a man whose time has come, the man for 1968, the Honor-able. . . ."

Nixon's demonstration was about equal to Rockefeller's. Hordes of noise, two cages of balloons, machine-gun drum-fire as they went out—no lift in the audience, no real lift. Nothing this night could begin to recall that sense of bar-barians about a campfire and the ecstasy of going to war which Barry Goldwater had aroused in '64.

Still the demonstrations gave another image of the three candidacies: Reagan's men had straight hair cropped short, soldiers and state troopers for Ronnie; so far as Republi-cans were swingers, so swingers marched with Rocky; and for Nixon—the mood on the floor was like the revel in the main office of a corporation when the Christmas Party is high.

More nominations. Harold Stassen for the seventh time. Senator Case of New Jersey, Governor Rhodes of Ohio, Senator Thurmond who immediately withdrew for Nixon. At 1:07 A.M., eight hours and seven minutes after the convention had opened for nomination, it was closed, and over the floor rested the knowledge that nothing had happened tonight. It had been Nixon on the first ballot from the beginning, and it was Nixon at the end. By the time Alabama, the first state, voted, 14 for Nixon, 12 for Reagan, the next to last doubt was dispelled, for *The New York Times* on Sunday had estimated only 9 solid for Nixon. When Florida came in with 32 out of 34, and Georgia with 21 where only 14 had seemed likely a few days before, there was no need to worry the issue. Wisconsin with 30 votes for Nixon carried it over—the total was 692. The rest had gone: Rockefeller 277, Reagan 182, Rhodes 55, Romney 50, Case 22, Carlson 20, W. Rockefeller 18, Fong 14, Stassen 2, Lindsay 1.

Filing out of the hall, there was the opportunity to see Nixon on television. Where in 1960 he had said, "All I am I owe to my mother and father, my family and my church . . ." he was considerably more of the professional strategist tonight as he spoke of his efforts to win the nomination while unifying the party. "You see," he said to the cameras, "the beauty of our contest this year was that we won the nomination in a way designed to win the election. We didn't make the mistake of breaking up the California delegation or breaking up the Ohio delegation or raiding the Michigan delegation. And in the State of New York also we respected the Rockefeller position, being the candidate for New York. And I think this will pay off in November. We're going to have a united party. Sure we've had a real fight . . . but we have won it in a way that we're going into the final campaign united." He was lucid, he was convincing, he said he felt perfectly "free" to choose his Vice President. "I won the nomination without having to pay any price, making any deal with any candidate or any individuals representing a candidate. . . . I [will] meet with delegates from all over the country . . . Southern delegates, the Northern delegates, the Midwestern delegates and the Western delegates. But I will make the decision based on my best judgment as to the man that can work best with me, and that will, I think perhaps, if he ever has to do that, serve as President of the United States."

In the old days, he had got his name as Tricky Dick because he gave one impression and acted upon another— later when his language was examined, one could not call him a liar. So he had literally not made any deal with any candidate, but he was stretching the subtle rubber of his own credibility when he claimed he would not have to pay any price. The rest of the night at the Miami Hilton would belong to the South.

15

But let us leave the convention with a look at Reagan. He had come forward immediately after the first ballot was in, and made a move that the nomination be unanimous. Reagan was smiling when he came up for his plea, he looked curiously more happy than he had looked at any point in the convention, as if he were remembering Barry Goldwater's renunciation of the nomination in 1960, and the profitable results which had ensued, or perhaps he was just pleased because the actor in his soul had issued orders that this was the role to play. For years in the movies he had played the good guy and been proud of it. If he didn't get the girl, it was because he was too good a guy to be overwhelmingly attractive. That was all right. He would grit his teeth and get the girl next time out. Since this was conceivably the inner sex drama of half of respectable America, he was wildly popular with Republicans. For a party which prided itself on its common sense, they were curiously, even outrageously, sentimental.

Now as Reagan made his plea for unity, he spoke with a mildness, a lack of charisma, even a simplicity, which was reminiscent of a good middle-aged stock actor's simplicity—well, you know, fellows, the man I'm playing is an intellectual, and of course I have the kind of mind which even gets confused by a finesse in bridge.

They cheered him wildly, and he looked happy, as if something had gone his way. There was much occasion to recollect him on Thursday when Agnew for Vice President was announced; as the story of this selection developed, the reporter was to think of a view of Reagan he had had on Tuesday afternoon after the reception Nixon had given for the delegates in the American Scene.

On Tuesday the reporter had found Reagan at the Di Lido in downtown Miami Beach where the Alabama and Louisiana delegations were housed. In with Louisiana in a caucus, the Governor came out later to give a quick press conference, pleading ignorance of his situation. Listening to him, it was hard to believe he was fifty-seven, two years older than Nixon, for he had a boy's face, no gray in his head—he was reputed to dye his hair—and his make-up (about which one could hear many a whisper) was too excellent, if applied, to be detected.

Still, unlike Nixon, Reagan was altogether at ease with the Press. They had been good to him, they would be good again—he had the confidence of the elected governor of a big state, precisely what Nixon had always lacked; besides, Reagan had long ago incorporated the confidence of an actor who knows he is popular with interviewers. In fact, he had a public manner which was so natural that his discrepancies appeared only slightly surrealistic: at the age of fifty-seven, he had the presence of a man of thirty, the deferential enthusiasm, the bright but dependably unoriginal mind, of a sales manager promoted for his ability over men older than himself. He also had the neatness, and slim economy of move, of a man not massive enough to be President, in the way one might hesitate, let us say, ever to consider a gentleman like Mr. Johnny Carson of television—whatever his fine intelligence—as Chief Executive of a Heavyweight Empire. It was that way with Reagan. He was somehow too light, a lightweight six feet one inch tall—whatever could he do but stick-and-move? Well, he could try to make Generals happy in order to show how heavy he really might be, which gave no heart to consideration of his politics. Besides, darkening shades of the surreal, he had a second personality which was younger than the first, very young, boyish, maybe thirteen or fourteen, freckles, cowlick, I-tripped-on-my-sneaker-lace aw shucks variety of confusion. For back on Tuesday afternoon they had been firing questions at him on the order of how well he was doing at prying delegates loose from Nixon, and he could only say over and over, "I don't know. I just don't know. I've been moving around so quickly talking to so many delegations in caucus that I haven't had time to read a paper."

"Well, what do the delegations say, Governor?"

"Well, I don't know. They listen to me very pleasantly and politely, and then I leave and they discuss what I've said. But I can't tell you if we're gaining. I think we are, but I don't know, I don't know. I honestly don't know, gentlemen," and he broke out into a grin, "I just don't know," exactly like a thirteen year old, as if indeed gentlemen he *really* didn't know, and the Press and the delegates listening laughed with him as if there were no harm in Ronald Reagan, not unless the lightning struck.

But in fact the storm was going on all day Tuesday, delegate-stealing flickering back and forth over all the camps, a nomination on the first ballot no longer secure for Richard Nixon, no longer altogether secure, because Reagan's announcement on Saturday of his switch from being a favorite son of California to an open candidate had meant that a great push was on to pull Southern delegates loose from Nixon in numbers sufficient to stop him on first ballot, then get more delegates loose on second ballot to forestall Nixon's strength among the favorite sons. It was a strategy which reasoned as follows: if Nixon could be stopped on the first two ballots, there was little which could keep the overwhelming majority of delegate votes in Alabama, Arizona, California, Florida, Georgia, Idaho, Louisiana, Mississippi, Montana, Nebraska, North Carolina, Oklahoma, South Carolina, South Dakota, Tennessee, Texas and Virginia away from support of Reagan and a possible total of close to 500. Potentially it was a powerful argument, doubly powerful because Reagan was the favorite of the South, and the reporter talking to a leader of the Louisiana caucus heard him say in courtly tones to a delegate, "It breaks my heart that we can't get behind a fine man like Governor Reagan, but Mr. Nixon is deserving of our choice, and he must receive it." Which was a splendid way to talk of a deal.

There were forces out in full panoply to hold Reagan down. Senator Strom Thurmond of South Carolina who ran for President on the Dixiecrat ticket in 1948, now defected from the Democrats and become a Republican was the first committed to Nixon. The wise money would emphasize he had nowhere to go if Nixon did not make it, because he could not return to the Democrats, was too old to go to the third party, and had to be without his new party if Rockefeller won. Thurmond's point of reasoning with Southern delegates was that Nixon was the best conservative they could get and still win, and he had obtained assurances from Nixon that no Vice-Presidential candidate intolerable to the South would be selected. All that long afternoon while Nixon shook hands with delegates and radiated serenity, the nomination was conceivably in doubt and hung for a few hours on the efforts of Thurmond and Goldwater and Tower and O'Donnell of Texas, and a number of other Southern state chairmen and was probably won on the quiet argument that if the South did not hold firm for Nixon, he might still win with Ohio and Michigan on the second ballot. Then the South would have nothing at all, indeed the South would have driven Nixon to the left.

That the South did hold for Nixon is why perhaps Reagan may have sounded confused. He must have been receiving the double affection of delegates that day who liked him and yet would not be ready to give him their vote, therefore loved him twice. Yet in tangible return, he could not count the gains. Reports conflicted on his team —as indeed they would—he did not know, he *really* did not know.

Nor did the reporter. Tuesday afternoon, watching Nixon with the delegations he had no sense the nomination was in difficulty, or no more sense than the knowledge absorbed from quick conversation with a Louisiana delegate that Lindsay would not be nominated for Vice President since Nixon had promised as much. It came as no pleasure, but no surprise. The Great Unifier would obviously begin by unifying the South. He could move to the Blacks only when they had been chastened by the absence of any remaining relation to power, which is to say, only after his election. It was a strategy which could work, or fail. If it failed, civil war and a police state were near. But finally he had no choice. The iron demand when one would unify a schism is to strengthen the near side first, since one can always offer less to the far side yet hold them—unless they are indeed ready to revolt—with the consolation they are not being entirely forgotten. Nixon could no more desert the South than would Rockefeller, if he had won, have been able to turn his back on Harlem. The reporter was beginning to recognize for the first time that profound theses to the side, there might be cloud-banks of depression in the way of getting up on election day to cast a vote.

16

For these reasons, the reporter had decided by Thursday morning that Nixon could only nominate a moderate from the South or a conservative from the North. No other arrangement would mollify the South. So he left for home with the confidence that Senator Howard Baker of Tennessee would be the nominee and was only mildly surprised when it went to Agnew. But that night covering the convention before his television set in his own home, he realized he had missed the most exciting night of the convention, at least on the floor, and was able to console himself only with the sad knowledge that he could cover it better on television than if he had been there. Of course he was to find out later that it was an evening which would end in the blackest depression, for many were convinced that Nixon had made a powerful error in picking a man as unknown as Agnew.

No one seemed pleased but Nixon. It occurred to the reporter on reflection that Nixon had not made the worst of moves for himself. The Vice-Presidential nominee was on the surface a man without large appeal and had been the first to say, "I am quite aware that Spiro Agnew is not a household name." Still he was reasonable on television, a big man, soft-spoken and alert. He would not be independent—a necessity to Nixon—he would be loyal, exorbitantly loyal as Nixon had once been exorbitantly loyal to Eisenhower, for there was no choice. So Agnew would give Nixon nourishment, and spare the cankers of considering that the Vice President was more popular than himself. If Nixon was growing, he was not yet so large as Father Christmas himself. Best of all, he would have no ideological balance to maintain, he could work on his own, scrambling broken-field from Right to Left and back again, no ideologue running with him to halt and complain.

The liberal press was quick to declare that Nixon had lost the election with that one move, and indeed he could not hide the fact that Thurmond and other Southerners had eliminated Lindsay, Percy and Hatfield. Yet Nixon had fulfilled his Southern debts with a minimum of—from his point of view—damage to himself, and Nixon would never have to sleep with the particular terror that some conceivable Left-wing maniac, finding the Vice President more tolerable than himself would hunt for a silver bullet . . . Nixon, on television, seemed cheerful with his choice. Of course, others were not.

Seen from the Americana on television, Rockefeller looked like he had had a few life-giving drinks in the middle of the afternoon. Sounding more than ever congruent to Spencer Tracy in the middle of new-found wounds, Rockefeller said huskily, "I have no comment on Mr. Agnew. I'm going for a swim. I need some sun, and I'm going for a swim."

"They say," said the interviewer, "that Mr. Nixon saw a hundred leading Republicans before making his choice."

"I guess," said Rocky, "that makes me, fella, the hundred and first."

But Nixon would seek to ride it out. As he came to Convention Hall for his acceptance speech, he was high with success and happy, cautious with reporters about Agnew, but benign about the attempt of the rebel moderates to run Romney in protest. Romney had gone down 186 votes to 1,128, the bitterness of being passed over for a man so inconsequential as Agnew all visible in the red of his face, the gray-green glow of his eyes, but Nixon had made a point of calling up Romney on his entrance so that he approached the podium with the Governor of Michigan on his arm. "It was good to have a floor fight," he told the reporters, "a healthy thing for the party, it helped to clear the air. We'll be more united afterward." Nixon was obviously tense with waiting to begin his speech, he was obviously going to make every effort to deliver the greatest speech of his life.

His ovation on introduction was large but in no way frantic, it was the formal massing of a large sound which the convention would give to its nominee, but for him up on the podium, it had to sound very good because it lasted for minutes, time for him to call up his wife and children, and Spiro Agnew and his wife and two of his girls (the third girl was a child, and his son was in Vietnam) there was time for Nixon to stand there alone and wave his hands on high and grin like a winner, time for him to canter over to the side of the speaker's platform and receive a kiss from the starchy old lady who had read the roll call of the states in the balloting last night and tonight, time for him to grin and grin again, time for him to reveal the austere moves of his decorum and the little mincing gestures distantly reminiscent of a certain dictator long gone. The enigma of the night in Joe the Bartender's returned—was Nixon a man who would prove strong enough, or was one to fear his weaknesses would make him prove too strong?

He began at last by waving the audience to silence, begging them for silence with smiles and laughter. Then he began the speech he had worked on for weeks, his major effort, written in large part it could be assumed by himself, for the flavor of the man, old and new, old tricks and new dreams, stale sentiment and hints of bright new thought were all in it, he was to touch every base and he played a game which had twenty bases. He began by talking of sixteen years ago when he stood "before this convention to accept your nomination as the running mate of one of the greatest Americans of our time or anytime—Dwight D. Eisenhower. . . ." Tonight, Ike was critically ill in Walter Reed Hospital. "There is nothing that would lift him more than for us to win in November. And I say, let us win this one for Ike."

He had probably expected a roar which would shiver the Secret Service men on the catwalks high above the hall, but the cheer was empty. Ike had been used and re-used and used again, Ike was the retread on the bandwagon, and echoes sour as the smell of a broken mood came in at the thought of Pat O'Brien saying, "Let's win this one for the Gipper," yes, Old Nixon had popped up first, copping his plea. Unhappy as old Scratch was New Nixon with Old Nixon, for the line surprisingly had not been delivered well. Where Old Nixon would have dropped the fly right on the yawping hollering mouths of a cheering multitude of Republicans conditioned like fish, New Nixon blew the cast, some unconscious embarrassment jerking the line. He had gotten smarter than his habits.

The speech went on. He talked of sending the power of government back from Washington to the states and the cities, he congratulated Rockefeller and Reagan and Romney for their hard fight, and knew they would fight even harder for the win in November. "A party that can unite itself will unite America," he said, and it was possible the remark was not without its truth, but he was still squeezed into the hard sell; one could all but hear the mother of that remark, "A family which prays together, stays together."

If he had been wooing old Republicans up to now with sure-fire vulcanized one-line zingers, he could hardly be unaware that millions of Independents, some of them young, were also watching. Therefore, he shifted over to the electorate at large. "As we look at America we see cities enveloped in smoke and flame. We hear sirens in the night. We see Americans dying on distant battlefields abroad. We see Americans hating each other, fighting each other, killing each other at home. . . . Did we come all this way for this? . . . die in Normandy and Korea and Valley Forge for this? Listen to the answers. . . ." And his voice had converted to the high dramatic-operatic of a radio actor's voice circa 1939 in a Norman Corwin play; we hear: ". . . the quiet voice in the tumult and the shouting . . . voice of the great majority of Americans, the forgotten Americans—the non-shouters; the non-demonstrators. They are not racists or sick; they're not guilty of the crime that plagues the land; they are Black, they are white"—and he pushed on with the forgotten Americans who worked in factories, ran businesses, served in government, were soldiers who died. "They give drive to the spirit of America . . . life to the American dream . . .

steel to the backbone of America . . . good people . . .
decent people . . . work and save . . ." (and watch their
television sets) "pay their taxes and they care . . . they
know this country will not be a good place for any of us
to live in unless it's a good place for all of us to live in."

He proceeded to attack the leaders who had wasted the
substance and the pride of America, mismanaged the wars,
and the economy and the city ". . . the time has come
for . . . complete reappraisal of America's policies in
every section of the world." That was incontestable. "I
pledge to you tonight . . . to bring an honorable end to
the war in Vietnam."

Now, whether he would underline it so, or not, Nixon
was calling for an end to Henry Luce's American Century.
"There are 200 million Americans and there are two bil-
lion people that live in the free world, and I say the time
has come for other nations . . . to bear their fair share."
Cheers. The old parched throats of Republican isolationism
gave an atrophied cheer. "To the leaders of the Communist
world, we say . . . the time has come for an era of negotiations"—now protecting his flank—"we shall always
negotiate from strength and never from weakness." More
cheers. Perfunctory cheers. But later: "We extend the hand
of friendship to all people. To the Russian people. To the
Chinese people . . . the goal of an open world, open sky,
open cities, open hearts, open minds." Yes, he would move
to the Right on civil rights and he would move to the Left
of the Democrats on foreign affairs, but he was careful to
invoke the heats of the patriotic heart: "My friends, we
live in an age of revolution in America and in the world
. . . let us turn to a revolution . . . that will never grow
old, the world's greatest continuing revolution, the American Revolution." And he went on to call for progress, and
reminded everyone that progress depended on order. He
was of course in these matters shameless, he had no final
passion for the incorruptible integrity of an idea; no,
ideas were rather like keys to him on which he might play
a teletype to program the American mind. And yet the
American mind was scandalously bad—the best educational system in the world had produced the most pervasive conditioning of mind in the history of culture just
as the greatest medical civilization in history might yet
produce the worst plagues. It opened the thought that if

the Lord Himself wished to save America, who else could he possibly use for instrument by now but Richard Nixon? Of course if the Devil wished to push America over the edge—well, for that, Humphrey would serve as well.

Another key on the teletype: "The first civil right of every American is to be free from domestic violence." A feint to the Right, a feint to the Left. "To those who say law and order is the code word for racism, here is a reply: Our goal is justice—justice for every American. . . . America is a great nation today not because of what government did for people, but because of what people did for themselves over 190 years in this country . . . what we need are not more millions on welfare rolls but more millions on payrolls. . . . The greatest engine of progress ever developed in the history of man—American private enterprise." Or did he mean American corporate enterprise. It had been locked in common-law marriage with government for thirty-five years.

But Nixon was off on the power of positive thinking, "Black Americans [want to have] an equal chance to own their own homes, to own their own businesses, to be managers and executives as well as workers, to have a piece"—and he looked like a YMCA secretary: here came the little quotes—"a piece of the 'action' in the exciting ventures of private enterprise." But of course he was not necessarily all wrong. Private enterprise, *small* private enterprise, was an entrance to existential life for the mediocre and the courageous.

He went into the peroration. The year 2000 was coming. A great period of celebration and joy at being alive in America was ahead. "I see a day" he began to say, as Martin Luther King had once said "I have a dream." Every orator's art which had lately worked would become Nixon's craft. So he said "I see a day" nine times. He saw a day when the President would be respected and "a day when every child in this land, regardless of his background has a chance for the best education . . . chance to go just as high as his talents will take him." Nixon, the Socialist! "I see a day when life in rural America attracts people to the country rather than driving them away . . ." Then came a day he could see of breakthrough on problems of slums and pollution and traffic, he could see a day when the value of the dollar would be preserved, a day of freedom

from fear in America and in the world . . . this was the
cause he asked them all to vote for. His speech was almost
done, but he took it around the track again. "Tonight I
see the face of a child . . . Mexican, Italian, Polish . . .
none of that matters . . . he's an American child." But
stripped of opportunity. What pain in that face when the
child awakes to poverty, neglect and despair. The ghost
of J.M. Barrie stirred in Nixon's voice, stirred in the wings
and on the catwalks and in the television sets. "Let's all
save Peter Pan," whispered the ghost. Then Nixon saw
another child tonight, "He hears a train go by. At night
he dreams of faraway places where he'd like to go . . . he
is helped on his journey through life . . . a father who
had to go to work before he finished the sixth grade . . . a
gentle Quaker mother with a passionate concern for peace
. . . a great teacher . . . a remarkable football coach
. . . courageous wife . . . loyal children . . . in his
chosen profession of politics, first there were scores, then
hundreds, then thousands, and finally millions who worked
for his success. And tonight he stands before you, nominated for President of the United States. You can see why
I believe so deeply in the American dream . . . help me
make that dream come true for millions to whom it's an
impossible dream today."

Yes, Nixon was still the spirit of television. Mass communication was still his disease—he thought he could use it
to communicate with masses. "Today I leave you. I go to
assume a greater task than devolved on General Washington. The Great God which helped him must help me. Without that great assistance I will surely fail. With it, I cannot fail." Somberly Nixon said, "Abraham Lincoln lost
his life, but he did not fail. The next President of the
United States will face challenges which in some ways will
be greater than those of Washington or Lincoln . . . not
only the problem of restoring peace abroad, but of restoring peace at home . . . with God's help and your help,
we shall surely succeed. . . . My fellow Americans, the
dark long night for America is about to end. . . . The
time has come for us to leave the valley of despair and
climb the mountain. . . ." (And now one could hear
Martin Luther King crying out in his last passionate church
utterance, "I have gone to the top of the mountain—I
have seen the top.") Nixon was certainly without shame

and certainly without fear; what demons to invoke!—"To
the top of the mountain so that we may see the glory of
the dawn of a new day for America, a new dawn for peace
and freedom to the world." And he was done, and who
would measure the good and bad, the strength and weakness, sincerity and hypocrisy of what he had said, and the
cage of balloons emptied—a union had charged 33 cents
to blow up each single balloon—and the cheers and applause came, and the band, and Nixon and his family
looked happy, and Agnew and his family looked bewildered
and happy, and the cheers came down, not large, not
small, cheers for Richard Nixon's greatest effort in oratory,
and a better speech could not have been written by any
computer in existence, not even Hal the super-computer in
2001, and out in Miami, six miles from Convention Hall,
in the area from 54th to 79th Streets, and Seventh Avenue
to Twenty-Seventh Avenue, the Negroes were rioting, and
three had been killed and five in critical condition as Miami
policemen exchanged gunfire with snipers: "firefights like
in Vietnam," said a police lieutenant and five hundred
armed National Guard were occupying one hundred square
blocks, and one hundred and fifty Blacks had been arrested
since Wednesday night when it had all begun, Governor
Kirk had gone with the Reverend Abernathy who said, "I
will lead you by the hand," to plead with the rioters. Tonight the Governor said, "Whatever force is needed," in
answer to how the uprising would be quelled. It was the
first major riot in the history of Miami.

The reporter was 1,500 miles away by then and could
hardly have covered it, but indeed he did not know if he
saw the need. There would be more of the same in Chicago.
Maybe Chicago would help him to see which horse might
be most deserving of backing into the greatest office on
earth. It occurred to him that the intelligent American
voter was now in the situation of the poor Southern Black
forced these last fifty years to choose his ballot between
the bad racist and the racist who might conceivably be not
all bad. Humphrey versus Nixon.

But this was poor species of wit by which to look into
the glazed eye of the problem—for in truth he was left by
the television set with the knowledge that for the first time
he had not been able to come away with an intimation of
what was in a politician's heart, indeed did not know if he

was ready to like Nixon, or detested him for his resolutely non-poetic binary system, his computer's brain, did not know if the candidate were real as a man, or whole as a machine, lonely in his sad eminence or megalomaniacal, humble enough to feel the real wounds of the country or sufficiently narcissistic to dream the tyrant's dream—the reporter did not know if the candidate was some last wry hope of unity or the square root of minus one, a rudder to steer the ship of state or an empty captain above a directionless void, there to loose the fearful nauseas of the century. He had no idea at all if God was in the land or the Devil played the tune. And if Miami had masked its answers, then in what state of mind could one now proceed to Chicago? He felt like an observer deprived of the privilege to witness or hold a chair.

II
The Siege of
Chicago

Chicago, August 24–29

Chicago is the great American city. New York is one of the capitals of the world and Los Angeles is a constellation of plastic, San Francisco is a lady, Boston has become Urban Renewal, Philadelphia and Baltimore and Washington wink like dull diamonds in the smog of Eastern Megalopolis, and New Orleans is unremarkable past the French Quarter. Detroit is a one-trade town, Pittsburgh has lost its golden triangle, St. Louis has become the golden arch of the corporation, and nights in Kansas City close early. The oil depletion allowance makes Houston and Dallas naught but checkerboards for this sort of game. But Chicago is a great American city. Perhaps it is the last of the great American cities.

The reporter was sentimental about the town. Since he had grown up in Brooklyn, it took him no time to recognize, whenever he was in Chicago again, that the urbanites here were like the good people of Brooklyn—they were simple, strong, warm-spirited, sly, rough, compassionate, jostling, tricky and extraordinarily good-natured because they had sex in their pockets, muscles on their back, hot eats around the corner, neighborhoods which dripped with the sauce of local legend, and real city architecture, brownstones with different windows on every floor, vistas for miles of red-brick and two-family wood-frame houses with balconies and porches, runty stunted trees rich as farmland in their promise of tenderness the first city evenings of spring, streets where kids played stick-ball and roller-hockey, lots of smoke and iron twilight. The clangor of the late nineteenth century, the very hope of greed, was in these streets. London one hundred years ago could not have looked much better.

Brooklyn, however, beautiful Brooklyn, grew beneath the skyscrapers of Manhattan, so it never became a great city, merely an asphalt herbarium for talent destined to cross the river. Chicago did not have Manhattan to preempt top branches, so it grew up from the savory of its neighborhoods to some of the best high-rise architecture in the world, and because its people were Poles and Ukrainians and Czechs as well as Irish and the rest, the city had Byzantine corners worthy of Prague or Moscow, odd tortured attractive drawbridges over the Chicago River, huge Gothic spires like the skyscraper which held the Chicago *Tribune,* curves and abutments and balconies in cylindrical structures thirty stories high twisting in and out of the curves of the river, and fine balustrades in its parks. Chicago had a North Side on Lake Shore Drive where the most elegant apartment buildings in the world could be found— Sutton Place in New York betrayed the cost analyst in the eye of the architect next to these palaces of glass and charcoal colored steel. In superb back streets behind the towers on the lake were brownstones which spoke of ironies, cupidities and intricate ambition in the fists of the robber barons who commissioned them—substantiality, hard work, heavy drinking, carnal meats of pleasure, and a Midwestern sense of how to arrive at upper-class decorum were also in the American grandeur of these few streets. If there was a fine American aristocracy of deportment, it was probably in the clean tough keen-eyed ladies of Chicago one saw on the streets off Lake Shore Drive on the near North Side of Chicago.

Not here for a travelogue—no need then to detail the Loop, in death like the center of every other American city, but what a dying! Old department stores, old burlesque houses, avenues, dirty avenues, the El with its nineteenth-century dialogue of iron screeching against iron about a turn, and caverns of shadow on the pavement beneath, the grand hotels with their massive lobbies, baroque ceilings, resplendent as Roman bordellos, names like Sheraton-Blackstone, Palmer House, red fields of carpet, a golden cage for elevator, the unheard crash of giant mills stamping new shapes on large and obdurate materials is always pounding in one's inner ear—Dreiser had not written about Chicago for nothing.

To the West of the Lake were factories and Ciceros, Mafia-lands and immigrant lands; to the North, the suburbs, the Evanstons; to the South were Negro ghettos of the South Side—belts of Black men amplifying each the resonance of the other's cause—the Black belt had the Blackstone Rangers, the largest gang of juvenile delinquents on earth, 2,000 by some count—one could be certain the gang had leaders as large in potential as Hannibal or Attila the Hun—how else account for the strength and wit of a stud who would try to rise so high in the Blackstone Rangers?

Further South and West were enclaves for the University of Chicago, more factories, more neighborhoods for Poles, some measure of more good hotels on the lake, and endless neighborhoods—white neighborhoods which went for miles of ubiquitous dingy wood houses with back yards, neighborhoods to hint of Eastern Europe, Ireland, Tennessee, a gathering of all the clans of the Midwest, the Indians and Scotch-Irish, Swedes, some Germans, Italians, Hungarians, Rumanians, Finns, Slovaks, Slovenes—it was only the French who did not travel. In the Midwest, land spread out; not five miles from the Loop were areas as empty, deserted, enormous and mournful by night as the outer freight yards of Omaha. Some industrial desert or marsh would lie low on the horizon, an area squalling by day, deserted by night, except for the hulking Midwestern names of the boxcars and the low sheds, the warehouse buildings, the wire fences which went along the side of unpaved roads for thousands of yards.

The stockyards were like this, the famous stockyards of Chicago were at night as empty as the railroad sidings of the moon. Long before the Democratic Convention of 1968 came to the Chicago Amphitheatre, indeed eighteen years ago when the reporter had paid his only previous visit, the area was even then deserted at night, empty as the mudholes on a battlefield after a war has passed. West of the Amphitheatre, railroad sidings seemed to continue on for miles, accompanied by those same massive low sheds larger than armories, with pens for tens of thousands of frantic beasts, cattle, sheep, and pigs, animals in an orgy of gorging and dropping and waiting and smelling blood.

In the slaughterhouses, during the day, a carnage worthy of the Disasters of War took place each morning and afternoon. Endless files of animals were led through pens to be stunned on the head by hammers, and then hind legs trussed, be hoisted up on hooks to hang head down, and ride along head down on an overhead trolley which brought them to Negroes or whites, usually huge, the whites most often Polish or Hunkies (hence the etymology of Honkie—a Chicago word) the Negroes up from the South, huge men built for the shock of the work, slash of a knife on the neck of the beast and gouts of blood to bathe their torso (stripped of necessity to the waist) and blood to splash their legs. The animals passed a psychic current back along the overhead trolley—each cut throat released its scream of death into the throat not yet cut and just behind, and that penultimate throat would push the voltage up, drive the current back and further back into the screams of every animal upside down and hanging from that clanking overhead trolley, bare electric bulbs screaming into the animal eye and brain, gurglings and awesome hollows of sound coming back from the open plumbing ahead of the cut jugular as if death were indeed a rapids along some underground river, and the fear and absolute anguish of beasts dying upside down further ahead passed back along the line, back all the way to the corrals and the pens, back even to the siding with the animals still in boxcars, back, who knew—so high might be the psychic voltage of the beast—back to the farm where first they were pushed into the truck which would take them into the train. What an awful odor the fear of absolute and unavoidable death gave to the stool and stuffing and pure vomitous shit of the beasts waiting in the pens in the stockyard, what a sweat of hell-leather, and yet the odor, no, the titanic stench, which rose from the yards was not so simple as the collective diarrhetics of an hysterical army of beasts, no, for after the throats were cut and the blood ran in rich gutters, red light on the sweating back of the red throat-cutters, the dying and some just-dead animals clanked along the overhead, arterial blood spurting like the nip-ups of a little boy urinating in public, the red-hot carcass quickly encountered another Black or Hunkie with a long knife on a long stick who would cut the belly from chest to groin and a stew and a stink of two hundred pounds of stomach, lungs, intestines, mucosities, spleen, exploded cowflop and pigshit, blood, silver lining, liver, mother-of-pearl tissue, and general gag-all would flop and slither over the floor, the man with the knife getting a good blood-splatting as he dug and twisted with his blade to liberate the roots of the organ, intestine and impedimenta still integrated into the meat and bone of the excavated existence he was working on.

Well, the smell of the entrails and that agonized blood electrified by all the outer neons of ultimate fear got right into the grit of the stockyard stench. Let us pass over into the carving and the slicing, the boiling and scraping, annealing and curing of the flesh in sugars and honeys and smoke, the cooking of the cow carcass, stamp of the inspector, singeing of the hair, boiling of hooves, grinding of gristle, the wax-papering and the packaging, the foiling and the canning, the burning of the residue, and the last slobber of the last unusable guts as it went into the stockyard furnace, and up as stockyard smoke, burnt blood and burnt bone and burnt hair to add their properties of specific stench to fresh blood, fresh entrails, fresh fecalities already all over the air. It is the smell of the stockyards, all of it taken together, a smell so bad one must go down to visit the killing of the animals or never eat meat again. Watching the animals be slaughtered, one knows the human case—no matter how close to angel we may come, the butcher is equally there. So be it. Chicago makes for hard minds. On any given night, the smell may go anywhere—down to Gary to fight with the smog and the coke, out to Cicero to quiet the gangs with their dreams of gung ho and mop-up, North to Evanston to remind the polite that *inter faeces et urinam* are we born, and East on out to Lake Michigan where the super felicities in the stench of such earth-bound miseries and corruptions might cheer the fish with the clean spermy deep waters of their fate.

Yes, Chicago was a town where nobody could ever forget how the money was made. It was picked up from floors still slippery with blood, and if one did not protest and take a vow of vegetables, one knew at least that life was hard, life was in the flesh and in the massacre of the flesh—one breathed the last agonies of beasts. So something of the entrails and the secrets of the gut got into the faces of native Chicagoans. A great city, a strong city with faces tough as leather hide and pavement, it was also a city where the faces took on the broad beastiness of ears which were dull enough to ignore the bleatings of the doomed, noses battered enough to smell no more the stench of every unhappy end, mouths—fat mouths or slit mouths—ready to taste the gravies which were the reward of every massacre, and eyes, simple pig eyes, which could look the pig truth in the face. In any other city, they would have found technologies to silence the beasts with needles, quarter them with machines, lull them with Muzak, and have stainless steel for floors, aluminum beds to take over the old overhead trolley—animals would be given a shot of vitamin-enrichment before they took the last ride. But in Chicago, they did it straight, they cut the animals right out of their hearts—which is why it was the last of the great American cities, and people had great faces, carnal as blood, greedy, direct, too impatient for hypocrisy, in love with honest plunder. They were big and human and their brother in heaven was the slaughtered pig—they did not ignore him. If the yowls and moans of his extinction was the broth of their strength, still they had honest guts to smell him to the end—they did not flush the city with Odorono or Pinex or No-Scent, they swilled the beer and assigned the hits and gave America its last chance at straight-out drama. Only a great city provides honest spectacle, for that is the salvation of the schizophrenic soul. Chicago may have beasts on the street, it may have a giant of fortitude for Mayor who grew into a beast—a man with the very face of Chicago—but it is an honest town, it does not look to incubate psychotics along an air-conditioned corridor with a vinyl floor.

2

If the face of Chicago might be reduced to a broad fleshy nose with nostrils open wide to stench, stink, power, a pretty day, a well-stacked broad, and the beauties of a dirty buck, the faces in the crowd of some 5,000 Eugene McCarthy

supporters out at Midway Airport to greet the Senator's
arrival on Sunday, August 25th, could have found their
archetype in any one of a number of fairly tall slim young
men in seersucker suits with horn-rimmed glasses, pale
complexions, thin noses, and thin—this was the center of
the common denominator—thin nostrils. People who are
greedy have extraordinary capacities for waste disposal—
they must, they take in too much. Whereas, the parsimo-
nious end up geared to take in too little—viz, Chicago
nostrils versus McCarthy nostrils. Of course, the parsimony
of the McCarthyites was of a special sort—they had hardly
been mean with funds in supporting their candidate, nor
small in the boldness of their attempt, and no one could
claim that the loyalty of their effort had been equalled in
many a year—certainly not since Adlai Stevenson, perhaps
not since Henry Wallace. No, like all crusaders, their stingi-
ness could be found in a ferocious lack of tolerance or
liaison to their left or right—the search for Grail seems
invariably to proceed in a straight line. It was no accident
that an extraordinary number of McCarthyites seemed to
drive Volkswagens (or was it that an extraordinary number
of Volkswagens bore the white and blue psychedelic flower?
—if psychedelic it could truly be called, since the blue was
too wan and the white too milky for the real sports of
psychedelia land). Support of Eugene McCarthy was, of
course, a movement whose strength was in the suburbs and
the academy—two bastions of that faith which would state
that a man must be allowed to lead a modest and reasonable life without interference by large forces. If corruption
in politics, opportunism, and undue ambition excited their
contempt, and injustice in race relations their disapproval
(because injustice was inflammatory to reason) the war in
Vietnam encouraged their most honorable suppressed fury
for it spoke of a large and outrageous outside force which
would sweep their lives away. In the suburbs and the academy, parents and children came together in detestation of
that war.

The moral powers of the vegetarian, the pacifist, and the
nationalist have been so refined away from the source of
much power—infantile violence—that their moral powers
exhibit a leanness, a keenness, and total ferocity which can
only hint at worlds given up: precisely those sensuous
worlds of corruption, promiscuity, fingers in the take, poli-

tical alliances forged by the fires of booze, and that sense of
property which is the fundament of all political relations.

Talk of that later—for now, at the airport, enough to
observe that the crowd of 5,000 at Midway waiting for Gene
McCarthy were remarkably homogeneous, young for the
most part, too young to vote, a disproportionate number of
babies in mother's arms—sly hint of middle-class Left
mentality here at work! (The middle-class Left would
never learn that workingmen in greasy dungarees make a
point of voting against the mother who carries the babe—
the righteous face of any such mother reminds them of
schoolteachers they used to hate!) Yes, the rally taking
place in a special reserved area of the parking lot at Midway
gave glimpses of faces remarkably homogeneous for a political rally. One could pass from heavy-set young men with
a full chop of beard and a fifty-pound pack on their back
to young adolescent poetesses, pale as Ophelia, prim as
Florence Nightingale, from college boys in sweaters with
hints of Hippie allegiance, to Madison Avenue types in side-
burns, straw hats, and a species of pill-taking panache;
through decent, mildly fanatic ranks of middle-class professionals—suggestion of vitiated blood in their complexion
—to that part of theater and show biz which dependably
would take up cause with the cleaner cadres of the Left.
One of their ranks, a pretty brunette in a red dress, was
leading a set of foot-tapping songs while the crowd waited
for the Senator's plane, the style of the lyrics out on that
soft shoulder between liberalism and wit, and so reminiscent of the sort of songs Adolph Green and Betty Comden
had been composing and Tom Lehrer singing for years.
"The special fascination of . . . we think he's just sensational . . . *Gene! ! !*" two notes sounding on "Gee-yene,"
so humorous in its vein, for the lyrics implied one was team
with a limited gang of humans who derived from Noel
Coward, Ogden Nash, and juke hill-billy—"Gee-yene! Gee-
yene!"

Song went on: "The GOP will cry in its beer, for here is
a man who will change the scene. Gee-yene! Gee-yene!"
Depression came over the reporter. Try as he would, he
could not make himself happy with McCarthy supporters.
Their common denominator seemed to be found in some
blank area of the soul, a species of disinfected idealism
which gave one the impression when among them of living

in a lobotomized ward of Upper Utopia. George Wallace, pay heed!

Of course, the reporter had been partisan to Bobby Kennedy, excited by precisely his admixture of idealism plus willingness to traffic with demons, ogres, and overloads of corruption. This had characterized the political style of the Kennedys more than once. The Kennedys had seemed magical because they were a little better than they should have been, and so gave promise of making America a little better than it ought to be. The reporter respected Mc-Carthy, he respected him enormously for trying the vengeance of Lyndon Johnson, his heart had been given a bit of life by the success of the New Hampshire primary campaign. If there had then been little to make him glad in the abrupt and unhappy timing of Bobby Kennedy's immediate entrance into the race for nomination, he had, nonetheless, remained Kennedy's man—he saw the battle between the two as tragic; he had hardly enjoyed the Kennedy-McCarthy debate on television before the California primary; he had not taken pleasure in rooting for Kennedy and being thereby forced to condemn McCarthy's deadness of manner, blankness of affect, and suggestion of weakness in each deep pouch beneath each eye. The pouches spoke of clichés —eyes sitting in sagging brassieres of flesh, such stuff. He knew that McCarthy partisans would find equal fault somewhere in Kennedy.

A few nights after this debate, the reporter was awakened from a particularly oppressive nightmare by the ringing of a bell. He heard the voice of an old drinking friend he had not seen in two years. "Cox," he shouted into the phone, "are you out of your skull? What do you mean calling at three A.M.?"

"Look," said the friend, "get the television on. I think you ought to see it. Bobby Kennedy has just been shot."

"No," he bellowed. "No! No! No!" his voice railing with an ugliness and pain reminiscent to his ear of the wild grunts of a wounded pig. (Where he had heard that cry he did not at the moment remember.) He felt as if he were being despoiled of a vital part of himself, and in the middle of this horror noted that he screamed like a pig, not a lion, nor a bear. The reporter had gone for years on the premise that one must balance every moment between the angel in oneself and the swine—the sound of his own voice shocked him therefore profoundly. The balance was not what he thought it to be. He watched television for the next hours in a state which drifted rudderless between two horrors. Then, knowing no good answer could come for days, if at all, on the possible recovery of Bobby Kennedy, he went back to bed and lay in a sweat of complicity, as if his own lack of moral *witness* (to the subtle heroism of Bobby Kennedy's attempt to run for President) could be found in the dance of evasions his taste for a merry life and a married one had become, as if this precise lack had contributed (in the vast architectonics of the cathedral of history) to one less piton of mooring for Senator Kennedy in his lonely ascent of those vaulted walls, as if finally the efforts of brave men depended in part on the protection of other men who saw themselves as at least provisionally brave, or sometimes brave, or at the least—if not brave— balanced at least on a stability between selflessness and appetite and therefore—by practical purposes—decent. But he was close to having become too much of appetite —he had spent the afternoon preceding this night of assassination in enjoying a dalliance—let us leave it at that— a not uncharacteristic way to have spent his time, and lying next to his wife now, TV news pictures of the assassination rocketing all over the bruised stone of his skull, he hated his wife for having ever allowed such a condition to come to be, hated her subtle complicity in driving him out, and then apart, and knew from the other side of his love that he must confess this afternoon now, as if that would be a warrant of magic to aid Senator Kennedy on the long voyage through the depth of the exploded excavations in his brain, and did not have the simple courage to confess, stopped in his mental steps as if confronting a bully in an alley and altogether unable to go on—the bully in the alley no less than his wife's illimitable funds of untempered redneck wrath. So he did what all men who are overweight must do—he prayed the Lord to take the price on his own poor mortal self (since he had flesh in surfeit to offer) he begged that God spare Senator Kennedy's life, and he would give up something, give up what?—give up some of the magic he could bring to bear on some one or another of the women, yes, give that up if the life would be saved, and fell back into the horror of trying to rest with the sense that his offer might have been given too late and by the wrong vein—confession to his wife was what the moral pressure had first demanded—and so fell asleep with some gnawing sense of the Devil there to snatch his offering after the angel had moved on in disgust.

Kennedy dead, he was doubly in gloom, passionate gloom for the loss of that fine valuable light—like everyone else he loved Bobby Kennedy by five times more in death than life—a few lives have the value to illumine themselves in their death. But he was also dull in dejection at what he might have given away that other night. For he believed a universe in which at stricken moments one could speak quietly to whichever manifest of God or Devil was near, had to be as reasonable a philosophical proposition as any assumption that such dialogues were deluded. So it was possible he had given something away, and for nothing: the massive irreversible damage to the Senator's brain had occurred before the spring of his own generosity had even been wet. Indeed! Who knew what in reality might have been granted if he had worked for the first impulse and dared offer confession on a connubial bed. A good could have come to another man and by another route.

He never knew for certain if something had been given up—he was working too hard in too many ways to notice subtle change. (Although it seemed to him that a piece of magic had probably been relinquished.) Who cared but the reporter? He was, in general, depressed; then he met Senator McCarthy at a cocktail party in Cambridge not a week after the assassination. McCarthy was in depression as well.

3

At this party, McCarthy looked weary beyond belief, his skin a used-up yellow, his tall body serving for no more than to keep his head up above the crowd at the cocktail party. Like feeder fish, smaller people were nibbling on his reluctant hulk with questions, idiotic questions, petulant inquiries he had heard a thousand times. "Why?" asked a young woman, college instructor, horn-rimmed glasses, "Why don't we get out of Vietnam?" her voice near hysterical, ringing with the harsh electronics of cancer gulch, and McCarthy looked near to flinching with the question and the liverish demand on him to answer. "Well," he said in his determinedly mild and quiet voice, last drop of humor never voided—for if on occasion he might be surrounded by dolts, volts, and empty circuits, then nothing to do but send remarks up to the angel of laughter. "Well," said Senator McCarthy, "there seem to be a few obstacles in the way."

But his pale green eyes had that look somewhere between humor and misery which the Creation might offer when faced with the bulldozers of boredom.

Years ago, in 1960, the reporter had had two glimpses of Eugene McCarthy. At the Democratic convention in Los Angeles which nominated John F. Kennedy, McCarthy had made a speech for another candidate. It was the best nominating speech the reporter had ever heard. He had written about it with the metaphor of a bullfight:

. . . he held the crowd like a matador . . . gathering their emotion, discharging it, creating new emotion on the wave of the last, driving his passes tighter and tighter as he readied for the kill. "Do not reject this man who made us all proud to be called Democrats, do not leave this prophet without honor in his own party." McCarthy went on, his muleta furled for the naturales. *"There was only one man who said let's talk sense to the American people. He said, the promise of America is the promise of greatness. This was his call to greatness . . . Do not forget this man . . . Ladies and gentlemen, I present to you not the favorite son of one state, but the favorite son of the fifty states, the favorite son of every country he has visited, the favorite son of every country which has not seen him but is secretly thrilled by his name." Bedlam. The kill. "Ladies and gentlemen, I present to you Adlai Stevenson of Illinois." Ears and tail. Hooves and bull. A roar went up like the roar one heard the day Bobby Thompson hit his home run at the Polo Grounds and the Giants won the pennant from the Dodgers in the third playoff game of the 1951 season. The demonstration cascaded onto the floor, the*

gallery came to its feet, the sports arena sounded like the
inside of a marching drum.

Perhaps three months later, just after his piece on that
convention had appeared, and election time was near, he
had met Senator McCarthy at another cocktail party on
Central Park West to raise money for the campaign of
Mark Lane, then running for State Assemblyman in New
York. The reporter had made a speech himself that day.
Having decided, on the excitements of the Kennedy candidacy and other excitements (much marijuana for one)
to run for Mayor of New York the following year, he gave
his maiden address at that party, a curious, certainly a
unique political speech, private, personal, tortured in metaphor, sublimely indifferent to issues, platform, or any
recognizable paraphernalia of the political process, and
delivered in much too rapid a voice to the assembled be-
wilderment of his audience, a collective (and by the end
very numb) stiff clavicle of Jewish Central Park West
matrons. The featured speaker, Senator McCarthy, was
to follow, and climbing up on the makeshift dais as he
stepped down, the Senator gave him a big genial wide-as-
the-open-plains Midwestern grin.

"Better learn how to breathe, boy," he whispered out of
the corner of his mouth, and proceeded to entertain the
audience for the next few minutes with a mixture of
urbanity, professional elegance, and political savvy. That
was eight years ago.

But now, near to eight years later, the hour was different,
the audience at this cocktail party in Cambridge with their
interminable questions and advice, their over-familiarity
yet excessive reverence, their desire to touch McCarthy,
prod him, *galvanize* him, seemed to do no more than drive
him deeper into the insulations of his fatigue, his very
disenchantment—so his pores seemed to speak—with the
democratic process. He was not a mixer. Or if he had ever
been a mixer, as he must have been years ago, he had had
too much of it since, certainly too much since primaries in
New Hampshire, Wisconsin, Indiana, Oregon, and California—he had become, or he had always been, too private
a man for the damnable political mechanics of mixing,
fixing, shaking the hands, answering the same questions
which had already answered themselves by being asked.

And now the threat of assassination over all, that too, that his death might come like the turn of a card, and could a man be ready? The gloomy, empty tomb-like reverberations of the last shot shaking rough waves doubtless through his own dreams, for his eyes, sensitive, friendly, and remote as the yellow eyes of an upper primate in a cage, spoke out of the weary, sagging face, up above the sagging pouches, seeming to say, "Yes, try to rescue me—but as you see, it's not quite possible." And the reporter, looking to perform the errand of rescue, went in to talk about the speech of 1960 in Los Angeles, and how it was the second best political speech he had ever heard.

"Oh," said McCarthy, "tell me, what was the best?"

And another questioner jostled the circle about McCarthy to ask another question, the Secret Service man in the gray suit at McCarthy's elbow stiffening at the impact. But McCarthy held the questioner at a distance by saying, "No, I'd like to listen for awhile." It had obviously become his pleasure to listen to others. So the reporter told a story about Vito Marcantonio making a speech in Yankee Stadium in 1948, and the Senator listened carefully, almost sadly, as if remembering other hours of oratory.

On the way out the door, in the press of guests and local party workers up to shake his hand before he was gone, a tall bearded fellow, massive chin, broad brow for broad horn-rimmed glasses, spoke out in a resonant voice marred only by the complacency of certain nasal intrigues. "Senator, I'm a graduate student in English, and I like your politics very much, but I must tell you, I think your poetry stinks."

McCarthy took it like a fighter being slapped by the referee across the forearms. "You see what it is, running for President," said the laughter in his eyes. If he worshipped at a shrine, it was near the saint of good humor.

"Give my regards to Robert Lowell," said the reporter. "Say to him that I read 'The Drunken Fisherman' just the other day."

McCarthy looked like the victim in the snow when the St. Bernard comes up with the rum. His eyes came alight at the name of the poem . . . "I will catch Christ with a greased worm," might have been the line he remembered. He gave a little wave, was out the door.

Yet the reporter was depressed after the meeting. Mc-

Carthy did not look nor feel like a President, not that tall tired man with his bright subtle eyes which could sharpen the razor's edge of a nuance, no, he seemed more like the dean of the finest English department in the land. There wasn't that sense of a man with vast ambition and sufficient character to make it luminous, so there was not that charisma which leaves no argument about the nature of the attempt.

4

If that meeting had been in the beginning of June, there were differences now by the end of August. McCarthy, at Midway Airport to greet his followers, looked big in his Presidential candidate's suit this sunny afternoon, no longer tired, happy apparently with the crowd and the air of his reception. He went down the aisle of friends and reporters who had managed to get ahead of the restraining rope for the crowd and shook hands, gave a confident wink or good twinkle there, "Whatever are you doing *here,* Norman?" he said with a grin, quick as a jab, and made his way up to the platform where a clump of microphones on spikes garnished the podium. But the microphones were dead. Which set McCarthy to laughing. Meanwhile posters waved out in the crowd: AMERICA'S PRIMARY HOPE; LUCIDITY, NOT LUNACY; MAKE MINE McCARTHY. He scanned the home-made posters, as if his sense of such language, after a decade and more, had become sufficiently encyclopedic to treasure every rare departure, and he laughed from time to time as he saw something he liked.

Finally, he called out to the crowd, *"They* cut the power line. *We're* trying to fix it." Great college moans at the depravity of the opposition—wise laughter at the good cheer of the situation. "Let's sing," said Gene McCarthy; a shout from the crowd. His standard was theirs: good wit could always support small horror. So they sang, This land is your land, this land is my land, and McCarthy moved along to another mike, much shifting of position in his entourage to be near him, then gave up and came back to the first mike. Things were now fixed. He introduced Senator Yarborough from Texas who would in turn introduce him. Yarborough looked like a florid genial iron-ribbed barrel of a British Conservative M.P., and spoke with a modest Texas accent; he told the audience that McCarthy had "won this campaign in the hearts of the American people." While he spoke, McCarthy sat next to his wife Abigail, a warm-colored woman with a pleasant face full of the arch curves of a most critical lady of the gentry. Something in her expression spoke of uncharitable wit, but she was elegant—one could see her as First Lady. Indeed! One could almost see him now as President. He had size, he had humor. He looked strong. When he got up to speak, he was in easy form. Having laughed at a poster which said, "Welcome to Fort Daley," he began by paying his respects to the Mayor of Chicago who is "watching over all of us."

"Big Brother," shouted a powerhouse in the crowd.

McCarthy talked for six or seven minutes. The audience was looking for a bust-out-of-the-corrals speech but the Senator was not giving it. He talked mildly, with his throwaway wit, his almost diffident assertion—"We can build a new society and a new world," said he at one point in the mildest tones of his mild register, and then added as if to take the curse off such intellectual presumption, "We're not asking for too much—just a modest use of intelligence."

"Too much," murmured a news-service man admiringly.

A good yell came up. Even a modest use of intelligence would forbid Vietnam.

McCarthy drew one more big cheer by declaring he was not interested in being Vice President. "I'm not here to compromise what we've all worked for," he said to cheers, and shortly after, to the crowd's disappointment, was done. The band played—Warren King's Brass Impact, four trombones, two guitars, drums, six trumpets, one tenor sax, two Negroes not very black among the musicians.

Yes, he had compromised nothing, not even the musicians. If he was at heart a conservative, and no great man for the Blacks, then damned if he would encourage harmoniums and avalanches of soul music. No, he had done it his way up to now, cutting out everyone from his councils who was interested in politicking at the old trough, no, his campaign had begun by being educational, and educational had he left it—he had not compromised an inch, nor played the demagogue for a moment, and it had given him strength, not strength enough perhaps to win, certainly not enough to win, but rectitude had laid the keel, and in that air of a campaign run at last for intelligent men, and give no alms to whores, he left.

It was no great meeting, but excitement was there, some thin weal of hope that victory, impossible to spring aloft, might still find wings. Take a good look, for it is the last of such pleasant occasions. Later that day, Hubert Humphrey came into O'Hare, but there was no crowd to receive him, just a few of the Humphrey workers. Hubert Humphrey had two kinds of workers. Some, with crew cut or straight combed hair, could have gone with Ronald Reagan. Others were out of that restaurant where Mafia shakes hands with the union. Let no one say that Hubert was unfriendly to the real people. But there is more to see of all these men.

5

Here, my friends, on the prairies of Illinois and the Middle West, we can see a long way in all directions . . . here there are no barriers, no defenses to ideas and to aspirations. We want none. We want no shackles on the mind or the spirit, no rigid patterns of thought and no iron conformity. We want only the faith and the convictions of triumph and free and fair contest.
(From an address by Adlai Stevenson, Governor of Illinois, to the Democratic Convention in Chicago in 1952.)

It may be time to attempt a summary of the forces at work upon the convention of 1968.

A similar consideration of the Republican convention never seemed necessary. The preliminaries to Miami Beach were simple: Nixon, by dint of an historical vacuum whose presence he was the first to discern, and by the profit of much hard work, early occupied the Republican center— the rest of the history resides in Rockefeller's attempts to clarify his own position to himself. Was he to respond only to a draft of Republicans desperate not to lose to Johnson, then to Kennedy, or was he to enter primaries, and divide the party? Since he was perfectly capable of winning the election with a divided Republican Party, because his presence as a nominee would divide the Democratic Party even further, the question was academic. But Rockefeller's history can not be written, for it is to be found in the timing of his advisers and the advice of his intimates, and they are not ready, one would assume, to hang themselves yet.

Where it is not to remain hidden, the Republican history was relatively simple and may be passed over. It is the Democratic which insists on presenting itself, for no convention ever had such events for prelude.

On March 31, on a night when the latest Gallup Poll showed LBJ to be in favor with only 36% of the American public (while only 23% approved his handling of the war) Johnson announced on national television that he would not seek nor "accept the nomination of my party as your President." On April 2, there was talk that Humphrey would run—McCarthy had taken the Wisconsin primary with 57% of the vote to Johnson's 35% (and it was estimated that if Johnson had not resigned, the vote would have been more like 64% to 28%).

On April 4, Martin Luther King, Jr. was assassinated by a white man, and violence, fire and looting broke out in Memphis, Harlem, Brooklyn, Washington, D.C., Chicago, Detroit, Boston and Newark over the next week. Mayor Daley gave his famous "shoot to kill" instruction to the Chicago police, and National Guard and U.S. troops were sent to some of these cities.

On April 23 Columbia students barricaded the office of a Dean. By another day the campus was disrupted, then closed, and was never to be comfortably open again for the rest of the semester. On May 10, as if indicative of a spontaneous world-wide movement, the students of the

Sorbonne battled the Paris police on barricades and in the streets. On the same day, Maryland was quietly pledging its delegates to Humphrey.

On June 3, Andy Warhol was shot. On June 4, after winning the California primary 45% to 42% for McCarthy, and 12% for Humphrey, RFK was shot in the head and died next day. The cannibalistic war of the McCarthy and Kennedy peace forces was at an end. McCarthy had been all but finished in Indiana, Nebraska, Iowa, and South Dakota; Kennedy had been badly mauled by his defeat in Oregon. Meanwhile Humphrey had been picking up delegates in states like Missouri, which did not have primaries, and the delegates in states which did, like Pennsylvania, after it had given 90% of its vote to McCarthy.

So went the month. Cleveland with its first Negro Mayor still had a riot. Spock, Goodman, Ferber and Coffin were sentenced to two years in jail. Kentucky with 46 delegates gave 41 to HHH, and the McCarthy supporters walked out. There were stories every other day of Humphrey's desire to have Teddy Kennedy for Vice President, and much comment in columns on the eagerness of the Democrats to move the convention from Chicago. Chicago had a telephone strike and the likelihood of a taxi strike and a bus strike. Chicago was to be unwilling host to a Yippie (Youth International Party) convention the week the Democrats would be there. Chicago had the massive bull temper of Mayor Daley for the Democratic Party to contend with— much work went on behind the scenes to move the convention to Miami where the telephone and television lines were in, and Daley would be out. But Daley was not about to let the convention leave his city. Daley promised he would enforce the peace and allow no outrageous demonstrations. Daley hinted that his wrath—if the convention were moved—might burn away whole corners of certain people's support. Since Hubert Humphrey was the one who could most qualify for certain people, he was in no hurry to offend the Mayor. Lyndon Johnson, when beseeched by interested parties to encourage Daley to agree to the move, was rumored to have said, "Miami Beach is not an American city."

The TV networks applied massive pressure to shift the convention. In Chicago, because of the strictures of the strike, their cameras would be limited to the hotels and to the Amphitheatre—they would not be able to take their portable generators out to the street and run lines to their color cameras. That would not be permitted. They were restricted to movie cameras, which would make them half a day late in reporting action or interviews in the streets (half a day late for television is equal to being a week late). How they must have focussed their pressure on Daley and Johnson. It is to the Mayor's curious credit that he was strong enough to withstand them. It should have been proof interior that Daley was no other-directed twentieth-century politician. Any such man would have known the powers of retaliation which resided in the mass media. One did not make an enemy of a television network for nothing; they could repay injury with no more than a chronic slur in the announcer's voice every time your deadly name was mentioned over the next twelve months, or next twelve years. Daley, however, was not a national politician, but a clansman—he could get 73% of the vote in any constituency made up of people whose ancestors were at home with rude instruments in Polish forests, Ukrainian marshes, Irish bogs—they knew how to defend the home: so did he. No interlopers for any network of Jew-Wasp media men were going to dominate the streets of his parochial city, nor none of their crypto-accomplices with long hair, sexual liberty, drug license and unbridled mouths. It was as if the primitive powers of the Mayor's lungs, long accustomed to breathing all variety of blessings and curses (from the wind of ancestors, constituents, and screaming beasts in the stockyards where he had once labored for a decade and more) could take everything into his chest, mighty barrel of a chest in Richard J. Daley, 200 pounds, 5 feet 8 inches tall. These blessings and curses, once prominently and in public breathed in, could be processed, pulverized, and washed into the choleric blood, defiance in the very pap and hemoglobin of it—"I'll swallow up their spit and shove it through," the Mayor could always bellow to his electorate. So Daley was ready to take on the electronic wrath of the semi-conductors of the world, his voter-nourished blood full of beef and curses against the transistorized communicatory cabals of the media. And back of him— no evidence will ever be produced to prove such a thought—must have been Lyndon

Johnson, great wounded secret shaman of the Democratic Party. If Teddy Roosevelt had once wrecked William Howard Taft and the Republican Party by running as a Bull Moose, so Lyndon Johnson was now a warlock of a Bull Moose, conceiving through all the months of June, July, and August how he would proceed to create a cursed convention, a platform, a candidate, and a party which would be his own as much as the nightmarish vision of a phantom ship is the soul of a fever; he would seek to rend his party, crack it in two—that party to which his own allegiance in near to forty years could hardly be questioned —because that party had been willing to let him go. In revenge he would create a candidate who need never run, for his campaign would be completed by the nomination. Conceive what he would have thought of a candidate who could attract more votes than himself.

6

"Politics is property," said Murray Kempton, delegate from New York, over the epiphanies of a drink, and never was a new science comprehended better by a young delegate. Lyndon Johnson was first preceptor of the key that politics-is-property so you never give something away for nothing. Convention politics is therefore not the art of the possible so much as the art of what is possible when you are dealing with property holders. A delegate's vote is his holding—he will give it up without return no more than a man will sign over his house entire to a worthy cause.

The true property-holder is never ambivalent about his land, he does not mock it, or see adjacent estates as more deserving than his own—so a professional in politics without pride in his holding is a defector. The meanest ward-heeler in the cheapest block of Chicago has his piece—he cannot be dislodged without leaving his curse nor the knotty untangling of his relations with a hundred job-holders in the area; he gives up tithes in the umbilical act of loyalty to his boss, he receives protection for his holding in return.

Such property relations are to be witnessed for every political sinecure in the land—judgeships, jobs, contracts, promises—it comes down to chairs in offices, and words negotiable like bonds: all of that is politics as simple property. Everybody in the game has a piece, and that piece is workable, it is equivalent to capital, it can be used to accrue interest by being invested in such sound conservative enterprises as decades of loyalty to the same Machine. So long as the system progresses, so will one's property be blessed with dividends. But such property can also be used as outright risk capital—one can support an insurgent movement in one's party, even risk the loss of one's primary holding in return for the possibility of acquiring much more.

This, of course, is still politics at city hall, county or state house, this is the politics of the party regular, politics as simple property, which is to say politics as concrete negotiable power—the value of their engagement in politics is at any moment just about directly convertible to cash.

Politics at national level can still be comprehended by politics-as-property provided one remembers that moral integrity (or the public impression of such) in a high politician is also property, since it brings power and/or emoluments to him. Indeed a very high politician—which is to say a statesman or leader—has no political substance unless he is the servant of ideological institutions or interests and the available moral passions of the electorate, so serving, he is the agent of the political power they bestow on him, which power is certainly a property. Being a leading anti-Communist used to be an invaluable property for which there was much competition—Richard Nixon had once gotten in early on the equivalent of an Oklahoma landgrab by staking out whole territories of that property. "End the war in Vietnam," is a property to some, "Let no American blood be shed in vain," is obviously another. A politician picks and chooses among moral properties. If he is quick-witted, unscrupulous, and does not mind a life of constant anxiety, he will hasten—there is a great competition for things valuable in politics—to pick up properties wherever he can, even if they are rival holdings. To the extent a politician is his own man, attached to his own search for his own spiritual truth—which is to say willing to end in any unpalatable position to which the character of his truth could lead him—then he is ill-equipped for the game of politics. Politics is property. You pick up as much as you can, pay the minimum for the holding, extract the maximum, and combine where you may—small geniuses like Humphrey saw, for example, that devout trade-unionism and devout anti-Communism might once have faced each other across no-man's-land but right after the second world war were ready to enrich each other into the tenfold of national respectability.

There is no need to underline Lyndon Johnson's ability to comprehend these matters. (For the higher game of international politics-is-property he was about as well-equipped as William F. Buckley, Eleanor Roosevelt, Barry Goldwater, George Patton, J. Edgar Hoover, Ronald Reagan, and Averill Harriman, but that is another matter.) Johnson understood that so far as a man was a political animal (and therefore not searching for some private truth which might be independent of politics) he was then, if deprived of his properties, close to being a dead man. So the true political animal is cautious—he never, except in the most revolutionary times, permits himself to get into a position where he will have to dare his political stake on one issue, one bet, no, to avoid that, he will even give up small pieces of his stuff for nothing, he will pay tribute, which is how raids are sometimes made, and how Barry Goldwater won his nomination. (For his followers promised political extermination with all dispatch to those marginal delegates not quite ready to come along.)

The pearl in the oyster of this proposition is that there is only one political job in America which has no real property attached to it, except for the fantastical property of promotion by tragedy, and that, of course, is the Vice Presidency. It is the only high office to which all the secondary characteristics of political property may adhere—comprehensive public awareness of the name, attention in the press to one's speeches, honory emoluments in the Senate, intimacy (of varying degree) with the President, junkets abroad. If you are very active as Vice President, everyone in America knows your name. But that is your only property. It is not the same thing as real power—more

like being a movie star. Taken in proportion to the size of
the office, the Vice President has less real holding than the
ward-heeler in his anteroom chair. The Vice President can
promise many things, but can be certain of delivering on
nothing. So he can never be certain of getting anything
back. It is not a job for a politician but a philosopher.

It is the thesis of this argument that Lyndon Johnson,
having recognized that he could not win the election in
1968 (and could win the nomination for a candidate of his
choice only by exploding his own party into two or more
fragments) nonetheless set out to make the party vindicate
him. The last property of political property is ego, ego in-
tact, ego burnished by institutional and reverential flame.
Not all men wish statues of themselves on their tomb, but
it is hard to think of LBJ with a plain stone—"Here lies a
simple fellow with many victories and one catastrophic
mistake"—Lyndon would carry his emoluments into the
debating chambers of Hell. He had had to live after all
through March and April and May with the possibility of
Bobby Kennedy winning the nomination, winning the election, the laughter of the Kennedys playing echoes off the
walls of his own bad dreams; Lyndon had learned during
the propertyless period of his own Vice Presidential days
how rapid could be the slide of your holdings, how soluble
the proud salts of your ego. How quickly might come his
deterioration if a Kennedy were again in office—his own
bleak death in such a case may have spoken to him already.
Men whose lives are built on ego can die of any painful
disease but one—they cannot endure the dissolution of
their own ego, for then nothing is left with which to face
emotion, nothing but the urge to grovel at the enemy's
feet. It is the primitive price one pays for holding onto
property which possesses no moral value. How much Johnson must have been ready to offer in March and April and
May in order that Bobby Kennedy be stopped. Perhaps
even his own vindication might have been sacrificed.

After the Senator's assassination, however, nomination
for Humphrey was empty for Johnson. If Humphrey
wished to win the election, his interest was to separate
himself from the President. Since this was counter to Johnson's interest, the torture of Hubert Humphrey began.

Mark it: politics is the hard dealing of hard men over
properties; their strength is in dealing and their virility.

Back of each negotiator is the magic of his collected properties—the real contention of the negotiation is: whose properties possess the more potent magic? A good politician then can deal with every kind of property-holder but a fanatic, because the fanatic is disembodied from his property. He conceives of his property—his noble ideal!—as existing just as well without him. His magic partakes of the surreal. That is why Lyndon Johnson could never deal with Ho Chi Minh, and why he could manipulate Hubert Humphrey with absolute confidence. Humphrey had had to live for four years with no basic property, and nobody knew better than the President what that could do to an animal as drenched in politics as Hubert. Humphrey could never make his move. Deprived for four years of his seat as Senator, deprived of constituency, and the power to trade votes, the small intricate nourishing marrow of being able to measure the profit or loss of concrete favors traded for concrete favors, the exchange of political affections based on solid property-giving, property-acquiring negotiations, forced to offer influence he now might or might not possess, Humphrey never knew where to locate himself in negotiations spoken or unspoken with Lyndon Johnson. So his feet kept slipping. Against the crusades of law and order building on the Right, his hope was to build a crusade on the Left, not to divide the Left. But to do that, he would have had to dare the enmity of Lyndon Johnson, have had to dare the real chance that he might lose the nomination, and that was the one chance he could not take for that would be the hollowest death of them all. He would be lost in retirement, his idle flesh would witness with horror the decomposition of his ego. A politician in such trouble can give away the last of his soul in order not to be forced to witness how much he has given away already.

Hubert Humphrey was the small genius of American politics—his horror was that he was wed to Lyndon Johnson, the domestic genius of us all. Humphrey could not find sufficient pride in his liver to ask for divorce. His liver turned to dread. He came to Chicago with nobody to greet him at the airport except a handful of the faithful—the Vice President's own poor property—those men whose salary he paid, and they were not many. Later, a group of a few hundred met him at the Sherman House, the boys and the Humphrey girls were out. In 1964 some of the

Goldwater girls had looked like hookers on horses, now in '68, some of the women for Humphrey looked like hookers. The Mafia loved Humphrey; they always loved a political leader who kept a well-oiled pair of peanuts in his pants, and there was big money behind Humphrey, $800,000 had been raised for him in one night in New York; he would be the perfect President—for a time—for every speculator who liked a government contract to anchor his line while he got off that touchdown pass. So Humphrey money was there in Chicago for convention frolics, and a special nightclub or cabaret in the Hilton called the Hubaret where you needed a scorecard to separate the trade-union leaders from the Maf, and the women —let us not insult women. Suffice it that the beehives were out, and every girl named Marie had a coif like Marie Antoinette. Every Negro on the take was there as well— some of the slickest, roundest, blackest swingers ever to have contacts in with everyone from Mayor Daley to the Blackstone Rangers. There was action at the Hubaret, and cheer for every late-night drinker. If Hubie got in, the after-hours joints would prosper; the politics of joy would never demand that all the bars be dead by four—who could argue with that?

Negroes in general had never been charmed with McCarthy. If he was the epitome of Whitey at his best, that meant Whitey at ten removes, dry wit, stiff back, two-and-a-half centuries of Augustan culture and their distillate— the ironic manners of the tightest country gentry; the Blacks did not want Whitey at his best and boniest in a year when they were out to find every justification (they were not hard to find) to hate the Honkie. But if the Black militant and the Black workingman would find no comfort or attraction in McCarthy, think then of how the Black mixer-dixer was going to look on Clean Gene. He wasn't about to make a pilgrimage up to some Catholic rectory in the Minnesota North woods where they passed one bean through the hot water for bean soup, no, he wanted some fatback in his hand. You couldn't take the kind of hard and sanctified little goat turds McCarthy was passing out for political marbles back to the Black homefolk when they were looking for you to spread the gravy around. So Hubie Humphrey came into Chicago with nine-tenths of the organized Democratic Party—Black support, labor support, Mafia support, Southern delegates support, and you could find it all at the Hubaret if you were looking, as well as a wet wash of delegates with buttons for Humphrey, the big bold HH with its unwitting—though who knew these days what was unwitting?—reference to barbed-wire fences, concentration camps, gas chambers. The letter H went marching to the horizon.

There were 1,400-1,500 delegates secured for Hubert Humphrey on the day he came to town—such was the hard estimate of the hardest heads on his staff, Larry O'Brien, Norman Sherman, Bill Connell; the figure was low, they were not counting on the favorite sons of the South, nor on the small reserve of uncommitted delegates. Still there were rumors up of gale warnings, and much anxiety—Mayor Daley had led the Illinois delegation into caucus on Sunday, and led them out again without committing a single one of the state's 118 votes to a single delegate and there were stories Daley wanted Teddy Kennedy. John Connally of Texas, furious that the unit rule was about to be abolished in this convention, gave threats on Sunday of nominating Lyndon Johnson.

Either the convention was sewed up for Humphrey or the convention was soft. No one really knew. Usually it was enough to come to conventions with less than a first ballot victory, even two hundred votes less, and you were certain of winning. The panic among delegates to get on the winning side at the last minute is always a stampede. It is as though your land will double in value. Humphrey came in with one hundred to two hundred votes more than he needed, yet he was not without his own panic; he took care to announce on "Meet the Press" before taking the plane to Chicago that he supported President Johnson's Vietnam policies because they were "basically sound." For two months he had been vacillating, giving hints one day that he was not far from the doves, rushing back the next to be close in tone to the Administration. It could be said, of course, that it was part of his political skill to keep the McCarthyites uncertain of his position; once convinced that he would take a line close to Lyndon Johnson on the war in Vietnam, they might look—McCarthy included—to induce Teddy Kennedy to run. So Humphrey played at being a dove as a way of holding the youngest Kennedy in Hyannis. But what was he to gain besides the approval of Lyndon Johnson? A liaison with McCarthy could even give him a chance for victory in November. Yet Humphrey engaged in massive safe play after massive safe play, paying court to the South, paying court to LBJ, to Daley, to Meany, to Connally; even then, he came to Chicago with his nomination insecure. He had 1,500 votes, but if something went wrong he did not know if he could count on a single one of them—they could all wash away in the night. Humphrey was staying at the Conrad Hilton, but his first act after landing at O'Hare was to proceed to the Sherman House to visit the Illinois delegation. Daley was working to induce Teddy Kennedy to run—once Teddy Kennedy ran and lost, he might have to accept a draft as Vice President. At the same time, once running, he might show huge strength— Daley would then be able to claim he stole the nomination from Humphrey and got it over to Kennedy. Daley could not lose. All the while he was encouraging Kennedy to run, Humphrey was promising Daley more and more treasures, obliged—since he had no political property of his own just yet—to mortgage future property. He was assigning future and double substance to Daley, to the unions, to the South, to business interests. His holding operations, his safe plays to guarantee the nomination once the nomination was already secure, became exorbitantly expensive. A joke made the rounds of the convention:

"What was Hubert able to keep?"

"Well, he was able to keep Muriel."

His dangers were absurdly small. McCarthy, three times unpopular with the delegates, for being right, for being proud that he was right, and for dealing only in moral property, had no chance whatsoever. Moreover, he was disliked intensely by the Kennedyites. If Bobby Kennedy and Gene McCarthy had been in the Sinn Fein together they would have carried their guns in holsters under opposite shoulders —they embodied the ultimate war of the Irish. McCarthy was reputed to carry volumes of Augustine and Aquinas in his suitcase; it is possible Bobby Kennedy thought one of the penalties of being Irish is that you could get lost in the *Summa Theologica*.

But Hubert Humphrey carried no gun and no tome.

Finally he was a hawk not a dove for the most visceral of reasons—his viscera were not firm enough to face the collective wrath of that military-industrial establishment he knew so well in Washington, that rifleman's schizophrenia one could see in the eyes of the clerks at the Pentagon, yes, his fear went beyond political common sense and a real chance to win, it went even beyond slavery to LBJ (because LBJ finally had also been afraid of the Pentagon) it came down to the simple fear that he was not ready to tell the generals that they were wrong. Peace they might yet accept, but not the recognition that they were somewhat insane— as quickly tell dragons to shift their nest.

7

It was a curious convention, all but settled before it began, except for the bile-bubbling fear of the nominee that he would lose; it was locked, yet extraordinarily unsettled, even if totally dominated by Lyndon Johnson. He had his men everywhere—Hale Boggs, Majority Whip of the House on the Platform Committee; Carl Albert, Majority Leader of the House as Chairman of the convention; John B. Connally, Governor of Texas, and Mayor Daley, Governor of Chicago, in front of the rostrum with their Texas and Illinois delegations, the rostrum indeed so layered about with Humphrey delegations that if one took a swing in semicircle through the states nearest to the podium, Minnesota, Utah, Kentucky, Tennessee, Texas, Rhode Island, the Virgin Islands, Illinois, Pennsylvania, West Virginia, Hawaii, Connecticut, New Jersey, Delaware and Florida, the final returns for Johnson's candidate were 730 votes out of a possible 834, and in none of those states did he have less than two-thirds of the delegates. To the rear of the Amphitheatre, in a semicircle through the seats farthest removed from the podium, Vermont, Puerto Rico, New York, California, Colorado, Virginia, Wisconsin, Arkansas, Oregon, Missouri, Mississippi, and New Hampshire, the vote for Humphrey was only 297 out of 720.

It could be asked to what end go such picayune preparations, and the answer is politics is property. A good seat at a convention, strong, central and down front, is as important as a good seat at a show. Politicians do not have egos which sleep far from their property; since they are all a hint psychopathic (their sense of the present being vastly more intense than their sense of the past) a poor seat depresses their view of themselves. This might have an effect of no more than one percent on the stout-hearted, but Lyndon Johnson, like the Mafia, worked on point spread and picked up nickels and dimes in every percentage.

The man who made the arrangements was John Criswell, Treasurer of the Democratic National Convention, an unknown until installed by the President; such a Johnson man, he even gave the Humphrey people a difficult time on small matters, which was precisely the way to remind a man like the Vice President that he was yet politically landless. Nonetheless, Humphrey contingents had front seats—they could boo the speaker or cheer him, threaten his delivery with the imminence of their presence, not insignificant when one had to look at Illinois goons humphing in concert with Daley. Some of them had eyes like drills; others, noses like plows; jaws like amputated knees; they combed their hair straight with a part to the side in imitation of the Mayor who from up close had a red skin with many veins and hair which looked like dirty gray silk combed out straight—at his worst, Daley looked in fact like a vastly robust old peasant woman with a dirty gray silk wig. (At his best, he looked respectable enough to be coach of the Chicago Bears.) At any rate, no small matter to have the Illinois delegation under your nose at the podium, all those hecklers, fixers, flunkies, and musclemen scanning the audience as if to freeze certain obstreperous faces, make them candidates for a contract and a hit. The guys with eyes like drills always acted this way, it was their purchase on stagecraft, but the difference in this convention were the riots outside, and the roughing of the delegates in the hall, the generator trucks on the perimeter of the stockyards ready to send voltage down the line of barbed wire, the police and Canine Corps in the marshes west of the Amphitheatre. Politics is property. Rush forward with your standard. Push and push. When you get near the podium, there is nothing to see but Daley and Connally. Take a look at Connally, Governor of Texas, who once sat across from John F. Kennedy in the Presidential limousine passing the Elm Street Book Depository. Connally is a handsome man, mean, mean right to the gum, he has wavy silver hair, is cocky as a dude, sports a sharp nose, a thin-lipped Texas grin, a confident grin—it spoke of teeth which knew how far they could bite into every bone, pie, nipple or tit. Connally belonged to the Texas pure-property school of politics: there were the Ins and the Outs, and the Outs had one philosophy. Get where the Ins are. The Ins had one philosophy. Keep the Outs out. That was politics. Your seat was very important.

It was also important because the microphones for the delegates were varied in their volume. The Illinois, Texas, Michigan, Ohio, and other Humphrey microphones were very clear. The New York, Wisconsin, and California microphones were weak in volume. In an emergency, in any attempt to gain the attention of the Chair, how much more difficult to yell from the rear, how much more futile to wave the standard. In any total emergency when all the mikes were dead—one hand on one switch could accomplish that—who would ever be heard in the rear if the front was demanding the floor? Yes, it was Lyndon's convention, and he controlled it with Criswell and Daley and the Andy Frain ushers, controlled it with plastic passes to enter the Amphitheatre—so specially magnetized, it was advertised in advance, that you had not only to insert them in a box when you went in, but were obliged to insert them again when you went out so that they might be demagnetized. What fury and ushers' fists fell on a delegate from New Hampshire who used a credit card to go in and out, and was detected the second time when he had a reporter to accompany him. But checks by every member of the Press who held a card in the Diners' Club revealed that they were precisely, micrometrically equal in size to the admission passes—what a preparation had obviously been made to load the galleries or floor if the need came. What an absence of real security! And in the interim, how difficult to get to the floor. Television, press, radio and periodicals were drastically restricted in the number of their passes. Whenever the convention came alive, it was next to impossible to reach the floor, so the amount of damage which could be done by keen press coverage was limited. It was not a practical objective, so much as the air of oppression of the convention itself. LBJ hated the Press by now, hated them for the freedom they took to criticize his heart, his good intentions, and his purchase on the truth. He hated them for showing the scar of his gall bladder operation on every front page, hated them for revealing the emptiness of his war in Vietnam, must have blamed them secretly for losing the war—it was no mystery that the Pentagon detested the Press by now, they were some curious fourth dimension in the solid three dimensions of old-fashioned politics-is-property, they opened the door to mockery of high office, gave eminence to Hippies, broadcast criticism of the war, and purveyed some indefinable nihilism. They sped the wrong things up. So Lyndon closed the convention down for them so far as he could; Daley was his arm.

Yet for all the power of his command on that convention floor, Johnson never appeared in person to speak, was rarely mentioned, and the convention sat without a photograph of him anywhere in sight. In Atlantic City in '64 there had been two photos four stories high from floor to upmost balcony. Whereas Lyndon's presence at this convention was felt more as a brain the size of a dirigible floating above the delegates in the smoke-filled air.

Yet for all that he controlled it, the convention was the wildest Democratic convention in decades, perhaps in more than forty years, and the bitterest, the most violent, the most disorderly, most painful, and in certain ways the most uncontrolled—so it was like his Administration: utterly controlled down to the last echo of his voice, and beyond was absolute chaos. At one end was Carl Albert, Chairman, taking his cue on what to do next by nods, fingers, and other signs from Daley's henchmen, transparent in their signification—"Let the boss speak" or "Shut that guy up"—to thirty million TV viewers. At the other end was the chaos of Michigan Avenue when the police fulfilled their Yippie christening and flailed at the forage like wild pigs. With it all was the comedy, sad, dim and sorrowful as a tender laugh, when Senator Daniel K. Inouye of Hawaii, a Johnson man, the keynoter, spent ten pages of his thirteen-page speech in describing the ills of the country. He was not supposed to do that. The keynote speech extols the glories of the party and the iniquities of the opposition. The keynote speech is pure and automatic dividend from collective holdings. It is like passing Go in Monopoly, $200 bucks, but the country was in straits so poor that even with a Johnson man on the podium, the keynoter was obliged to dwell on America's crisis and deliver a troubled and most literate speech.

There was the unit rule fight which had Connally sufficiently furious to be ready to nominate Johnson. There were the credentials fights which reached such a peak of fury at two-thirty of Tuesday morning with the first Monday night session not yet done, that the Chair was booed for many minutes. Tuesday evening when the Georgia delegation by voice acclamation was seated in a great hurry to establish a split, half to Maddox, half to Julian Bond, broader comedy was played. "I had my seat taken away from me," complained a thin boyish white delegate from Georgia, "without their even asking me, notifying me, or the Chair even deigning or condescending to have a vote. That was the way they took my seat away from me. Very high-handed, I call it," said the Georgia delegate in a whining voice like a car singing through the gears. "That was my seat, and they never had no right to it. I feel kind of funny now not having my seat." Yes, politics went right back through the multiplicities of its negotiation and barter to the primal seat in the family ring around the kitchen table and if Older Brother or Sis has taken your seat, then cause for complaint. But when Mom is gone, or any authority to whom you can appeal, well, politics has ceased to exist, Southern politics at any rate.

"Yes sir," said the delegate from Georgia, "I'm going back home to think for awhile, and then I might just decide to work for Mr. Wallace."

"Then, sir," said the interviewer, "you do not plan to work for the Democratic nominee?"

"How can I, sir? They took my seat."

8

Tuesday morning, the California delegation met in the Grand Ballroom of the LaSalle to hear an impromptu debate between Senator McCarthy, Hubert Humphrey, and Senator McGovern. There had been another debate planned for television between Humphrey and McCarthy, but it had never taken place. When McGovern and Lester Maddox announced their candidacies, they insisted at the same time on joining the debate. In the confusion, Humphrey had withdrawn.

Now he was back, however. The onus of refusing to debate McCarthy would no longer be his—besides it was too late to gain or lose more than a few votes by this kind of activity, and indeed, McGovern who was to do very well this particular morning, probably did not gain a total of twenty extra delegates from his efforts. Politics is property, and to fall in love with a man's voice sufficiently to vote for him next day is not to get much return for your holding—besides, the votes McGovern stole were in the main from McCarthy, who was not going to give much return either.

The Grand Ballroom of the LaSalle was on the nineteenth floor, and a noble room, perhaps fifty feet wide, three times as long, with an arched ceiling thirty feet high. Nearly a thousand delegates, guests and newspapermen were to crowd into its space, a hunger for confrontation feeding not only the crowds of students and Yippies in the streets below, but the delegates and the Press themselves, as if the frustration of listening to Johnson and Humphrey defend the war for more than four years had begun unconscious dialogues in many a man and woman not accustomed to muttering to themselves on the street— indeed with proper warning twenty thousand tickets could have been sold in a day for this meeting of the three men.

Yet, it proved curiously anti-climactic. If the atmosphere of the Ballroom was tense, theatrical, even *historical*, no great debate ensued. The technologies of television and convention politics were often curious, they seemed calculated to work to the deterrence of dramatic possibility, and nowhere was this more evident than in the format arrived

at (perhaps hammered out by Humphreyites, for it bene-
fited no one else) since it left each man to make a ten-
minute opening statement, then threw the meeting open
to questions from the delegates. Each candidate who was
asked a question could reply for three minutes, his opponents could comment for two minutes. At the end a
short summation was in order for each. It was a decorous
format, designed precisely to inhibit the likelihood of a
continuing confrontation between the principals, since any
quarrel which started could hardly continue beyond the
time allotted to each question. Politics is property, and
Humphrey's property here was twenty years of service in
the Senate and the Administration—he wasn't about to
limit debate to a slug-fest on Vietnam, no, he would sit on
his seat and let the format cover other subjects as well,
legislative service, the Supreme Court, willingness to support Democratic candidates; they got to talk about Vietnam for a few minutes. That was later, however. The
beginnings were not altogether congenial. Scheduled to
begin at 10:00 A.M., McGovern came in at 10:05, McCarthy at 10:13. Humphrey, following the logic of champion-
ship fights which keeps the contender waiting in the ring,
did not appear in any hurry. At 10:26, McCarthy left the
platform and moved slowly toward the door, shaking hands
with friends and talking. He looked about ready to leave.

But a winner cannot have bad timing. Humphrey came
into the room at 10:30, and the debate, half an hour late,
was on. McCarthy was the first to speak, and something of
the testiness of defeat had gotten into his presentation. He
spoke in his cool, offhand style, now famous for its lack
of emphasis, lack of power, lack of dramatic concentration,
as if the first desire of all men must be not the Presidency,
but the necessity to avoid any forcing of one's own person
(as if the first desire of the Devil might be to make you the
instrument of your own will). He had insisted over all these
months of campaigning that he must remain himself, and
never rise to meet any ocasion, never put force into his presentation because external events seemed to demand that
a show of force or oratorical power would here be most
useful. No, McCarthy was proceeding on the logic of the
saint, which is not to say that he necessarily saw himself as
a saint (although there must have been moments!) but that
his psychology was kin: God would judge the importance

of the event, not man, and God would give the tongue to
speak, if tongue was the organ to be manifested. He would
be good when the Lord chose him to be good, powerful
when the Lord needed power, dominating when that was
God's decision. To attempt to carry the day by the energy
of his own means would be vanity, an exercise for the devil
in oneself, perhaps an offering to the Devil. Everything in
McCarthy's manner, his quiet voice, his resolute refusal to
etch his wit with any hint of emphasis, his offhand delivery
which would insist that remarks about the future of the
world were best delivered in the tone you might employ for
buying a bottle of aspirin, gave hint of his profound conservatism. He was probably, left to his own inclinations,
the most serious conservative to run for nomination since
Robert Taft—yes, everything in McCarthy's manner spoke
out in profound detestation of the Romantic impulse. Man
was not his own project, not his own creation to be flung
across the void in the hope that a thread of gray matter he
might be carrying would end as a bridge right over the
abyss, no, man was probably damned and where not
damned, a damn fool, and so must always distrust the bold-
est and most adventurous of his own impulses. That Mc-
Carthy was also a Romantic could hardly be denied—only
a Romantic would have dared the incalculable wrath
aroused in Lyndon Johnson by the disruption of his volcanic properties, but McCarthy reaching out with his left
hand for the taboo would restrain himself by the right. It
was one thing to run, another to betray one's principles by
running. The central requirement was to remember that all
the filth and all the mess of all the world had come from
men extending themselves further than their means, mar-
shalling emotions they did not quite feel, pushing the stuff
of the heart into theatrical patterns which sought to manipulate others—*there* was the very TNT of spiritual damna-
tion. So McCarthy was damned if he would move a phony
finger for any occasion.

The occasion today in the Grand Ballroom called for an
heroic historic set of speeches which would demolish Humphrey, smelt him down to the suet at the center of his seat,
but there were no false moves for the Senator. The fire to
kill, the fire to condemn, the fury to wield the saint's own
sword was nowhere in him today. Defeat hung over his
cause. Teddy Kennedy would not be nominated, nor any

favorite sons from the South. The months of campaigning were all but over. The Romantic in his own heart, which must have hoped against all gray irons of restraint in his intelligence that somehow, somewhere, the politics of the party would prove not property but spirit, was as dead as the taste of death today—he spoke with the quiet controlled bitterness of a man whose greatest vice was bitterness. If there was a grave flaw in McCarthy, it came out of some penury of his own spirit: too bitter even to express his bitterness, it leaked out of the edges of his wit, turned as punishment upon his own people in the determined bland tone of his presentation in a dramatic hour, and leaking, seemed to get into the very yellow of his skin, his single most unattractive feature.

He was not furious so much at losing as at the lack of recognition given by his party for the isolation and stamina of his performance; he was furious at the indifference, even antipathy, of the bulk of the Kennedy cadres; he was hurt probably more than he could admit even to himself at the entrance of Senator George McGovern, now running on a set of issues almost identical to his own, but softer, more compromising. He had to be icy with wrath at McGovern's comments in the Nebraska caucus yesterday. McGovern had said of McCarthy that he "has taken the view that a passive and inactive Presidency is in order, and that disturbs me. Solving our domestic problems will be much more difficult and that will require an active and compassionate President."

So McCarthy now in his opening remarks to the California delegation spent but a word on Vietnam, even emphasizing that he did not wish to restate his case, and then —no man a match for the glide and slash of McCarthy's wit, the shark in the man could best show here—he said in speaking of criticism of him, ". . . Most recently the suggestion that I would be a passive President. Well, I think a little passivity in that office is all right, a kind of balance, I think. I have never quite known what active compassion is. Actually, compassion, in my mind, is to suffer with someone, not in advance of him." He paused, "Or not in public necessarily." He paused again. Here came the teeth. The voice never altered. "But I have been, whether I have been passive or not, the most active candidate in the party this year."

He had been a baseball pitcher once for a minor league team—he had learned presumably to throw two or three kinds of pitch off the same delivery; some of his pitches could take a man's head off. He went on to talk of New Hampshire in the cold and snow, Wisconsin in the ice, "raising issues all the way"—there was ice enough in his soul now—"They say I was impersonal, I want you to know I am the only candidate who said he would get rid of J. Edgar Hoover and that is a person."

McGovern was next. McGovern was friendly. McGovern was the friendliest man in Chicago. He was a reasonably tall, neatly built man, with an honest Midwestern face, a sobriety of manner, a sincerity of presentation, a youthfulness of intent, no matter his age, which was reminiscent of Henry Fonda. Now, he was making his amends to McCarthy. "I will say to my friend and colleague, Gene McCarthy, that I appreciate what he has done in moving out first in this Presidential race to help turn the course of American policy in Southeast Asia." But he was friends with everyone, "and I don't have a short memory. I remember Vice President Humphrey as one who for twenty years has carried the standard of civil and human justice in our own country." McGovern gave his sweet smile. "What I am trying to say here this morning is that I am no fan of Richard Nixon." He was to win the audience over both hours in just such a way. Now he ended his opening remarks by suggesting that we "tame the savageness of man and make gentle the life of the world." A Christian sweetness came off him like a psychic aroma—he was a fine and pleasant candidate but for that sweetness. It was excessive. Not artificial, but excessive, as the smell of honeysuckle can be excessive.

He had spoken one-and-a-half times as long as McCarthy. Humphrey spoke three times as long, trudging through an imprecision of language, a formal slovenliness of syntax which enabled him to shunt phrases back and forth like a switchman who locates a freight car by moving everything in the yard.

"I happen to believe that one of the unique qualities of the Democratic Party is its leadership over the years—recognizing its fallibility, recognizing its inadequacies, because it is a human instrument—is the capacity of this country to come to this party and its leadership, to come to

grips with change, and to be responsive to the future."
Where Lyndon Johnson spoke and wrote in phrases which
could be hyphenated like Mayor Daley's temporary fences
on the way to the Amphitheatre, making you keep your eye
off the weeds in the vacant lot, and on the dual highway
ahead, so Hubert Humphrey's phrases were like building
plots in sub-developments, each little phrase was a sub-
property—the only trouble was that the plots were all in
different towns, little clichés from separate speeches made
on unrelated topics in distinctly different years were now
plumped down next to each other in the rag-bag map of his
mind. He went on for many minutes planting shrubs in each
separate little plot, saying sweet things about his opponents,
talking of the difficulties of the twentieth century, and the
honor of his own record, the unflagging fight he had made,
the need for unity. His voice had a piping cheerfulness
which seemed to come from the very act of exercising the
faculty of speech; once the current of air started to move
out from his lungs, he was as vibrant as a set of organ pipes
—the thing for him to do was keep striking notes off those
pipes, it did not matter which precise music came out. So
he went on and on, and by the time he was done, close to
half the debate was gone.

Finally the question of Vietnam came up. A delegate
got the floor—doubtless he had it arranged with Jesse Unruh
in advance, why not?

Delegate: "Mr. Vice President, specifically, in what ways,
if at all, do you disagree with President Johnson's position
with reference to Vietnam?"

Humphrey took his time going to the podium. It was a
question he had obviously been ready to expect, and yet he
seemed agitated. It is one thing to know that some day we
will die, it is another to wake in the middle of the night and
hear your heart. Humphrey tried to be grand in his reply;
but the organ pipes had a mote—he was a crack squeaky.
"Would you mind," he asked, "if I just stated my position
on Vietnam?"

"No," the crowd shouted. "No! No!"

"Because," he went on in his little determined voice, "the
President of the United States is not a candidate and I did
not come here to repudiate the President of the United
States. I want that made quite clear."

They shouted no, there were hints of boos, cries of muted

disgust. A professional round of applause from his supporters in the audience came to back him up, a sort of
peremptory we-run-the-meeting-and-we-salute-the-flag was
in the sound. Actually, his supporters did not run this meeting. It was the California delegation, led by Jesse Unruh,
pledged once to Bobby Kennedy, now more or less split
between McCarthy and McGovern, which held the power
here, but there was enough authority in the heavy medicine-
ball palms of the Humphrey hand-beaters to remind the
crowd of other meetings the hand-beaters had run, and
meetings they would yet run again. The sound of the Machine was in the percussion-effects of their skin.

So Humphrey was delivered of any need to delineate
separation of Lyndon Johnson's position on Vietnam from
his own. And proceeded to give his characteristic little
talk—the one which had been losing him the love of the
liberal Left for the last three years. They had, of course,
never had much taste, or they would never have admired
him so much in the first place, but then they had never
had an opportunity before to recognize in intimate continuing detail that Hubert Humphrey simply could not
attach the language of his rhetoric to any reality; on the
contrary, he was perfectly capable of using the same word,
"Freedom" let us say, to describe a ward fix in Minneapolis
and a gathering of Quakers. So he still spoke of our presence in Vietnam as "there to prevent the success of an
aggression." It would do no good to tell him that one
million American and South Vietnamese troops were fighting the aggression of 200,000 or 250,000 Vietcong and
North Vietnamese. If he said there was aggression, then
aggression became his reality—the figures had nothing to
do with it. So "Democracy in South Vietnam" was established because the use of the word by Lyndon Johnson and
himself had established it. The radiance of the sensation
of democracy came from the word itself, "Democracy!"
Halos in his eyes. "When you look over the world scene,
those elections [in South Vietnam] stand up pretty well
and the basis of the Government today is a broader-based
Government." Earlier he had actually said, "We have not
sought to impose a military solution. Regrettably, wars
have their built-in escalation." One would have to be a
great novelist to dare to put this last remark in the mouth
of a character so valuable as Humphrey. "The roadblock

to peace, my dear friends, is not in Washington, D.C. It is in Hanoi, and we ought to recognize it as such."

The medicine-balls gave him a good hand, and he was pleased with himself when he stepped down. He had given a warm sincere little speech which he obviously believed, or rather, had actually experienced. While he spoke, the sensation of truth quivered about him like a nimbus. He must have felt bathed in light. He had the same kind of truth that an actor has while playing Napoleon—with the lights on him, he *is* Napoleon. So with the lights on Hubert, democracy did exist in South Vietnam, and our inability to end the war was indeed Hanoi's fault (even though we had never declared war on North Vietnam and were still bombing half of everything which moved). Hubert Humphrey loved America. So the madness of America had become his own madness. He was a lover after all.

It was McCarthy's turn to speak. Everyone leaned forward. The confrontation was at hand. But McCarthy, receiving no inner voice, drinking some bitter cup of rejection or despair, a simple distaste for the whole human race backing up in him, contented himself with remarking in his most penurious tones, "The people know my position." Perhaps his silence was meant to convey some absolute contempt for Humphrey's remarks, or some absolute statement of his political belief that one must not move without an inner sanction no matter what the occasion; it was still an extraordinary abstention.

Dull anger passed through the audience—but, of course! This was exactly why McCarthy had not been able to win the candidacy. Indeed had he ever wanted to win it, or had he moved like some sinister stalking-horse over the paths of new possibility? Or was he just in a thoroughgoing Irish miff because McGovern was obviously everyone's pet? Once again, the gulf between the answer on one side of the question and the other was greater than the question itself. If Nixon had been an enigma, McCarthy was a larger one.

McGovern picked up all the chips. "Coming in as late as I did," he said in reference to his candidacy, "I can't afford to give up any free time." And he gave an angelic grin. The crowd roared. They were his. They were waiting for an answer to Humphrey.

If a casting director in Hollywood had to find a Boy

Scout leader who could play Romantic lead in a ten-million-dollar movie, McGovern would be his find. There was nobody nicer or cleaner than George McGovern in the city of Chicago. And he made all the points in his sweet troubled vibrant honest good guy Good Christian missionary voice. "I think we Democrats bear a special burden before the American people in 1968 in that four years ago we sought their votes, we sought their confidence on a rallying cry of 'No wider war.'" The house broke down. Wild cheers. Hints of an impromptu demonstration. "It is all very well and good," said McGovern, riding the energy of this enthusiasm, "to talk about the recent election in Vietnam, but let's remember that one of the most honorable candidates in that election, Presidential candidate Chu, was recently sent to jail for five years at hard labor for the single crime of advocating what Senator McCarthy and George McGovern and others have advocated, and that is a 'negotiated end of this war.' Thank you very much."

They gave him a standing ovation. They were delighted. They loved him. He was not really a big enough man to think of him seriously as President, he had more than a hint of that same ubiquitous sweetness which had finally melted away Humphrey's connection between the simplest fact and his own dear brain, but McGovern had years to go before he would sing *castrat'*. He would even—if he had entered earlier, but of course he had not, no accident he had not—have done modestly well in taking delegates from McCarthy, he offered everything McCarthy did not, including the pleasure of watching Hubert Humphrey smile like a roasted cherub at the standing ovation given the speaker who had just demolished his speech. What a passion was in the air to tell Humphrey of the fury of the doves.

They had been squeezed, squashed, gunned down, outmaneuvered, driven in rout from the summits of power at this convention, had seen their party escape from them and race to the abyss with the Fool for their unwanted candidàte—so it was their one opportunity to shout into his face, and they took it. Fool!

When this ovation was done, the debate went on, anticlimactic but for a later speech by McCarthy, a speech in which he as much as said farewell to those who had hopes for him in this room, and in that land of suburbs and television sets where his crusade had first been cheered. Asked if he would throw his support "to another person who has similar views," he began quietly, proceeded quietly, but his metaphor on this occasion was equal to his bitterness, his pride, and his high sense of the standards. He brought the curtain down with that dignity which was his most unique political possession. ". . . many stood on the sidelines, as I said earlier, on the hilltops, dancing around the bonfires. Few came down into the valley where the action was. And I said then that if one challenged the President he had to be prepared to be President. It is like striking at the King—it is a dangerous thing." How dangerous only he could know. Only he could know how far a pressure could push a terror, and how many mutations might a nightmare produce, yes, he had had to face Lyndon Johnson at eight in the morning and three in the morning, in the fatigue of five o'clock on a hard-working afternoon and after midnight in the effulgence of a full moon—only he had had to face Lyndon Johnson with such thoughts after Bobby Kennedy was dead. Perhaps there was bitterness so justifiable a man's mouth could pucker at the invitation to speak. "I said early in New Hampshire, during the New Hampshire primary—I was asked whether I could support Senator Robert Kennedy if he should become the nominee and his views were the same as my views. I said I could. . . . I have been waiting for them to say the same thing about me." He turned, started to go away, then came back. "One other thing. I said that I could not support a Democratic candidate whose views did not come close to what mine are."

Now he was gone, now back in his seat, the hand of applause started slowly, continued, built in volume. It grew for a surprising time, never wild in its force nor released in its enthusiasm, but it went on. The force of respect was also source for a modest ovation.

9

Later that day, early in the evening, McCarthy went into a meeting with Steve Smith, Teddy Kennedy's brother-in-law, and told him that he was willing to withdraw from the race if Kennedy would enter, and that he would instruct his delegates that they were free; further, he would suggest that they give their support to Kennedy.

Would there be anything he desired in return?

No, he was not asking for anything in victory or defeat. (McCarthy was obviously a fanatic—he was seeking to destroy politics-is-property.)

Smith thanked him, told him he would relay his message to Teddy Kennedy, made some comment on the munificence of the offer, perhaps thinking to himself that it came a little late, and left.

Perhaps two hours after this, the reporter encountered McCarthy by chance in a Chicago restaurant on the North Side.

The Senator, sitting at a long table in the corner of the main dining room, a modest room (for the restaurant was situated in a brownstone) had his back comfortably to the wall, and was chatting over the coffee with his guests. The atmosphere was sufficiently relaxed for the reporter and his friend, another reporter who had been doing a story on McCarthy for *Look*, to come up past the Secret Service without great strain and greet the Senator. Neither of the reporters was to know anything about the meeting with Steve Smith until some days later, but it was likely McCarthy had come to some decision—at the least, he was more relaxed than at any time the reporter had seen him in Chicago. Perhaps it was the friends he was with, big Irishmen like himself for the most part, a couple of them present with their wives, or at least such was the reporter's impression, for he was introduced to more than a half-dozen people in the aftermath of meeting the Senator and some were big genial Irishmen with horn-rimmed glasses and some were lean Irishmen with craggy faces, and one was an Irishman from Limerick with a Dublin face, one-third poet, one-third warrior, one-third clerk. Perhaps it was the company, but the reporter had never seen McCarthy in such a mood. The benign personality of the public meetings, agreeable but never compelling, was gone—the personality which suggested that serious activity had something absurd about it—gone. The manner which declared, "I'm a nice guy, and look what I got into"—gone!

Speaking with the license a man has when his dinner is interrupted, McCarthy struck back to the conversation twelve weeks earlier in a living room in Cambridge, "Still waiting for me to repeat that 1960 speech?"

"Well, Senator," said the reporter—he was trying to become sufficiently presumptuous to say, "if you could make a speech like that on the war in Vietnam tonight when the peace plank is debated . . ."

But McCarthy cut him off. "That was then. We don't retain all our abilities necessarily. Once the ability leaves you, how do you regain it?" It was impossible to tell if he was mocking the reporter or mocking himself. "I used to be angry then," he said across the table with an evil look of amusement, as if recording these remarks for posterity as well, his yellow eyes gleaming in the light, "but I can't seem to get angry again. It's a gift to get angry when you wish to get angry, Mailer."

"A grace I would say, sir."

If the table had been laughing at McCarthy's sallies, they chuckled now with his. The Senator's friends looked tough and were tough-minded, but they were obviously open to wit from any corner.

"Then you also want to ask yourself if you should get people angry." McCarthy went on in a voice of the hardest-tempered irony. "Once you get them angry, you've got to get them quieted down. That's not so easy. Lyndon, for instance, has never understood the problem. He thinks politicians are cattle, whereas in fact most politicians are pigs. Now, Norman, there's a little difference between cattle and pigs which most people don't know. Lyndon doesn't know it. You see, to get cattle started, you make just a little noise, and then when they begin to run, you have to make more noise, and then you keep driving them with more and more noise. But pigs are different. You have to start pigs running with a great deal of noise, in fact the best way to start them is by reciting Latin, very loudly, that'll get them running—then you have to quiet your voice bit by bit and they'll keep moving. Lyndon has never understood this."

These gnomic remarks now concluded, the reporter had no idea precisely what the Senator was talking about. He had been expanding a metaphor, and images of the stockyards, the convention, the war on the streets, the expression on the face of Humphrey delegates and McCarthy delegates, and some tidal wave of contempt at the filthy polluted plumbing of things was in the remark. In the laughter which followed, the reporter was silent.

"It's a funny thing about pigs," McCarthy went on. "They have an odd way of keeping warm in winter if they find themselves outside. You see, pigs don't know if they're cold, provided their nose is warm. So they stand around in a circle with their nose between the hind legs of the pig in front of them. Wouldn't you call that a curious relationship?"

"Oh, Senator, I would call that a Satanic relationship."

McCarthy joined in the laughter. Hard was his face, hard as the bones and scourged flesh of incorruptibility, hard as the cold stone floor of a monastery in the North Woods at five in the morning. The reporter leaned forward to talk into his ear.

"You see, sir," he said, "the tragedy of the whole business is that you should never have had to run for President. You would have been perfect for the Cabinet." A keen look back from McCarthy's eye gave the sanction to continue. "Yessir," said the reporter, "you'd have made a perfect chief for the F.B.I!" and they looked at each other and McCarthy smiled and said, "Of course, you're absolutely right."

The reporter looked across the table into one of the hardest, cleanest expressions he had ever seen, all the subtle hints of puffiness and doubt sometimes visible in the Senator's expression now gone, no, the face that looked back belonged to a tough man, tough as the harder alloys of steel, a merciless face and very just, the sort of black Irish face which could have belonged to one of the hanging judges in a true court of Heaven, or to the proper commissioner of a police force too honest ever to have existed.

The reporter left. But the memory of McCarthy at this

table persisted. And the memory of his presence, harder than the hardest alloys of steel. But not unjust. What iron it must have taken to be annealed in Lyndon's volcanic breath. Yes, the reporter had met many candidates, but McCarthy was the first who felt like a President, or at least felt like a President in that hard hour after he had relinquished the very last of his hopes, and so was enjoying his dinner.

10

We have been present until now at an account of the Democratic Convention of 1968. It has not, however, been a description of the event. The event was a convention which took place during a continuing five-day battle in the streets and parks of Chicago between some of the minions of the high established, and some of the nihilistic of the young. But if we had begun with a description of this superb battle, it might not have been automatic to transfer interest to the convention, since the greatest excitement in the Amphitheatre was often a reflection of the war without.

Yet, let us hesitate for one last patriot's cry before slogging to the front. It is from the speech of Governor Lester G. Maddox of Georgia which announced his candidacy for the Democratic nomination on August 17, 1968. Since we will see the Governor but once again, and he is a fellow of pithy comment, let us describe him pithily: Governor Maddox has the face of a three-month-old infant who is mean and bald and wears eyeglasses.

From our Governor's speech:

I am proud to be an American. Aren't you?
I love my country and its flag and I regard defending them as a privilege as well as a duty. Don't you?
I . . . when I sing God Bless America, I mean it with all of my heart.

. . . the problems which confront us are the direct result of our failure to insist that our leaders put first things first . . . the safety of law-abiding citizens ahead of the safety of law-defying citizens. . . .

Politics is property; property relations are law-abiding. Even seizure of property can be accomplished legally. So the history of a convention must concern itself with law-abiding citizens; conversely, a study of law-defying citizens who protested the deliberations of this convention in the street ought to find them propertyless, therefore not in politics. In fact, it does not. Not quite. There were two groups to the army of young people who assembled in Chicago; one could divide them conveniently as socialists and existentialists. The socialists, you can be certain, believed in every variety of social and revolutionary idea but membership in the Socialist Party, which of course, being young people, they detested; for the most part they were students of the New Left who belonged to SDS, the Resistance (a movement of confirmed draft resisters) and a dozen or more peace organizations. While their holdings were almost entirely in moral property, it would take a strong country mind to claim that socialists have no property relations in their own politics, since indeed there are ideologies among these sissies, Governor Maddox, which have passed down like a family trust through the generations, and the war for control of a radical committee will often revolve around the established seat of the Chairman.

Emphasis, however, on the New Left is directed away from power struggles; the old Marxist splinter groups reduced all too many old radical admirals to command of leaking rowboats, or, to maintain our corporate metaphor of property, squires in command of chicken coops. The New Left was interested for the most part in altering society (and being conceivably altered themselves—they were nothing if not Romantic) by the activity of working for a new kind of life out in the ghettoes, the campuses, and the anti-war movement. If one would still refer to them generically as socialists, it is because the product of their labor was finally, one must fear, ideological: their experience would shape their ideas, and ideally these ideas would serve to clarify the experience of others and so bring them closer to the radical movement. While they detested almost to a man the repressive, obsessive and finally—they were modern minds—the anally compulsive oppressions of Russian Communism (as much as they detested the anally retentive ideologies of the corporation) there were many among them who were all for the Czechoslovakian Communists, for Che Guevara, for Castro, for Tito up to a point, for Rumania, and for the North Vietnamese. Some of them even made a point of carrying the flags of the NLF in meetings and marches. A number, devoted to the memory of Che, were elevated as well to militant ideals of revolution. A few had come to Chicago ready to fight the police. (We can be certain that their counterparts in Eastern Europe and the Soviet were being attacked and imprisoned by all the Russian bureaucrats who look like Spiro Agnew, Dick Nixon, and Hubert Humphrey.)

First organized for this action in Chicago back on March 23 in a YMCA camp in Lake Villa, Illinois, in a conference of about one hundred anti-war groups, the project had then seemed a direct action capable of attracting large numbers, for Johnson was still in office, and the war in Vietnam showed no sign of ending. Plans, more or less under the aegis of the National Mobilization to End the War in Vietnam (the same clearing house organization which had led the march on the Pentagon) were made for mass demonstrations to protest the nomination of Lyndon Johnson. Since the President was to announce a week later that he would not run again, and the start of the Paris peace talks soon followed, many of the members of the anti-war groups were distracted, and efforts for this huge mobilization under the leadership of David Dellinger, editor of *Liberation* and chief architect of the march on the Pentagon, Rennie Davis, who headed the Center for Radical Research, and Vernon Grizzard, a Boston draft-resistance leader, were lost in the move of many of the younger workers to the Kennedy and McCarthy campaigns. The dream of a broad front of radical groups to meet in Chicago seemed no longer practical. So more modest plans were consolidated between Rennie Davis and Tom Hayden, perhaps the outstanding young leader of the New Left now that Jerry Rubin was a Yippie and Mario Savio was relatively quiescent. Between Hayden, Davis, and Dellinger, the

Mobilization would function. Where aims were similar to the Yippies, led by Abbie Hoffman, Paul Krassner—editor of *The Realist*—and Jerry Rubin there would even be cooperation. Rubin, a former associate of Dellinger on the march to the Pentagon, had been working since December 1967 with a vision of bringing one hundred thousand kids to Chicago to hold a Youth Festival which by a sheer mixture of music, witchcraft, and happy spontaneous disruption would so exacerbate the anxiety of the Establishment that Johnson would have to be nominated under armed guard and real Texas guns. Needless to say, plans of the Yippies had also suffered from Johnson's withdrawal.

Nonetheless, by mid-summer, the wings of the MOB and Yippie army were more or less ready. On one flank was the New Left, still generically socialist, believing in a politics of confrontation, intelligent programmatic warriors, Positivists in philosophy, educational in method, ideological in their focus—which is to say a man's personality was less significant than his ideas; on the other flank, Yippies, devoted to a politics of ecstasy (we will avoid comparisons with Hubert Humphrey's politics of joy) programmatic about drug-taking, Dionysiacs, propagandists by example, mystical in focus. (Rubin had once burned some money in a debate with a Trotskyist.) By the summer of 1968 each group had however so influenced the other on campus, via street activity and in demonstrations, that their differences were no longer significant. Indeed under the impact of Rubin's ideas, the emphasis was much on a politics of confrontation which searched to dramatize the revolution as theater.

But let them speak for themselves. Here is a quotation from Tom Hayden of the New Left:

> . . . The overdevelopment of bureaucracy and technology can lead to a breakdown. A clock can be wound too tight. The super-carrier Forrestal was destroyed by one of its own rockets. In Chicago this week, the military and security machinery . . . might devour its mother the Democratic Party. . . .
> Consider the dilemmas facing those administering the . . . apparatus. They are centralized, suited to confront (or negotiate with) a centralized opposition, but poorly prepared for spontaneous waves of action. . . . They cannot distinguish "straight" radicals from newspapermen or

observers from delegates. . . . They cannot distinguish rumors about demonstrations from the real thing. They cannot be certain whether bomb threats are serious no matter how much they have "sanitized" the hotels and Amphitheatre . . .

We always knew that storming or physically disrupting the convention, or conducting guerrilla war in strange territory, was insane. The perspective has been to show the unrepresentative character of the political system by exposing its essentially repressive response to human need and protest. . . .

. . . Twenty-five thousand troops are being brought here not to stop "disrupters"—no amount of security can stop an assassin or bomber—but because the rulers . . . are relying on coercion. . . . We are forced into a military style not because we are "destructive" and "nihilistic" but because our normal rights are insecure. . . .

Here is a quotation from Ed Sanders, characteristic of the visionary aspects of Hippie prose:

Gentlemen, joy, nooky, circle groups, laughing, dancing, sharing, grass, magic, meditation, music, theatre, and weirdo mutant-jissomed chromosome-damaged ape-chortles have always been my concern for Lincoln Park.

Yours for the power of the lob-throb.

The more practical—by Abbie Hoffman in *The Realist:*

A Constitutional Convention is being planned . . . visionary mind-benders who will for five long days and nights address themselves to the task of formulating the goals and means of the New Society.

It will be a blend of technologists and poets, of artists and community organizers, of anyone who has a vision. We will try to develop a Community of Consciousness.

There will be a huge rock-folk festival for free . . . theater groups from all over the country are pledged to come. They are an integral part of the activities. . . .

Workshops in a variety of subjects such as draft resistance, drugs, commune development, guerrilla theater and underground media will be set up. . . .

There will probably be a huge march across town to haunt the Democrats.

People coming to Chicago should begin preparations for five days of energy-exchange. Do not come prepared to sit down and watch and be fed and cared for. . . . If you don't have a thing to do, stay home, you'll only get in the way.

All of these plans are contingent on our getting a permit, and it is toward that goal that we have been working. A permit is a definite contradiction in philosophy since we do not recognize the authority of the old order, but tactically it is a necessity.

We are negotiating, with the Chicago city government, a six-day treaty. All of the Chicago newspapers as well as various pressure groups have urged the city of Chicago to grant the permit. They recognize full well the huge social problem they face if we are forced to use the streets of Chicago for our action. . . . We have had several meetings, principally with David Stahl, Deputy Mayor of Chicago, and it remains but to iron out the terms of the treaty—suspension of curfew laws, regulations pertaining to sleeping on the beach, etc.—for us to have a bona fide permit on our hands.

The possibility of violence will be greatly reduced. There is no guarantee that it will be entirely eliminated. This is the United States, 1968, remember. If you are afraid of violence you shouldn't have crossed the border.

This matter of a permit is a cat-and-mouse game. The Chicago authorities do not wish to grant it too early, knowing this would increase the number of people that descend on the city. They can ill afford to wait too late, for that will inhibit planning on our part and create more chaos.

It is not our wish to take on superior armed troops who outnumber us on unfamiliar enemy territory. It is not their wish to have a Democrat nominated amidst a major bloodbath. The treaty will work for both sides.

The Yippies like the Hippies were famous for their optimism. The permit was not granted by Stahl or Daley. In turn, an offer by Daley on August 21 to allow a march from 1 PM to 4 PM in a part of Chicago miles away from the convention was rejected by the Mobilization. Hayden said that marchers coming to Chicago "by the tens of thousands" preferred to be at the Amphitheatre. So the city got ready for a week of disorders its newspapers had advised it to avoid. One can only divine the expression on Daley's face when he read literature like the following—it comes from a throwaway in Lincoln Park, given out on Sunday afternoon August 25:

YIPPIE!

Lincoln Park

VOTE PIG IN 68

Free Motel
"come sleep with us"

REVOLUTION TOWARDS A FREE SOCIETY: YIPPIE!

By A. Yippie

1. An immediate end to the War in Vietnam. . . .

2. Immediate freedom for Huey Newton of the Black Panthers and all other black people. Adoption of the community control concept in our ghetto areas. . . .

3. The legalization of marihuana and all other psychedelic drugs. . . .

4. A prison system based on the concept of rehabilitation rather than punishment.

5. . . . abolition of all laws related to crimes without victims. That is, retention only of laws relating to crimes in which there is an unwilling injured party, i.e. murder, rape, assault.

6. The total disarmament of all the people beginning with the police. This includes not only guns, but such brutal devices as tear gas, MACE, electric prods, blackjacks, billy clubs, and the like.

7. The Abolition of Money. The abolition of pay housing, pay media, pay transportation, pay food, pay education, pay clothing, pay medical help, and pay toilets.

8. A society which works toward and actively promotes the concept of "full unemployment." A society in which people are free from the drudgery of work. Adoption of the concept "Let the Machines do it."

9. . . . elimination of pollution from our air and water.

10. . . . incentives for the decentralization of our crowded cities . . . encourage rural living.

11. . . . free birth control information . . . abortions when desired.

12. A restructured educational system which provides the student power to determine his course of study and allows for student participation in over-all policy planning. . . .

13. Open and free use of media . . . cable television as a method of increasing the selection of channels available to the viewer.

14. An end to all censorship. We are sick of a society which has no hesitation about showing people committing violence and refuses to show a couple fucking.

15. We believe that people should fuck all the time, anytime, whomever they wish. This is not a program to demand but a simple recognition of the reality around us.

16. . . . a national referendum system conducted via television or a telephone voting system . . . a decentralization of power and authority with many varied tribal groups. Groups in which people exist in a state of basic trust and are free to choose their tribe.

17. A program that encourages and promotes the arts. However, we feel that if the Free Society we envision were to be fought for and achieved, all of us would actualize the creativity within us. In a very real sense we would have a society in which every man would be an artist.

. . . Political Pigs, your days are numbered. We are the Second American Revolution. We shall win. Yippie!

But let us go to Lincoln Park on this Sunday afternoon.

11

A moment:

The following is a remark by Dino Valente, an electric guitarist. It ran as the headline in an advertisement in the *East Village Other* for an album of his records.

> "You take this electrical power out of the wall and you send it through the guitar and you bend it and shape it and make it into something, like songs for people and that power is a wonderful thing."

Yes, the Yippies were the militant wing of the Hippies, Youth International Party, and the movement was built on juice, not alcoholic juice which comes out of the mystery of fermentation—why, dear God, as fruits and grains begin to rot, does some distillate of this art of the earth now in decomposition have the power to inflame consciousness and give us purchase on visions of Heaven and Hell?—no, rather, we are speaking of the juice which comes from another mystery, the passage of a metallic wire across a field of magnetism. That serves to birth the beast of all modern technology, electricity itself. The Hippies founded their temple in that junction where LSD crosses the throb of an electric guitar at full volume in the ear, solar plexus, belly, and loins. A tribal unity had passed through the youth of America (and half the nations of the world) a far-out vision of orgiastic revels stripped of violence or even the differentiation of sex. In the oceanic stew of a non-violent, tribal ball on drugs, nipples, arms, phalluses, mouths, wombs, armpits, short-hairs, navels, breasts and cheeks, incense of odor, flower and funk went humping into Breakthrough Freak-out Road together, and children on acid saw Valhalla, Nepenthe, and the Taj Mahal. Some went out forever, some went screaming down the alleys of the mad where cockroaches drive like Volkswagens on the oilcloth of the moon, gluttons found vertigo in centrifuges of consciousness, vomitoriums of ingestion; others found love, some manifest of love in light, in shards of Nirvana, sparks of satori—they came back to the world a twentieth-century tribe wearing celebration bells and filthy garments. Used-up livers gave their complexions a

sickly pale, and hair grew on their faces like weeds. Yet
they had seen some incontestable vision of the good—the
universe was not absurd to them; like pilgrims they looked
at society with the eyes of children: society was absurd.
Every emperor who went down the path was naked, and
they handed flowers to policemen.

It could hardly last. The slum in which they chose to
live—for they were refugees in the main from the suburbs
of the middle class—fretted against them, fretted against
their filth, their easy casual cohabiting, their selflessness
(which is always the greatest insult to the ghetto, for selflessness is a luxury to the poor, it beckons to the spineless,
the undifferentiated, the inept, the derelict, the drowning—
a poor man is nothing without the fierce thorns of his ego).
So the Hippies collided with the slums, and were beaten
and robbed, fleeced and lashed and buried and imprisoned,
and here and there murdered, and here and there successful, for there was scattered liaison with bikers and Panthers
and Puerto Ricans on the East Coast and Mexicans on the
West. There came a point when, like most tribes, they
divided. Some of the weakest and some of the least attached went back to the suburbs or moved up into com-
merce or communications; others sought gentler homes
where the sun was kind and the flowers plentiful; others
hardened, and like all pilgrims with their own vision of
a promised land, began to learn how to work for it, and
finally, how to fight for it. So the Yippies came out of the
Hippies, ex-Hippies, diggers, bikers, drop-outs from college, hipsters up from the South. They made a community
of sorts, for their principles were simple—everybody, obviously, must be allowed to do (no way around the next
three words) his own thing, provided he hurt no one doing
it—they were yet to learn that society is built on many
people hurting many people, it is just who does the hurting
which is forever in dispute. They did not necessarily understand how much their simple presence hurt many good
citizens in the secret velvet of the heart—the Hippies and
probably the Yippies did not quite recognize the depth of
that schizophrenia on which society is built. We call it
hypocrisy, but it is schizophrenia, a modest ranch-house
life with Draconian military adventures; a land of equal
opportunity where a white culture sits upon a Black; a

horizontal community of Christian love and a vertical hierarchy of churches—the cross was well-designed! a land of family, a land of illicit heat; a politics of principle, a politics of property; nation of mental hygiene with movies and TV reminiscent of a mental pigpen; patriots with a detestation of obscenity who pollute their rivers; citizens with a detestation of government control who cannot bear any situation not controlled. The list must be endless, the comic profits are finally small—the society was able to stagger on like a 400-lb. policeman walking uphill because living in such an unappreciated and obese state it did not at least have to explode in schizophrenia—life went on. Boys could go patiently to church at home and wait their turn to burn villages in Vietnam. What the Yippies did not recognize is that their demand for all-accelerated entrance into twentieth-century Utopia (where modern mass man would have all opportunities before him at once and could thus create and despoil with equal conscience—up against the wall mother-fucker, let me kiss your feet) whether a vision to be desired or abhorred, was nonetheless equal to straight madness for the Average Good American, since his liberated expression might not be an outpouring of love, but the burning of his neighbor's barn. Or, since we are in Chicago, smashing good neighbor's skull with a brick from his own back yard. Yippies, even McCarthyites, represented nothing less by their presence than the destruction of every saving hypocrisy with consequent collision for oneself—it is not so easy to live every day of your life holding up the wall of your own sanity. Small wonder the neighborhood whites of Chicago, like many small-town whites in other places, loved Georgie Wallace—he came in like cavalry, a restorer of every last breech in the fort.

Somber thoughts for a stroll through Lincoln Park on a Sunday afternoon in summer, but the traffic of the tourists and the curious was great; one had to leave the car six blocks away. Curiosity was contained, however, in the family automobile: the burghers did not come to the park. Young tourists and cruisers were there in number, tough kids, Polish and Irish (not all plainclothesmen) circulating around the edges of the crowd, and in the center of the southern part of Lincoln Park where the Yippies had chosen to assemble on an innocuous greensward undistinguished from similar meadows in many another park, a folk-rock group was playing. It was an orderly crowd. Some-where between one and two thousand kids and young adults sat on the grass and listened, and another thousand or two thousand, just arrived, or too restless to sit, milled through an outer ring, or worked forward to get a better look. There was no stage—the entrance of a flatbed truck from which the entertainers could have played had not been permitted. so the musicians were half hidden, the public address system —could it work off batteries?—was not particularly clear. For one of the next acts it hardly mattered—a young white singer with a cherubic face, perhaps eighteen, maybe twenty-eight, his hair in one huge puff ball teased out six to nine inches from his head, was taking off on an inter-planetary, then galactic, flight of song, halfway between the space music of Sun Ra and "The Flight of the Bumblebee," the singer's head shaking at the climb like the blur of a buzzing fly, his sound an electric caterwauling of power come out of the wall (or the line in the grass, or the wet plates in the batteries) and the singer not bending it, but whirling it, burning it, flashing it down some arc of con-sciousness, the sound screaming up to a climax of vibra-tions like one rocket blasting out of itself, the force of the noise a vertigo in the cauldrons of inner space—it was the roar of the beast in all nihilism, electric bass and drum driving behind out of their own non-stop to the end of mind. And the reporter, caught in the din—had the horns of the Huns ever had noise to compare?—knew this was some variety of true song for the Hippies and adolescents in the house, in this enclave of grass and open air (luxury apartments of Lake Shore Drive not five football fields away) crescendos of sound as harsh on his ear, ear of a generation which had danced to "Star Dust," as to drive him completely out of the sound, these painted dirty under-twenties were monsters, and yet, still clinging to recognition in the experience, he knew they were a generation which lived in the sound of destruction of all order as he had known it, and worlds of other decomposition as well; there was the sound of mountains crashing in this holocaust of the decibels, hearts bursting, literally bursting, as if this were the sound of death by explosion within, the drums of physiological climax when the mind was blown, and forces of the future, powerful, characterless, as insane and scalding as waves of lava, came flushing through the urn of all acquired culture and sent the brain like a foundered carcass smashing down a rapids, revolving through a whirl of demons, pool of uproar, discords vibrating, electric crescendo screaming as if at the electro-mechanical climax of the age, and these children like filthy Christians sitting quietly in the grass, applauding politely, whistles and cries of mild approval when the song was done, and the reporter as affected by the sound (as affected by the recognition of what nihilisms were calmly encountered in such musical storm) as if he had heard it in a room at midnight with painted bodies and kaleidoscopic sights, had a certainty which went through gangs and groups and rabble, tourists and consecrated saints, vestal virgins with finger bells, through the sight of Negroes calmly digging Honkie soul, sullen Negroes showing not impressed, but digging, cool on their fringe (reports to the South Side might later be made) through even the hint of menace in the bikers, some beaks alien to this music, come to scoff, now watching, half turned on by noise so near to the transcendencies of some of their own noise when the whine of the gears cohabited with the pot to hang them out there on the highway singing with steel and gasoline, yeah, steel and gasoline exactly equal to flesh plus hate, and blood plus hate; equations were pure while riding the balance of a machine, yes, even the tourists and the college boys who would not necessarily be back contributed nonetheless to the certainty of his mood. There was a mock charade going on, a continuation of that celebration of the Yippie Convention yet to come, when Pigasus, a literal pig, would be put in nomination. Vote Pig in '68, said the Yippie placards, and now up at the stage, music done, they announced another candidate to a ripple of mild gone laughter across the grass, Humphrey Dumpty was the name, and a Yippie clown marched through the crowd, a painted egg with legs, "the next President of the United States," and in suite came a march of the delegates through an impromptu aisle from the stage to the rear of the crowd. A clown dressed like a Colorado miner in a fun house came first; followed Miss America with hideous lip-sticked plastic tits, stars of rouge on her cheeks; Mayor

Daley's political machine—a clown with a big box horizontal to his torso, big infant's spoon at the trough on top of the box, and a green light which went on and off was next; then the featured delegate, the Green Beret, a clown with a toy machine gun, soot, and red grease on his face, an Australian bush hat on his head. Some sort of wax vomit pop-art work crowned the crown. Yes, the certainty was doubled. Just as he had known for one instant at the Republican Gala in Miami Beach that Nelson Rockefeller had no chance of getting the nomination, so he knew now on this cool gray Sunday afternoon in August, chill in the air like the chill of the pale and the bird of fear beginning to nest in the throat, that trouble was coming, serious trouble. The air of Lincoln Park came into the nose with that tender concern which air seemed always ready to offer when danger announced its presence. The reporter took an unhappy look around. Were these odd unkempt children the sort of troops with whom one wished to enter battle?

12

The justifications of the March on the Pentagon were not here. The reporter was a literary man—symbol had the power to push him into actions more heroic than himself. The fact that he had been marching to demonstrate against a building which was the living symbol of everything he most despised—the military-industrial complex of the land —had worked to fortify his steps. The symbol of the Pentagon had been a chalice to hold his fear; in such circumstances his fear had even flavored his courage with the sweetest emotions of battle.

But in Chicago, there was no symbol for him. Not the Amphitheatre in the stockyards, for he had a press pass to enter, and had entered indeed—it did not seem as much of a protest to march to a building he had entered already.

Besides, the city would not allow a march: one was offered then the choice to be tear-gassed or abstain. Of course, there was the Conrad Hilton for a convenient symbol, but it was Democratic Party Headquarters and Press Headquarters, and he had a room in the Hilton, in fact it was the only Hilton Hotel he did not dislike, for it was old, not new, and had thousands of little rooms, or so it seemed, like the St. George in Brooklyn, plus a dingy rear twenty-five stories high with the sad legend, "World's Largest and Friendliest Hotel" painted in black and white on the weary color-dead elephantine brick. There was Lincoln Park, and anyone who wished to protest the horrors of the continuing war in Vietnam, or the horrors of this Democratic convention which would choose the candidate least popular and least qualified by strength, dignity, or imagination to lead, could bed down in Lincoln Park. The city, we may remember, had refused to issue a permit to the Yippies. So they could not sleep in the park. They had been ordered to vacate it by eleven. Their leaders had even told them to vacate it.

Paul Krassner:

"Sleeping in Lincoln Park after 11 P.M. isn't as important as living our revolution there the rest of the day (the park opens at 6 A.M.)."

Jerry Rubin:

". . . Chicago is a police state, and we must protect ourselves. The cops want to turn our parks into graveyards. But we, not them, will decide when the battle begins."

In fact, as everyone knew, many were not going to vacate the park, they were going to force the police to drive them out; so one could protest with one's body, one could be tear-gassed—with what unspoken later damage to the eyes had never necessarily been decided—and one could take a crack on the head with a policeman's stick, or a going-over by plainclothesmen. The reporter had an aversion to this. Besides, he was afraid of his *own* violence. It was not that he was such a good fighter, but he was not altogether courteous either—he had broken a man's jaw in a fight not so long before, and was not certain the end of that was yet heard; it had left him nervous and edgy about fights. He was not afraid of his own violence because he necessarily thought it would be so heinous to break a policeman's jaw, good law-abiding citizen that he was! It was more that he was a little concerned with what the policeman's friends and associates might do to him immediately afterward. He had taken a hint of a bad beating once or twice in his life; he was, conceivably, ready to take much more, but he could not pretend that he welcomed it.

So he went that night—after the visit to the park on Sunday afternoon—to a party, and from there to the Hilton and a quick visit on impulse to Humphrey's private headquarters, where, late at night, there was nobody to receive him but six or eight young Secret Servicemen or F.B.I. with bullet-faces, crew cuts, and an absurd tension at the recognition of his name.

The mission to see Humphrey fruitless as he had known it would be, he had merely wanted to look at the style of Humphrey's cops, he then went down a few floors and to bed, and did not know until the morning that there had been a battle already in Lincoln Park, and the Yippies driven out long after the 11 P.M. curfew with tear gas, and what was more sensational some reporters and photographers showing press cards had been beaten with the rest.

Monday night, the city was washed with the air of battle. Out at the stockyards, some hours after the convention had begun, the streets were empty but for patrol cars and police barricades at every approach. The stench of the yards was heavy tonight, and in a district nearby where the Mayor lived like the rest of his neighbors in a small wooden frame house, the sense of Chicago as a city on the plains (like small railroad cities in North Dakota and Nebraska) was clear in image, and in the wan streetlights, the hushed sidewalks, for almost no one was out in this area, the houses looked ubiquitously brown, the fear within almost palpable outside. The average burgher of Chicago, cursed with the middling unspiked culture of that flat American midcult which lay like a wet rag on the American mind, was without those boulevards and mansions and monuments of the mind which a thoroughgoing culture can give to paranoia for enrichment; no, the Chicagoan hiding this Monday night (as he was to hide Tuesday night, Wednesday night, Thursday night) inside his home was waiting perhaps for an eruption of the Blacks or an avalanche of

Yippies to storm the chastity of his family redoubts. So fear was in these empty streets, and the anger of the city at its own fear, an anger which gave promise not soon to be satisfied by measures less than tyranny.

Seven miles to the northeast, just so far as from Greenwich Village to the middle of Harlem, the air of men ready for combat was up in Lincoln Park. It was after eleven, even close to midnight, and police cars were everywhere, and platoons of policemen every few hundred feet, enough for a parade. In the meadow in the angle between North Clark Street and LaSalle Drive, where the reporter had heard the music the afternoon before, there were now a few hundred people milling about. In the dark, there was no way to count, perhaps a few thousand in all of the park, youths up for an event with every muted mix of emotion, fear as clean as skiers before a steep downhill run, and vigorous crazy gaiety in the air like college pranksters before a panty raid; with it, the night nonetheless not without horror, very much not without horror, as if a fearful auto accident had taken place but ten minutes before and people wandered about now in the dark with awareness that bodies wrapped in bloodstained blankets might be somewhere off a shoulder of the road. In the near distance, the blue light of a police car was revolving through the dark, the menacing blue light turning 360 degrees around and around again, and a white-silver light pierced the retina in alternation, lighting up the faces of boys not twenty-two, not twenty, some of them in Indian blankets or ponchos, others in white shirts and khaki pants, sleeves rolled up, some with jackets, some with bikers' helmets, others with football helmets, a fencing jacket or two, and the hint of a few with private weapons, spade cats drifting in and out, emitting that high smoke of action carried from night to night in the electrified cool of the blood.

Twenty or thirty of the kids were building a barricade. They brought in park benches and picnic tables, and ran it a distance of fifty feet, then a hundred feet. A barricade perhaps six feet high. It made no sense. It stood in the middle of a field and there were no knolls nor defiles at the flanks to keep the barricade from being turned—the police cars would merely drive around it, or tear-gas trucks would push through it.

It was then the reporter decided to leave. The park was cool, it was after midnight, and if the police had not come yet, they might not come for hours, or perhaps not at all—perhaps there were new orders to let the kids sleep here—he simply did not know. He only knew he did not wish to spend hours in this park. For what was one to do when the attack came? Would one leave when asked—small honor there—why wait to offer that modest obedience. And to stay—to what end?—to protest being ejected from the park, to take tear gas in the face, have one's head cracked? He could not make the essential connection between that and Vietnam. If the war were on already, if this piece of ground were essential to the support of other pieces of ground . . . but this ridiculous barricade, this symbolic contest with real bloody heads—he simply did not know what he thought. And he had a legitimate excuse for leaving. One of his best friends was with him, a professional boxer, once a champion. If the police ever touched him, the boxer would probably be unable to keep himself from taking out six or eight men. The police would then come near to killing the boxer in return. It was a real possibility. He had the responsibility to his friend to get him out of there, and did, even encountering Allen Ginsberg, William Burroughs, Jean Genet, Richard Seaver and Terry Southern on the way in. They had the determined miserable look of infantrymen trudging to the front; and Ginsberg, who had no taste for the violence ahead, and no conception whatsoever of looking for a way to avoid it, gave him a friendly salute, free of prejudice, and shuffled on forward to the meadow while Genet, large as Mickey Rooney, angelic in appearance, glanced at him with that hauteur it takes French intellectuals at least two decades to acquire. Burroughs merely nodded. Nothing surprised him favorably or unfavorably.

There was, of course, now every pressure to return but he would not—there was the real (if most fortuitous) danger of exposing the boxer; there was his own decision. He was either being sensible, militarily sensible, revolutionary in the hard way of facing into twenty years of a future like this, and the need for patience till the real battles came; or he was yellow. And he did not know. Fear was in him, but he had acted boldly in the past with much more fear than this. He could not decide whether he was in danger of deteriorating, or becoming sufficiently tough to be able to take a backward step.

And enjoyed the party he went to after this, enjoyed himself until the morning when he discovered the attack by the police had been ferocious, and Ginsberg had been tear-gassed, his throat so injured he could hardly speak—and since the chanting of his Hindu hymns was a spiritual manna for Ginsberg, how the injury to his voice would hurt. And worse. Seventeen newsmen had been attacked by police, a photographer for the Washington *Post*, two reporters for the Chicago *American*, one for the Chicago *Daily News*, two photographers and a reporter for the Chicago *Sun-Times*, a reporter and a photographer for *Life*, cameramen for three television networks, and three reporters and a photographer for *Newsweek* magazine. But since the reporter was not there, let us quote from the Washington *Post* in a story by Nicholas von Hoffman:

> The attack began with a police car smashing the barricade. The kids threw whatever they had had the foresight to arm themselves with, rocks and bottles mostly. Then there was a period of police action before the full charge.
>
> Shrieks and screams all over the wooded encampment area while the experienced militants kept calling out, "Walk! Walk! For Chrissakes don't run." There is an adage among veteran kids that "panicky people incite cops to riot."
>
> Rivulets of running people came out of the woods across the lawn area, the parking lots toward Clark Street. Next, the cops burst out of the woods in selective pursuit of news photographers. Pictures are unanswerable evidence in court. They'd taken off their badges, their name plates, even the unit patches on their shoulders to become a mob of identical, unidentifiable club swingers.
>
> . . . There is the scene at Henrotin Hospital with editors coming in to claim their wounded. Roy Fischer of the Chicago Daily News, Hal Bruno of Newsweek. Television guys who took a special clobbering waiting in the anteroom describing what happened and looking angry-eyed at the cops hanging around with the air of guys putting in a routine night.

The counterrevolution had begun. It was as if the police had declared that the newspapers no longer represented the true feelings of the people. The true feelings of the people, said the policemen's clubs, were with the police.

13

Next day was Johnson's birthday, which the President celebrated on the ranch. Three thousand youths went to the Chicago Coliseum, an old and crumbling convention hall to attend an anti-birthday party, sponsored by the Mobilization to End the War in Vietnam, and the Holocaust No-Dance Band played at total volume; speeches were made; a song called "Master of Hate" was dedicated to LBJ. It went:

> Suicide is an evil thing
> But at times it is good
> If you've been where the master lives
> I think you surely should.

Phil Ochs sang: "It's always the old who lead us to war; it's always the young who fall," and the crowd rose, held their hands high in a V for Victory sign, and chanted, "No, no, we won't go."

Burroughs and Genet spoke of the police as mad dogs, statements were read for Terry Southern and Allen Ginsberg, and Dick Gregory gave the last speech. "I've just heard that Premier Kosygin has sent a telegram to Mayor Daley asking him to send 2,000 Chicago cops immediately."

The reporter was not present at the Coliseum. He had been covering the convention in the stockyards, expecting the debate to take place that night on the majority versus the minority plank on Vietnam, but the convention adjourned after midnight with the debate postponed for the next afternoon. Little had happened that night worth reporting. So he drove up to Lincoln Park about one-thirty in the morning, and everything seemed calm. A few police were still about, and one or two boys walked along holding wet handkerchiefs to their mouths. The streets were acrid with old tear gas. The reporter did not know that the worst battle of the week had taken place not an hour ago. Let us read a long account but an excellent one by Steve Lerner in the *Village Voice:*

. . . Around midnight on Tuesday some four hundred clergy, concerned local citizens, and other respectable gentry joined the Yippies, members of Students for a Democratic Society, and the National Mobilization Committee to fight for the privilege of remaining in the park. Sporting armbands decorated with a black cross and chanting pacifist hymns, the men of God exhorted their radical congregation to lay down their bricks and join in a nonviolent vigil.

Having foreseen that they could only wage a symbolic war with "little caesar Daley," several enterprising clergymen brought with them an enormous wooden cross which they erected in the midst of the demonstrators under a street lamp. Three of them assumed heroic poses around the cross, more reminiscent of the Marines raising the flag over Iwo Jima than any Christ-like tableau they may have had in mind.

During the half-hour interlude between the arrival of the clergy and the police attack, a fascinating debate over the relative merits of strict non-violence versus armed self-defense raged between the clergy and the militants. While the clergy was reminded that their members were "over thirty, the opiate of the people, and totally irrelevant," the younger generation was warned that "by calling the police pigs and fighting with them you become as bad as they are." Although the conflict was never resolved, everyone more or less decided to do his own thing. By then the demonstrators, some eight hundred strong, began to feel the phalanx of police which encircled the park moving in; even the most militant forgot his quibbles with "the liberal-religious sellout" and began to huddle together around the cross.

When the police announced that the demonstrators had five minutes to move out before the park was cleared, everyone went into his individual kind of panic. One boy sitting near me unwrapped a cheese sandwich and began to stuff it into his face without bothering to chew. A girl standing at the periphery of the circle who had been alone all evening walked up to a helmeted boy with a mustache and ground herself into him. People all over the park were shyly introducing themselves to each other as if they didn't want to die alone. "My name is Mike Stevenson from

Detroit; what got you into this?" I heard someone asking behind me. Others became increasingly involved in the details of survival: rubbing Vaseline on their face to keep the Mace from burning their skin, buttoning their jackets, wetting their handkerchief and tying it over their nose and mouth. "If it's gas, remember, breathe through your mouth, don't run, don't pant, and for Christsake don't rub your eyes," someone thoughtfully announced over the speaker. A boy in the center of the circle got up, stepped over his seated friends, and made his way toward the woods. "Don't leave now," several voices called in panic. The boy explained that he was just going to take a leak.

Sitting in a cluster near the main circle, Allen Ginsberg, Jean Genet, William Burroughs, and Terry Southern were taking in the scene. Ginsberg was in his element. As during all moments of tension during the week, he was chanting OM in a hoarse whisper, occasionally punctuating the ritual with a tinkle from his finger cymbals. Burroughs, wearing a felt hat, stared vacantly at the cross, his thin lips twitching in a half smile. Genet, small, stocky, baldheaded, with the mug of a saintly convict rubbed his nose on the sleeve of his leather jacket. I asked him if he was afraid. "No, I know what this is," he replied. "But doesn't knowing make you more afraid?" I asked. He shook his head and started to speak when the sky fell on us.

It happened all in an instant. The night which had been filled with darkness and whispers exploded in a fiery scream. Huge tear-gas canisters came crashing through the branches, snapping them, and bursting in the center of the gathering. From where I lay, groveling in the grass, I could see ministers retreating with the cross, carrying it like a fallen comrade. Another volley shook me to my feet. Gas was everywhere. People were running, screaming, tearing through the trees. Something hit the tree next to me, I was on the ground again, someone was pulling me to my feet, two boys were lifting a big branch off a girl who lay squirming hysterically. I couldn't see. Someone grabbed onto me and asked me to lead them out of the park. We walked along, hands outstretched, bumping into people and trees, tears streaming from our eyes and mucus smeared across our faces. I flashed First World War doughboys caught in no-man's-land during a mustard gas attack. I felt sure I was going to die. I heard others choking around me. And then everything cleared.

Standing on the sidewalk at the edge of the park I looked back at a dozen little fires which lit up the woods, still fogged with gas. The police were advancing in a picket line, swatting at the stragglers and crumpled figures;

huge trucks, usually used for cleaning the streets, swept toward us spraying more gas. Kids began ripping up the pavement and hurling snowball-size chunks at the truck windows. Then they flooded out into the streets, blocking traffic, fighting with plainclothesmen who awaited our exodus from the park, and bombarding hapless patrol cars which sped through the crowds.

The ragged army split up into a series of mobs which roamed through the streets breaking windows, setting trash cans on fire, and demolishing at least a dozen patrol cars which happened to cruise down the wrong street at the wrong time. Smoke billowed from a house several blocks from me and the fire engines began arriving. A policeman ran from an angry brick-throwing mob, lost his cap, hesitated, and ran away without it. At the intersection of Clark and Division, four cop cars arrived simultaneously and policemen leapt out shooting in the air. From all four sides the demonstrators let them have it; most of the missiles were overthrown and hit their comrades or store windows on the other side of the street. Diving down into the subway, I found a large group of refugees who had escaped the same way. The tunnel looked like a busy bomb shelter; upstairs the shooting continued.

14

They were young men who were not going to Vietnam. So they would show every lover of war in Vietnam that the reason they did not go was not for lack of the courage to fight; no, they would carry the fight over every street in Old Town and the Loop where the opportunity presented itself. If they had been gassed and beaten, their leaders arrested on fake charges (Hayden, picked up while sitting under a tree in daylight in Lincoln Park, naturally protested; the resulting charge was "resisting arrest") they were going to demonstrate that they would not give up, that they were the stuff out of which the very best soldiers were made. Sunday, they had been driven out of the park, Monday as well, now Tuesday. The centers where they slept in bedrolls on the floor near Lincoln Park had been broken into by the police, informers and provocateurs were everywhere; tonight tear-gas trucks had been used. They were still not ready to give up. Indeed their militancy may have increased. They took care of the worst of their injured and headed for the Loop, picking up fellow demonstrators as they went. Perhaps the tear gas was a kind of catharsis for some of them, a letting of tears, a purging of old middle-class weakness. Some were turning from college boys to revolutionaries. It seemed as if the more they were beaten and tear-gassed, the more they rallied back. Now, with the facility for underground communication which seemed so instinctive a tool in their generation's equipment, they were on their way to Grant Park, en masse, a thousand of them, two thousand of them, there were conceivably as many as five thousand boys and girls massed in Grant Park at three in the morning, listening to speakers, cheering, chanting, calling across Michigan Avenue to the huge brooding façade of the Hilton, a block wide, over twenty-five stories high, with huge wings and deep courts (the better to multiply the number of windows with a view of the street and a view of Grant Park). The lights were on in hundreds of bedrooms in the Hilton, indeed people were sleeping and dreaming all over the hotel with the sound of young orators declaiming in the night below, voices rising twenty, twenty-five stories high, the voices clear in the spell of sound which hung over the Hilton. The Humphrey headquarters were here, and the McCarthy headquarters. Half the Press was quartered here, and Marvin Watson as well. Postmaster General and Presidential trouble-shooter, he had come to bring some of Johnson's messages to Humphrey. His suite had a view of the park. Indeed two-thirds of the principals at the convention must have had a view early this morning, two and three and four A.M. of this Tuesday night, no, this Wednesday morning, of Grant Park filled across the street with a revolutionary army of dissenters and demonstrators and college children and McCarthy workers and tourists ready to take a crack on the head, all night they could hear the demonstrators chanting, "Join us, join us," and the college bellow of utter contempt, "Dump the Hump! Dump the Hump!" all the fury of the beatings and the tear-gassings, all the bitter dis-

appointments of that recently elapsed bright spring when
the only critical problem was who would make a better
President, Kennedy or McCarthy (now all the dread of
a future with Humphrey or Nixon). There was also the
sense that police had now entered their lives, become an
element pervasive as drugs and books and sex and music
and family. So they shouted up to the windows of the
Hilton, to the delegates and the campaign workers who
were sleeping, or shuddering by the side of their bed, or
cheering by their open window; they called up through the
night on a stage as vast and towering as one of Wagner's
visions and the screams of police cars joined them, pulling
up, gliding away, blue lights revolving, lines of police hundreds long in their sky-blue shirts and sky-blue crash helmets, penning the demonstrators back of barriers across
Michigan Avenue from the Hilton, and other lines of
police and police fences on the Hilton's side of the street.
The police had obviously been given orders not to attack
the demonstrators here, not in front of the Hilton with half
the Democratic Party watching them, not now at three in
the morning—would anyone ever discover for certain what
was to change their mind in sixteen hours?

Now, a great cheer went up. The police were being relieved by the National Guard. The Guard was being
brought in! It was like a certificate of merit for the demonstrators to see the police march off and new hundreds of
Guardsmen in khaki uniforms, helmets, and rifles take up
post in place, army trucks coughing and barking and filing
back and forth on Michigan Avenue, and on the side streets
now surrounding the Hilton, evil-looking jeeps with barbed-
wire gratings in front of their bumpers drove forward in
echelons, and parked behind the crowd. Portable barbed-
wire fences were now riding on jeeps.

Earlier in the week, it had been relatively simple to get
into the Hilton. Mobs of McCarthy workers and excited
adolescents had jammed the stairs and the main entrance
room of the lobby chanting all day, singing campaign
songs, mocking every Humphrey worker they could recognize, holding station for hours in the hope, or on the
rumor, that McCarthy would be passing through, and the
cheers had the good nature and concerted rhythmic steam
of a football rally. That had been Saturday and Sunday
and Monday, but the police finally had barricaded the kids

out of the lobby, and now at night covered the entrances to the Hilton, and demanded press passes, and room keys, as warrants of entry. The Hilton heaved and staggered through a variety of attacks and breakdowns. Like an old fort, like the old fort of the old Democratic Party, about to fall forever beneath the ministrations of its high shaman, its excruciated warlock, derided by the young, held in contempt by its own soldiers—the very delegates who would be loyal to Humphrey in the nomination and loyal to nothing in their heart—this spiritual fort of the Democratic Party was now housed in the literal fort of the Hilton staggering in place, all boilers working, all motors vibrating, yet seeming to come apart from the pressures on the street outside, as if the old Hilton had become artifact of the party and the nation.

Nothing worked well in the hotel, and much didn't work at all. There was no laundry because of the bus strike, and the house phones usually did not function; the room phones were tapped so completely, and the devices so over-adjacent, that separate conversations lapped upon one another in the same earpiece, or went jolting by in all directions like three handballs at play at once in a four-wall handball court. Sometimes the phone was dead, sometimes it emitted hideous squawks, or squeals, or the harsh electronic displeasure of a steady well-pulsed static. Sometimes one got long distance by taking it through the operator, sometimes one got an outside line only by ringing the desk and demanding it, sometimes one could get the hotel operator only by dialing the outside line. All the while, a photograph of Mayor Daley the size of a postage stamp was pasted on the cradle of the phone. "Welcome to the 1968 National Democratic Convention," it said. Often, one could not even extract a whimper from the room phone. It had succumbed. Sometimes the phone stayed dead for hours. Success in a convention is reduced to success in communications, as the reporter was yet to learn; communications in the headquarters of the largest party in the nation most renowned for the technology of its communications was breaking apart under strikes, pressure, sabotage, security, security over-check, overdevelopment and insufficient testing of advanced technical devices: at the base of the pyramid, sheer human inefficiencies before the combined onslaught of pressure and street war.

The elevators worked abominably. On certain floors the signal did not seem to ring. One could wait a half hour for an elevator to stop on the way down. After a time everybody went up to the top in order to be able to go down. Yet one could not use the stairs, for Secret Servicemen were guarding them. It could, at worst, demand an hour to go to one's room and go down again. So it might have been better to live in a hotel across the Loop; but then there were traffic jams and police lines and demonstrators every night, demonstrators marching along with handkerchiefs to their noses.

This night with the demonstrators up and aroused in Grant Park, tear gas was blowing right into the hotel. The police had tried to gas the kids out of the park when they first arrived in numbers from Lincoln Park, but the wind blew the wrong way, blew the tears across the street into the air conditioning of the Hilton lobby, and delegates and Press and officials walked about with smarting eyes, burning throats, and the presentiment that they were going to catch a cold. The lobby stunk. Not from the tear gas, but from stink bombs, or some advanced variety of them, for the source of the odor was either mysterious, or unremovable, or had gotten into the very entrails of the air-conditioning since it got worse from day to day and drenched the coffee shop and the bars and the lobby with a stench not easily forgettable. Standing near someone, the odor of vomit always prevailed from the bombs—no, it was worse than vomit, rather like a truly atrocious body odor which spoke of the potential for sour vomit in every joint of a bad piece of psychic work. So personal relations were curious. One met attractive men or women, shook hands with them, chatted for a time, said good-bye. One's memory of the occasion was how awful it had smelled. Delegates, powerful political figures, old friends, and strangers all smelled awful.

So nothing worked well in the hotel, and everything stank, and crowds—those who could get in—milled about, and police guarded the entrance, and across the street as the reporter moved through the tight press of children sitting packed together on the grass, cheering the speakers, chanting "Join us! Join us!" and "Dump the Hump" the smell of the stink bombs was still present, but different now, equally evil and vomitous but from a faded odor of

Mace. The nation divided was going to war with stinks; each side would inflict a stink upon the other. The years of sabotage were ahead—a fearful perspective: they would be giving engineering students tests in loyalty before they were done; the F.B.I. would come to question whoever took a mail order course in radio. It was possible that one was at the edge of that watershed year from which the country might never function well again, and service in American hotels would yet be reminiscent of service in Mexican motels. Whatever! the children were alive with revolutionary fire on this fine Tuesday night, this early Wednesday morning, and the National Guard policing them was wide-awake as well. Incidents occurred. Flare-ups. A small Negro soldier started pushing a demonstrator with his rifle, pushing him in sudden fury as at the wild kickoff of a wild street fight; the demonstrator—who looked to be a kindly divinity student—aghast at what he had set off; he had not comprehended the Negro wished no special conversation from him. And a National Guard officer came running up to pull the Negro back. (On the next night, there would be no Negroes in the line of National Guards.)

The kids were singing. There were two old standards which were sung all the time. An hour could not go by without both songs. So they sang "We Shall Overcome" and they sang "This Land Is Your Land," and a speaker cried up to the twenty-five stories of the Hilton, "We have the votes, you have the guns," a reference to the polls which had shown McCarthy to be more popular than Hubert Humphrey (yes, if only Rockefeller had run for the Democrats and McCarthy for the Republicans this would have been an ideal contest between a spender and a conservative) and then another speaker, referring to the projected march on the Amphitheatre next day, shouted, "We're going to march without a permit—the Russians demand a permit to have a meeting in Prague," and the crowd cheered this. They cheered with wild enthusiasm when one speaker, a delegate, had the inspiration to call out to the delegates and workers listening in the hundreds of rooms at the Hilton with a view of the park, "Turn on your lights, and blink them if you are with us. If you are with us, if you are sympathetic to us, blink your lights, blink your lights." And to the delight of the crowd, lights began to blink in the Hilton, ten, then twenty, perhaps so many as fifty lights were blinking at once, and a whole bank of lights on the fifteenth floor and the twenty-third floor went off and on at once, off and on at once. The McCarthy headquarters on the fifteenth and the twenty-third were blinking, and the crowd cheered. Now they had become an audience to watch the actors in the hotel. So two audiences regarded each other, like ships signalling across a gulf of water in the night, and delegates came down from the hotel; a mood of new beauty was in the air, there present through all the dirty bandaged kids, the sour vomit odor of the Mace, the sighing and whining of the army trucks moving in and out all the time, the adenoids, larynxes, wheezes and growls of the speakers, the blinking of lights in the Hilton, yes, there was the breath of this incredible crusade where fear was in every breath you took, and so breath was tender, it came into the lungs as a manifest of value, as a gift, and the children's faces were shining in the glow of the headlights of the National Guard trucks and the searchlights of the police in front of the Hilton across Michigan Avenue. And the Hilton, sinking in its foundations, twinkled like a birthday cake. Horrors were coming tomorrow. No, it is today. It is Wednesday already.

15

If Wednesday was nominating day, it was also the afternoon when the debate on the Vietnam peace plank took place. Indeed, it was also the evening when the Massacre of Michigan Avenue occurred, an extraordinary event: a massacre, equal on balance to some of the old Indian raids, yet no one was killed. Of course, a great many people were hurt. And several hundred delegates started to march back from the stockyards, early Thursday morning after the nomination, carrying lit candles in protest. It was obviously one of the more active days in the history of any convention.

Worn out by his portentous Southern sense of things to come, Lester Maddox, the fourth candidate, Governor of Georgia, even resigned his candidacy Wednesday morning. We quote from Walter Rugaber of the *New York Times:*

> His wife, Virginia, sat beside him weeping softly as Mr. Maddox ended his 11-day fling with a last news conference in the brightly lit Grand Ballroom of the Conrad Hilton Hotel.
> He talked about misinformed socialist and power-mad politicians. He assailed the Democrats as the party of "looting, burning, killing and draft-card burning. What's more," he said, "I denounce them all."

Then he caught a plane back to Atlanta. Who would declare that the chanting in Grant Park through the long hours of Tuesday night and the semi-obscene shouts— Dump the Hump!—had done nothing to accelerate his decision?

Originally, the debate on the Vietnam plank had been scheduled for Tuesday night, but the convention went on past midnight, so the hawks attempted to have it early in the morning. It was their hope to begin at 1 A.M. New York time, and thus obtain the pleasure of denying the doves a large television audience. But the doves raised a post-midnight demonstration on the floor which became progressively more obstreperous until Mayor Daley made the mistake of rising to remonstrate with the gallery, warning that they would be cleared out of their seats if they did not quiet down. "Let's act like ladies and gentlemen, and let people be heard," said Daley to the convention and to millions on television, looking for all the world like the best b.o. ever to come out of *Guys and Dolls*. But it was obvious the greater share of the noise came from behind Daley on the floor, from the rear where McCarthy and McGovern delegates from New York, California, South Dakota, Massachusetts, Wisconsin and Oregon were placed far from the podium. At any rate, the Administration forces lost their play. It was one thing for them to cut off a discussion—that was simply accomplished. One had only to give a signal, then make a quick motion which could as quickly be recognized by the Chairman who would whip in a lightning move for a voice-vote. "The ayes . . . the nays . . . The ayes have it," he would say, and rap his gavel, walk off the podium, close the session. But here, after midnight, the hawks were not trying to cut off a discussion, rather they wished to begin one; the doves had nothing to lose by a noisy non-stop protest. Moves for silence, whacks of the gavel by Carl Albert looking poisonous for being ignored, loud music of the band to drown out the rear delegation. Nothing worked. The television cameras were focussed on the doves who were protesting the lateness of the hour. The hawks could insist on their move, but they would look like the worst of the cattle gang on television. So a signal was passed to Daley by an Administration spokesman who drew his finger across his throat, an unmistakable sign to cut off conversation for the night. Daley, looking like he had just been stuffed with a catfish, stood up, got the floor, made a move to adjourn. Immediately recognized by Carl Albert. The little Chairman was now sufficiently excited to start to say Mayor Daley of the Great State of Chicago. He recovered quickly, however, quick enough to rap his gavel, and declare that the Chair accepted the motion, snapping it through with a slick haste, as if it had been his idea all along! The debate was postponed until Wednesday afternoon.

The debate, however, proved anti-climactic. There had been hopes that McCarthy would speak, idle dreams he might make a great speech; but it was rumored that the Senator, weighing the imponderable protocol of these profoundly established convention manners, had decided he would not enter debate unless Lyndon Johnson came to the Amphitheatre for his birthday party. Johnson, however, was not in the hall; he was still in Texas where he would remain (on the advice of his best wise men since they could not guarantee the character of his reception in the Amphitheatre, nor the nature of the stimulation it might give the streets). Therefore, McCarthy, respecting the balance, was not present either.

The hawks had first proposed fifteen minutes for the debate, than thirty. An hour was the maximum obtainable by the doves. On the greatest national issue any convention had faced since the second world war, debate would provide an hour of speech for each side. Moreover, the sides would make alternate speeches. Thus, no massive presentation of argument nor avalanche of emotion would ever result.

These restrictions having limited the outcome before they began, Rep. Philip Burton of California spoke first for the minority, then Senator Muskie of Maine for the majority. Burton asked that we "heed the voices of men and women of good will who across the land call for peace," Muskie went through the differences in the majority and minority planks, and the similarities, and then concluded that the majority protected our soldiers, whereas the minority was too quick to desire peace at any price.

The speakers came on. They seemed careful to abstain from rich, extravagant, or passionate language. No one got up to say that one million men on our side could not dominate a quarter million men on the other, for that would have been unpatriotic (which for a politician is sacrilege equal to burning money or flooding property) no, the best of the majority roamed mean and keen over the legalities, the technicalities of commitment, the safety of American soldiers, the tempo for establishing representative government; they spoke in styles sometimes reminiscent of the eminent sanity of Dean Rusk; he was always a model of sanity on every detail but one: he had a delusion that the war was not bottomless in its lunacy. Of course, words like lunacy were not for the floor of the convention. Muskie; Sen. McGee of Wyoming; Governor Hearnes of Missouri; Mrs. Geri Joseph of Minnesota; David Pryor of Arkansas; Rep. Ed Edmondson of Oklahoma; Mayor Wilson Wyatt of Louisville; Rep Zablocki of Wisconsin, and Rep. Hale Boggs of Louisiana, Chairman of the Platform Committee, spoke for the majority long enough to put in nitpicking points and intone against Communism. The whine in one American's nasal passages obviously stimulated something in the inner canal of other American ears when Communism was given its licks. The hawks then extolled the dove-like nature of the majority plank. The doves, however, came back by way of Senator Morse to reply that the "majority report stripped of its semantics is nothing but a naked proposal to continue the failures of our policy in Vietnam." Also speaking for the doves: Paul O'Dwyer of New York; Ken O'Donnell of Massachusetts; John Gilligan of Ohio; Senator Gore of Tennessee; Ted Sorensen of New York, and Pierre Salinger of California.

For those who are curious let us give excerpts of a few speeches.

Senator Edmund Muskie: "The choice is this: A negotiated settlement with, or a negotiated settlement without safeguards to protect free elections. . . . A bombing halt with, or a bombing halt without consideration of the air protection for our troops against military risks arising north of the demilitarized zone. . . . Mr. Chairman, I urge the adoption of the majority plank." (Muskie was obviously a contented rooster.)

Theodore Sorensen: "We call for an end to the bombing now—they call for an end if and when and maybe.

"Second, we call for a mutual withdrawal of all U.S. and North Vietnamese troops now. . . . The majority plank says maybe, sometime, if all Vietcong hostilities can somehow cease first.

"Third, we call, as Ted Kennedy called, for letting the South Vietnamese decide for themselves the shape of their own future. They call for the United States to stay and conform the Vietnamese to our political and economic standards.

"Fourth, we call for a reduction of American troops now. . . . They call for a reduction in troops only when the South Vietnamese Army can take over. . . ."

Governor Warren Hearnes: ". . . many of the decisions that are being made here in this convention hall by we politicians have been dictated by the prospects of victory or defeat. Victory or defeat in November.

". . . For God's sake, if you adopt the minority report, you are going to jeopardize the lives of the servicemen in Vietnam."

Kenneth O'Donnell: ". . . we were forced to watch a Congress of the United States . . . cut the budget $6-billion in the last Congress, and they cut it out of all the programs affecting the lives of every single American, out of the programs of health, in education and the problems that face our children . . . we will not have the money unless we are able in some fashion to disengage ourselves from the expeditures not only of our best treasure, the young men, but the fact that we are spending $30-billion a year in a foreign adventure in South Vietnam. It must end."

Representative Hale Boggs: "Can General Abrams supply an answer to me on this question, and I pose the question:

"Is there any possibility of your providing even an approximate estimate of the additional casualties we would take if we stopped the bombing of North Vietnam unilaterally and unconditionally?

"And the answer came back and here I read it to you—these are not my words, these are the words of General Abrams: 'If the bombing in North Vietnam now authorized were to be suspended unilaterally, the enemy in ten days to two weeks could develop a capability in the DMZ area in terms of scale, intensity, and duration of combat on the order of five times what he now has.'

"I cannot agree. I cannot agree to place our forces at the risk which the enemy's capability would then pose. That, my friends, concludes our debate." (Hale Boggs was the hawk's own tern.)

The Administration was taking no chances on birds. A confidential White House briefing had been thrown into the shot-load for this debate, and by the time the last speaker had his word, the military were concluding the debate, that same military which had been giving expert guesses for years on just how many troops and just how many bombs would be necessary to guarantee victory in exactly so many weeks or exactly so many months; the party was still buying just such expert advice. "Scale, intensity, and duration of combat on the order of five times." The Texas delegation up front cheered. Put a big man in a big uniform, let him recite big figures, and they would take the word of no priest or pope. In America the uniform always finished first, the production expert second, and Christ was welcome to come in third. So the vote came out as 1,567¾ to 1,041½—the majority plank was passed. Lyndon Johnson was vindicated by the same poor arguments which had originally implicated him. Politics was property, and the gravitational power of massive holdings was sufficient to pull you out of your own soup.

But the floor would not rest. The New York and California delegations began to sing "We Shall Overcome." Quickly, the Platform was passed; still the New York delegation sang. Now Wisconsin stood on its seats. The rear of the floor booed the front of the floor. A few hundred posters, STOP THE WAR, quickly printed a couple of hours earlier for this occasion, were held up. Defeated delegates yelled, "Stop the War," in the fierce frustration of knowing that the plank was Lyndon Johnson's and the party was still his. The convention recessed. Still the New York delegation sang, "We Shall Overcome," standing on their seats. The convention band across the way tried to drown them out. It played in ever-increasing volume "We Got a Lot of Living to Do."

The managers of the convention turned the New York microphones down, and amplified the public address system for the band. So on the floor of the convention, the doves were drowned in hostile sound, but on the television sets, the reception was opposite, for the networks had put their own microphones under the voices of the delegates, and they sang in force across the continent. Thus a few thousand people on the floor and the gallery heard little of the doves —all the rest of America heard them well. Politics-is-property had come to the point of fission. He who controlled the floor no longer controlled the power of public opinion. Small wonder the old party hands hated the networks—it was agitating to have mastered the locks and keys in the house of politics and discover that there was a new door they could not quite shut. In disgust the hawk delegations left the floor. The doves continued to sing "We Shall Overcome." Now, the orchestra played "Happy Days Are Here Again."

The demonstrators chanted, "We want peace! We want peace!" "I'm Looking Over a Four-Leaf Clover," the orchestra offered, then rejected, then switched over to "If You Knew Suzy," then they gave up. The demonstrators began to sing the "Battle Hymn of the Republic." New York, California, Oregon, Wisconsin, South Dakota and other delegations marched around the empty floor. It was half an hour after the convention had recessed. Still they sang. It had been a long war to lose.

16

Meanwhile, a mass meeting was taking place about the bandshell in Grant Park, perhaps a quarter of a mile east of Michigan Avenue and the Conrad Hilton. The meeting was under the auspices of the Mobilization, and a crowd of ten or fifteen thousand appeared. The Mayor had granted a permit to assemble, but had refused to allow a march. Since the Mobilization had announced that it would attempt, no matter how, the march to the Amphitheatre that was the first purpose of their visit to Chicago, the police were out in force to surround the meeting.

An episode occurred during the speeches. Three demonstrators climbed a flag pole to cut down the American flag and put up a rebel flag. A squad of police charged to beat them up, but got into trouble themselves, for when they threw tear gas, the demonstrators lobbed the canisters back, and the police, choking on their own gas, had to fight their way clear through a barrage of rocks. Then came a much larger force of police charging the area, overturning benches, busting up members of the audience, then heading for Rennie Davis at the bullhorn. He was one of the coordinators of the Mobilization, his face was known, he had been fingered and fingered again by plainclothesmen. Now urging the crowd to sit down and be calm, he was attacked from behind by the police, his head laid open in a three-inch cut, and he was unconscious for a period. Furious at the attack, Tom Hayden, who had been in disguise these last two days to avoid any more arrests for himself, spoke to the crowd, said he was leaving to perform certain special tasks, and suggested that others break up into small groups and go out into the streets of the Loop "to do what they have to do." A few left with him; the majority remained. While it was a People's Army and therefore utterly unorganized by uniform or unity, it had a variety of special troops and regular troops; everything from a few qualified Kamikaze who were ready to charge police lines in a Japanese snake dance and dare on the consequence, some vicious beatings, to various kinds of small saboteurs, rock-throwers, gauntlet-runners—some of the speediest of the kids were adept at taunting cops while keeping barely out of range of their clubs—not altogether alien to running the bulls at Pamplona. Many of those who remained, however, were still nominally pacifists, protesters, Gandhians—they believed in non-violence, in the mystical interposition of their body to the attack, as if the violence of the enemy might be drained by the spiritual act of passive resistance over the years, over the thousands, tens of thousands, hundreds of thousands of beatings over the years. So Allen Ginsberg was speaking now to them.

The police looking through the plexiglass face shields they had flipped down from their helmets were then obliged to watch the poet with his bald head, soft eyes magnified by horn-rimmed eyeglasses, and massive dark beard, utter his words in a croaking speech. He had been gassed Monday night and Tuesday night, and had gone to the beach at dawn to read Hindu Tantras to some of the Yippies, the combination of the chants and the gassings had all but burned out his voice, his beautiful speaking voice, one of the most powerful and hypnotic instruments of the Western world was down to the scrapings of the throat now, raw as flesh after a curettage.

"The best strategy for you," said Ginsberg, "in cases of hysteria, overexcitement or fear, is still to chant 'OM' together. It helps to quell flutterings of butterflies in the belly. Join me now as I try to lead you."

The crowd chanted with Ginsberg. They were of a generation which would try every idea, every drug, every action—it was even possible a few of them had made out with freaky kicks on tear gas these last few days—so they would chant OM. There were Hindu fanatics in the crowd, children who loved India and scorned everything in the West; there were cynics who thought the best thing to be said for a country which allowed its excess population to die by the millions in famine-ridden fields was that it would not be ready soon to try to dominate the rest of the world. There were also militants who were ready to march. And the police there to prevent them, busy now in communication with other detachments of police, by way of radios whose aerials were attached to their helmets, thereby giving them the look of giant insects.

A confused hour began. Lincoln Park was irregular in shape with curving foot walks; but Grant Park was indeed not so much a park as a set of belts of greenery cut into files by major parallel avenues between Michigan Avenue and Lake Michigan half a mile away. Since there were also cross streets cutting the belts of green perpendicularly, a variety of bridges and pedestrian overpasses gave egress to the city. The park was in this sense an alternation of lawn with superhighways. So the police were able to pen the crowd. But not completely. There were too many bridges, too many choices, in effect, for the police to anticipate. To this confusion was added the fact that every confrontation of demonstrators with police, now buttressed by the National Guard, attracted hundreds of newsmen, and hence began a set of attempted negotiations between spokesmen for the demonstrators and troops the demonstrators finally tried to force a bridge and get back to the city. Repelled by tear gas, they went to other bridges, still other bridges, finally found a bridge lightly guarded, broke through a passage and were loose in the city at six-thirty in the evening. They milled about in the Loop for a few minutes, only to encounter the mules and three wagons of the Poor People's Campaign. City officials, afraid of provoking the Negroes on the South Side, had given a permit to the Reverend Abernathy, and he was going to march the mules and wagons down Michigan Avenue and over to the convention. An impromptu march of the demonstrators formed behind the wagons immediately on encountering them and ranks of marchers, sixty, eighty, a hundred in line across the width of Michigan Avenue began to move forward in the gray early twilight of 7 P.M.; Michigan Avenue was now suddenly jammed with people in the march, perhaps so many as four or five thousand people, including onlookers on the sidewalk who jumped in. The streets of the Loop were also reeking with tear gas—the wind had blown some of the gas west over Michigan Avenue from the drops on the bridges, some gas still was penetrated into the clothing of the marchers. In broken ranks, half a march, half a happy mob, eyes red from gas, faces excited by the tension of the afternoon, and the excitement of the escape from Grant Park, now pushing down Michigan Avenue toward the Hilton Hotel with dreams of a march on to the Amphitheatre four miles beyond, and in the full pleasure of being led by the wagons of the Poor People's March, the demonstrators shouted to everyone on the sidewalk, "Join us, join us, join us," and the sidewalk kept disgorging more people ready to march.

But at Balbo Avenue, just before Michigan Avenue reached the Hilton, the marchers were halted by the police. It was a long halt. Perhaps thirty minutes. Time for people who had been walking on the sidewalk to join the march, proceed for a few steps, halt with the others, wait, get bored, and leave. It was time for someone in command of the hundreds of police in the neighborhood to communicate with his headquarters, explain the problem, time for the dilemma to be relayed, alternatives examined, and orders conceivably sent back to attack and disperse the crowd. If so, a trap was first set. The mules were allowed to cross Balbo Avenue, then were separated by a line of police from the marchers, who now, several thousand compressed in this one place, filled the intersection of Michigan Avenue and Balbo. There, dammed by police on three sides, and cut off from the wagons of the Poor People's March, there, right beneath the windows of the Hilton which looked down on Grant Park and Michigan Avenue, the stationary march was abruptly attacked. The police attacked with tear gas, with Mace, and with clubs, they attacked like a chain saw cutting into wood, the teeth of the saw the edge of their clubs, they attacked like a scythe through grass, lines of twenty and thirty policemen striking out in an arc, their clubs beating, demonstrators fleeing. Seen from overhead, from the nineteenth floor, it was like a wind blowing dust, or the edge of waves riding foam on the shore.

The police cut through the crowd one way, then cut through them another. They chased people into the park, ran them down, beat them up; they cut through the intersection at Michigan and Balbo like a razor cutting a channel through a head of hair, and then drove columns of new police into the channel who in turn pushed out, clubs flailing, on each side, to cut new channels, and new ones again. As demonstrators ran, they reformed in new groups only to be chased by the police again. The action went on for ten minutes, fifteen minutes, with the absolute ferocity of a tropical storm, and watching it from a window on the nineteenth floor, there was something of the detachment of studying a storm at evening through a glass, the light was a lovely gray-blue, the police had uniforms of sky-blue, even the ferocity had an abstract elemental play of forces of nature at battle with other forces, as if sheets of tropical rain were driving across the street in patterns, in curving patterns which curved upon each other again. Police cars rolled up, prisoners were beaten, shoved into wagons, driven away. The rain of police, maddened by the uncoiling of their own storm, pushed against their own barricades of tourists pressed on the street against the Hilton Hotel, then pressed them so hard—but here is a quotation from J. Anthony Lukas in *The New York Times:*

> Even elderly bystanders were caught in the police onslaught. At one point, the police turned on several dozen persons standing quietly behind police barriers in front of the Conrad Hilton Hotel watching the demonstrators across the street.
>
> For no reason that could be immediately determined, the blue-helmeted policemen charged the barriers, crushing the spectators against the windows of the Haymarket Inn, a restaurant in the hotel. Finally the window gave way, sending screaming middle-aged women and children backward through the broken shards of glass.
>
> The police then ran into the restaurant and beat some of the victims who had fallen through the windows and arrested them.

Now another quote from Steve Lerner in *The Village Voice:*

> When the charge came, there was a stampede toward the sidelines. People piled into each other, humped over each other's bodies like coupling dogs. To fall down in the crush was just as terrifying as facing the police. Suddenly I realized my feet weren't touching the ground as the crowd pushed up onto the sidewalk. I was grabbing at the army jacket of the boy in front of me; the girl behind me had a stranglehold on my neck and was screaming incoherently in my ear.

Now, a longer quotation from Jack Newfield in *The Village Voice.* (The accounts in *The Voice* of September 5 were superior to any others encountered that week.)

> At the southwest entrance to the Hilton, a skinny, long-haired kid of about seventeen skidded down on the sidewalk, and four overweight cops leaped on him, chopping strokes on his head. His hair flew from the force of the blows. A dozen small rivulets of blood began to cascade down the kid's temple and onto the sidewalk. He was not crying or screaming, but crawling in a stupor toward the gutter. When he saw a photographer take a picture, he made a V sign with his fingers.
>
> A doctor in a white uniform and Red Cross arm band began to run toward the kid, but two other cops caught

him from behind and knocked him down. One of them jammed his knee into the doctor's throat and began clubbing his rib cage. The doctor squirmed away, but the cops followed him, swinging hard, sometimes missing.

A few feet away a phalanx of police charged into a group of women, reporters, and young McCarthy activists standing idly against the window of the Hilton Hotel's Haymarket Inn. The terrified people began to go down under the unexpected police charge when the plate glass window shattered, and the people tumbled backward through the glass. The police then climbed through the broken window and began to beat people, some of whom had been drinking quietly in the hotel bar.

At the side entrance of the Hilton Hotel four cops were chasing one frightened kid of about seventeen. Suddenly, Fred Dutton, a former aide to Robert Kennedy, moved out from under the marquee and interposed his body between the kid and the police.

"He's my guest in this hotel," Dutton told the cops.

The police started to club the kid.

Dutton screamed for the first cop's name and badge number. The cop grabbed Dutton and began to arrest him, until a Washington *Post* reporter identified Dutton as a former RFK aide.

Demonstrators, reporters, McCarthy workers, doctors, all began to stagger into the Hilton lobby, blood streaming from face and head wounds. The lobby smelled from tear gas, and stink bombs dropped by the Yippies. A few people began to direct the wounded to a makeshift hospital on the fifteenth floor, the McCarthy staff headquarters.

Fred Dutton was screaming at the police, and at the journalists to report all the "sadism and brutality." Richard Goodwin, the ashen nub of a cigar sticking out of his fatigued face, mumbled, "This is just the beginning. There'll be four years of this."

The defiant kids began a slow, orderly retreat back up Michigan Avenue. They did not run. They did not panic. They did not fight back. As they fell back they helped pick up fallen comrades who were beaten or gassed. Suddenly, a plainclothesman dressed as a soldier moved out of the shadows and knocked one kid down with an overhand punch. The kid squatted on the pavement of Michigan Avenue, trying to cover his face, while the Chicago plainclothesman punched him with savage accuracy. Thud, thud, thud. Blotches of blood spread over the kid's face. Two photographers moved in. Several police formed a closed circle around the beating to prevent pictures. One of the policemen then squirted Chemical Mace at the photographers, who dispersed. The plainclothesman melted into the line of police.

Let us escape to the street. The reporter, watching in safety from the nineteenth floor, could understand now how Mussolini's son-in-law had once been able to find the bombs he dropped from his airplane beautiful as they burst, yes, children, and youths, and middle-aged men and women were being pounded and clubbed and gassed and beaten, hunted and driven, sent scattering in all directions by teams of policemen who had exploded out of their restraints like the bursting of a boil, and nonetheless he felt a sense of calm and beauty, void even of the desire to be down there, as if in years to come there would be beatings enough, some chosen, some from nowhere, but it was as if the war had finally begun, and this was therefore a great and solemn moment, as if indeed even the gods of history had come together from each side to choose the very front of the Hilton Hotel before the television cameras of the world and the eyes of the campaign workers and the delegates' wives, yes, there before the eyes of half the principals at the convention was this drama played, as if the military spine of a great liberal party had finally separated itself from the skin, as if, no metaphor large enough to suffice, the Democratic Party had here broken in two before the eyes of a nation like Melville's whale charging right out of the sea.

A great stillness rose up from the street through all the small noise of clubbing and cries, small sirens, sigh of loaded arrest vans as off they pulled, shouts of police as they wheeled in larger circles, the intersection clearing further, then further, a stillness rose through the steel and stone of the hotel, congregating in the shocked centers of every room where delegates and wives and Press and campaign workers innocent until now of the intimate working of social force, looked down now into the murderous paradigm of Vietnam there beneath them at this huge intersection of this great city. Look—a boy was running through the park, and a cop was chasing. There he caught him on the back of the neck with his club! There! The cop is returning to his own! And the boy stumbling to his feet is helped off the ground by a girl who has come running up.

Yes, it could only have happened in a meeting of the

Gods, that history for once should take place not on some back street, or some inaccessible grand room, not in some laboratory indistinguishable from others, or in the sly undiscoverable hypocrisies of a committee of experts, but rather on the center of the stage, as if each side had said, "Here we will have our battle. Here we will win."

The demonstrators were afterward delighted to have been manhandled before the public eye, delighted to have pushed and prodded, antagonized and provoked the cops over these days with rocks and bottles and cries of "Pig" to the point where police had charged in a blind rage and made a stage at the one place in the city (besides the Amphitheatre) where audience, actors, and cameras could all convene, yes, the rebels thought they had had a great victory, and perhaps they did; but the reporter wondered, even as he saw it, if the police in that half hour of waiting had not had time to receive instructions from the power of the city, perhaps the power of the land, and the power had decided, "No, do not let them march another ten blocks and there disperse them on some quiet street, no, let it happen before all the land, let everybody see that their dissent will soon be equal to their own blood; let them realize that the power is implacable, and will beat and crush and imprison and yet kill before it will ever relinquish the power. So let them see before their own eyes what it will cost to continue to mock us, defy us, and resist. There are more millions behind us than behind them, more millions who wish to weed out, poison, gas, and obliterate every flower whose power they do not comprehend than heroes for their side who will view our brute determination and still be ready to resist. There are more cowards alive than the brave. Otherwise we would not be where we are," said the Prince of Greed.

Who knew. One could thank the city of Chicago where drama was still a property of the open stage. It was quiet now, there was nothing to stare down on but the mules, and the police guarding them. The mules had not moved through the entire fray. Isolated from the battle, they had stood there in harness waiting to be told to go on. Only once in a while did they turn their heads. Their role as actors in the Poor People's March was to wait and to serve. Finally they moved on. The night had come. It was dark. The intersection was now empty. Shoes, ladies' handbags, and pieces of clothing lay on the street outside the hotel.

17

There have been few studies on the psychological differences between police and criminals, and the reason is not difficult to discover. The studies based on the usual psychological tests fail to detect a significant difference. Perhaps they are not sufficiently sensitive.

If civilization has made modern man a natural schizophrenic (since he does not know at the very center of his deliberations whether to trust his machines or the imperfect impressions still afforded him by his distorted senses and the more or less tortured messages passed along by polluted water, overfertilized ground, and poisonously irritating air) the average man is a suicide in relation to his schizophrenia. He will suppress his impulses and die eventually of cancer, overt madness, nicotine poisoning, heart attack, or the complications of a chest cold. It is that minority—cop and crook—which seeks issue for violence who now attract our attention. The criminal attempts to reduce the tension within himself by expressing in the direct language of action whatever is most violent and outraged in his depths; to the extent he is not a powerful man, his violence is merely antisocial, like self-exposure, embezzlement, or passing bad checks. The cop tries to solve his violence by blanketing it with a uniform. That is virtually a commonplace, but it explains why cops will put up with poor salary, public dislike, uncomfortable working conditions and a general sense of bad conscience. They know they are lucky; they know they are getting away with a successful solution to the criminality they can taste in their blood. This taste is practically in the forefront of a cop's brain; he is in a stink of perspiration whenever he goes into action; he can tolerate little in the way of insult, and virtually no contradiction; he lies with a simplicity and quick confidence which will stifle the breath of any upright citizen who encounters it innocently for the first time. The difference between a good cop and a bad cop is that the good cop will at least do no more than give his own salted version of events— the bad cop will make up his version. That is why the police arrested the pedestrians they pushed through the window of the Haymarket Inn at the Conrad Hilton: the guiltier the situation in which a policeman finds himself, the more will he attack the victim of his guilt.

There are—it is another commonplace—decent policeman. A few are works of art. And some police, violent when they are young, mellow into modestly corrupt, humorous and decently efficient officials. Every public figure with power, every city official, high politician, or prominent government worker knows in his unspoken sentiments that the police are an essentially criminal force restrained by their guilt, their covert awareness that they are imposters, and by a sprinkling of career men whose education, rectitude, athletic ability, and religious dedication make them work for a balance between justice and authority. These men, who frighten the average corrupt cop as much as a priest frightens a choirboy, are the thin restraining edge of civilization for a police force. That, and the average corrupt cop's sense that he is not wanted that much by anyone.

What staggered the delegates who witnessed the attack —more accurate to call it the massacre, since it was sudden, unprovoked and total—on Michigan Avenue, was that it opened the specter of what it might mean for the police to take over society. They might comport themselves in such a case not as a force of law and order, not even as a force of repression upon civil disorder, but as a true criminal force, chaotic, improvisational, undisciplined, and finally- -sufficiently aroused--uncontrollable.

Society was held together by bonds no more powerful proportionately than spider's silk; no one knew this better than the men who administered a society. So images of the massacre opened a nightmare. The more there was disorder in the future, the more there would be need for larger numbers of police and more the need to indulge them. Once indulged, however, it might not take long for their own criminality to dominate their relation to society. Which spoke then of martial law to replace them. But if the

Army became the punitive force of society, then the Pentagon would become the only meaningful authority in the land.

So an air of outrage, hysteria, panic, wild rumor, unruly outburst, fury, madness, gallows humor, and gloom hung over nominating night at the convention.

18

The Amphitheatre was the best place in the world for a convention. Relatively small, it had the packed intimacy of a neighborhood fight club. The entrances to the gallery were narrow as hallway tunnels, and the balcony seemed to hang over each speaker. The colors were black and gray and red and white and blue, bright powerful colors in support of a ruddy beef-eating Democratic sea of faces. The standards in these cramped quarters were numerous enough to look like lances. The aisles were jammed. The carpets were red. The crowd had a blood in their vote which had traveled in unbroken line from the throng who cheered the blood of brave Christians and ferocious lions. It could have been a great convention, stench and all—politics in an abattoir was as appropriate as license in a boudoir. There was *bottom* to this convention: some of the finest and some of the most corrupt faces in America were on the floor. Cancer jostled elbows with acromegaly, obesity with edema, arthritis with alcoholism, bad livers sent curses to bronchiacs, and quivering jowls beamed bad cess to puffed-out paunches. Cigars curved mouths which talked out of the other corner to cauliflower ears. The leprotic took care of the blind. And the deaf attached their hearing aid to the voice-box of the dumb. The tennis players communicated with the estate holders, the Mob talked bowling with the Union, the principals winked to the principals, the honest and the passionate went hoarse shouting through dead mikes.

Yet the night was in trouble and there was dread in the blood, the air of circus was also the air of the slaughter-house. Word ripped through delegations of monstrosities unknown. Before the roll call was even begun, Peterson of Wisconsin, Donald Peterson, McCarthy man from the winning primary in Wisconsin, was on his feet, successful in obtaining the floor. (Since he was surrounded by TV, radio, and complements of the Press, the Chair knew it would be easier to accede than to ignore his demand for a voice.) Peterson wanted . . . Peterson wanted to have the convention postponed for two weeks and moved to another hall in some city far away, because of the "surrounding violence" and the "pandemonium in the hall." Before a mighty roar could even get off the ground, the Chair had passed to other business, and nominations were in order and so declared to a round of boos heavy as a swell of filthy oil. The sense of riot would not calm. Delegates kept leaving the floor to watch films on TV of the violence, McCarthy was reported to have witnessed the scene from his window and called it "very bad." McGovern described the fighting he saw as a "blood bath" which "made me sick to my stomach." He had "seen nothing like it since the films of Nazi Germany."

But that was the mood which hung over the hall, a revel of banquetry, huzzah and horror, a breath of gluttony, a smell of blood. The party had always been established in the mansions and slaughterhouses of society; Hyde Park and the take from policy, social legislation and the lubri-cating jelly of whores had been at the respective ends of its Democratic consensus, the dreams and the nose for power of aristocrat and gentry were mixed with beatings in the alley, burials at sea in concrete boots, and the poll tax with the old poll-tax rhetoric. The most honorable and the most debauched had sat down at table for Democratic luncheons. Now, the party was losing its better half, and the gang in the gashouse couldn't care less. They were about to roll up their sleeves and divide the pie, the local pie—who cared that the big election was dead? They had been pallbearers to moral idealism for too many years. Now they would shove it in the ground. The country was off its moorings and that was all right with them—let the ship of state drift into its own true berth: let patriotism and

the fix cohabit in the comfort for which they were designed
and stop these impossible collaborations.

So episodes popped up all over the place. The police
dragged a delegate from the floor when a sergeant-at-arms
told him to return to his seat and the delegate refused and
exchanged words. Paul O'Dwyer, candidate for the Senate
from New York, was pulled from the hall as he hung onto
him. Mike Wallace of CBS was punched on the jaw when
he asked some questions——they went out in a flurry of cops
quickly summoned, and rumors raced into every corner.
Clear confidence in the location of the seat of power was
gone. A delegate had now to face the chimera of arrest by
the police, then incarceration. Who would get him out?
Did Daley have the power or Johnson? Would Humphrey
ever be of use? Should one look for the U.S. Marines? A
discomfiture of the fundamental cardinal points of all location was in the rumblings of the gut. A political man
could get killed in this town by a cop, was the general
sentiment, and who would dare to look the Mayor in the
eye? If politics was property, somebody had tipped the plot:
West was now up in the North! To the most liberal of the
legislators and delegates on the floor must have come the
real panic of wondering: was this how it felt with the Nazis
when first they came in, the fat grin on the face of that
cigar who had hitherto been odious but loyal? Hard suppressed guffaws of revelry rumbled among the delegates
with the deepest greed and the most steaming bile. There
was the sense of all centers relocated, of authority on a ride.

The nominations took place in muted form. The Democrats had declared there would be no demonstrations at
their convention. The Democrats! Famous for their demonstrations. But they were afraid of maniacal outbursts for
McCarthy, fist fights on the floor, whole platoons of political
warriors grappling rivals by the neck. So each candidate
would merely be put in nomination, his name then cheered,
seconding speeches would follow, the roll would be called,
the next nominated.

McCarthy was put in by Governor Harold Hughes of
Iowa, Humphrey by Mayor Alioto of San Francisco. Let
us listen to a little of each——they are not uncharacteristic
of their men. Hughes said:

We are in the midst of what can only be called a revolution in our domestic affairs and in our foreign policy as well.

And as the late President Kennedy once said: "Those who would make peaceful revolution impossible make violent revolution inevitable."

. . . We must seek a leader who can arrest the polarization in our society, the alienation of the blacks from the whites, the haves from the have-nots and the old from the young.

We must choose a man with the wisdom and the courage to change the direction of our foreign policy before it commits us for an eternity to a maze of foreign involvements without clear purpose or moral justification.

But most of all the man we nominate must embody the aspirations of all those who seek to lift mankind to its highest potential. He must have that rare intangible quality that can lift up our hearts and cleanse the soul of this troubled country.

Gene McCarthy is such a man.

Mayor Alioto said:

I came here to talk to you about the man who has been for twenty years, right up to the present time, the articulate exponent of the aspirations of the human heart—for the young, for the old, and for those of us in between.

I'm not going to read to you, but I am going to ask you to project yourselves to Jan. 20, 1969, to project yourselves to the steps of the great Capitol of Washington, and in your mind's eyes to picture a man standing on those steps with his hands raised pledging that he will execute the office of the President of the United States and that he will in accordance with his ability preserve, protect and defend the Constitution of the United States, so help him God.

That man will look down on a country that is gripped in an earnest desire to find its way out of the confusion and the frustration that now infect this country. And the people at that moment will be looking for a decisive leader.

Let me put it directly to you—that man on Jan. 20 of 1969 is going to have to be an extraordinary man. And if he isn't an extraordinary man, the burdens of that office will crack him and the turbulence of the times will overwhelm us.

McGovern was nominated by Ribicoff, Senator Abraham Ribicoff of Connecticut, formerly Governor, a Ken-

nedy man for many years—his career had prospered with
the Kennedys. He was not a powerful looking man. He had
wings of silver gray hair, dark eyebrows, a weak mouth
which spoke of the kind of calculation which does not take
large chances. He had a slim frame with a hint of paunch.
He was no heavyweight. He had gotten along by getting
along, making the right friends. He was never famous as
a speaker, but he began by saying, "Mr. Chairman . . . as
I look at the confusion in this hall and watch on television
the turmoil and violence that is competing with this great
convention for the attention of the American people, there
is something else in my heart tonight, and not the speech
that I am prepared to give."

It was a curious beginning, but as he went on, the speech
became boring despite the force of a few of the phrases:
"500,000 Americans in the swamps of Vietnam." Ribicoff
droned, he had no flair, he was indeed about as boring as a
Republican speaker. There were yawns as he said:

> George McGovern is not satisfied that in this nation
> of ours, in this great nation of ours, our infant mortality
> rate is so high that we rank twenty-first in all the nations
> of the world.
> We need unity and we can only have unity with a new
> faith, new ideas, new ideals. The youth of America rally
> to the standards of men like George McGovern like they
> did to the standards of John F. Kennedy and Robert
> Kennedy.
> And with George McGovern as President of the United
> States we wouldn't have those Gestapo tactics in the
> streets of Chicago.
> With George McGovern we wouldn't have a National
> Guard.

Seconds had elapsed. People turned to each other. Did
he say, *"Gestapo tactics in the streets of Chicago"*? But he
had. His voice had quavered a hint with indignation and
with fear, but he had said it, and Daley was on his feet,
Daley was shaking his fist at the podium, Daley was mouth-
ing words. One could not hear the words, but his lips were
clear. Daley seemed to be telling Ribicoff to go have carnal
relations with himself.

There was a roundhouse of roars from the floor, a buzz
from the gallery. Daley glowered at Ribicoff and Ribicoff
stared back, his ordinary face now handsome, dignified

with some possession above itself. Ribicoff leaned down from the podium, and said in a good patrician voice, "How hard it is to accept the truth."

Perhaps it was Ribicoff's finest moment. Later, backstage, in McGovern Headquarters, he looked less happy, and considerably less in possession of himself as people came up to congratulate him for his speech. Indeed, Ribicoff had the winded worried heart-fatigued expression of a lightweight fighter who had just dared five minutes ago in the gym to break off a jab which broke the nose of a middleweight champ who had been working out with him. Now the lightweight would wake up in the middle of the night, wondering how they were going to pay him in return. Let us think of the man rather in his glory.

The balloting was finally begun. There were no surprises expected and none arrived. North Dakota actually said, "North Dakota which modestly admits to being cleaner and greener in the summer and brighter and whiter in the winter, casts 25 votes, 18 for Hubert Humphrey, 7 for Gene McCarthy." Then Ohio gave 94, Oklahoma was 37½, the floor began to shout. Pennsylvania offered up 103¾ of 130 and Humphrey was in. It was the state where McCarthy had gotten 90% of the primary vote. The deed was completed. The future storefront of the Mafia was now nominated to run against the probable prince of the corporation. In his hotel suite at the Hilton, Humphrey kissed Mrs. Fred R. Harris, wife of the Oklahoma Senator and co-chairman of his campaign; then as if to forestall all rumors, and reimpose propriety in its place, he rushed to the television screen and kissed the image of his own wife, which was then appearing on the tube. He was a politician; he could kiss babies, rouge, rubber, velvet, blubber and glass. God had not given him oral excellence for nothing.

Then the phone calls came. President Johnson, to whom Humphrey said with Southern grace, "Bless your heart," Mrs. Johnson, Lynda Bird and Luci; then Dick Nixon who congratulated him for winning the nomination earlier on the roll call than himself. Nixon was reported to have said that he enjoyed watching Mrs. Humphrey and the Humphrey family on television.

The vote when tabulated went like this: Humphrey, 1,761¾; McCarthy 601; McGovern 146½; Channing Philips (first Negro to be nominated for the Presidency)

67½; Dan Moore 17½; Edward Kennedy (without nomination) 12¾; James H. Gray ½; Paul E. "Bear" Bryant, coach of Alabama, 1½; and George C. Wallace, ½. George C. Wallace would do a lot better in November.

19

The disease was beneath the skin, the century was malignant with an illness so intricate that the Yippies, the Muslims, and the rednecks of George Wallace were all in attack upon it. They might eat each other first, but that was merely another facet of the plague—cannibalism was still the best cure for cancer.

If these were the medical reveries of the reporter after the nomination, the counterpart was to be seen in the faces of the delegates who exhibited the depression people show on leaving a bad fight: basic emotion has been aroused for too little.

A company of delegates, several hundred in number from New York, California, Wisconsin, Oregon, and a few of the other delegations, were going to meet in one of the caucus rooms to discuss immediate strategy. They were obviously not a happy gang, but since the characteristic tone of McCarthy supporters predominated—academics with horn-rimmed glasses in seersucker suits or pale generally lean politicians with hard bitten integrity on their lips, and the women for the most part too wholesome, some looked as if they had not worn lipstick in years—the cynical wonder intruded itself how they would celebrate a victory. Defeat was built into the integrity of their characters. Vinegar was the aphrodisiac of their diet.

Paul O'Dwyer was talking to them now. Candidate for the Senate against Jacob Javits in the coming election, he would make a fine opponent for that most worthy Senator —O'Dwyer was a small man with white hair, black eyebrows, an honest well-cut Irish look, an accent still clear with the tone of County Mayo, and a working-class sense of humor. He was also a gentleman. He had a natural elegance. So he would make a fine candidate. He was talking to the caucus now about the bitterness of the defeat, working to take the sting out of it. A man who had obviously been in many political battles, some of which he had won and many lost, he had learned how to discover the balanced mixture between indignation and hope so necessary to getting up off the defeat and looking for a new contest. So he fed their losers' fury first by commenting on the convention—"an unbelievable stifling of the democratic process," he said, and then proceeded to laud the group for their devotion, their hard work, their confidence, and the fact they could know that the voters out there were really with them, and that was a power which time would prove. He grinned. "If we keep working and do this for a few years, I think in the next convention it's the other side that will have its caucus here in Room 2." They cheered him happily for this, almost a little hysterically, as if close to the recognition that their best happiness often came when they felt hope in the midst of defeat. It is an emotion shared by the noblest of meat-eaters and the most confirmed vegetarians.

O'Dwyer was the spirit of this caucus, and when he did not speak, gloom came in again. Congressman Bill Ryan of New York talked for five minutes about his meeting with Daley. He spun it out properly, telling how he went down the aisle to speak to the Mayor of Chicago, expecting an appropriate show of courtesy since they were both, after all, of the same party, and he was a Congressman (and they were both Irish—which Ryan didn't quite get to say, although he phumphered on the edge) and finally after five minutes of dramatic preparation for this incisive private piece of information about to be delivered of some new and intimate villainy by Richard J., Mayor Daley, the end of the story could be delayed no longer and Ryan confessed: Daley had looked at him and said, "Get back to your delegation." An unbelievable stifling of the democratic process.

The reporter discovered an impulse in himself to get drunk. This caucus was composed of naught but honorable people, anxious now, even dedicated to the desire to find some way of protesting the nomination, the brutality of the police, the sheer disjointedness of the time—they were in politics because the philosophical anguish of brooding upon a problem which might not be soluble—exactly what gave unique dignity to McCarthy—was not near to them. They needed an action to fit every ill, they were the dearest descendants of Eleanor, the last of Roosevelt hygiene; now out of their passion to act, act even this night, act especially this night, they came up with a proposal to march in vigil from the Amphitheatre to the Conrad Hilton. It would be a way of expressing their concern for the victims of the police. They even had candles. Richard Goodwin, assistant to McCarthy, prepared for everything on this nominating night, had brought in a thousand tapers in case they wished to protest on the floor and the lights would be cut off. Now they could be used for the march through the dark lonely streets of Chicago.

O'Dwyer laughed unhappily. "How far is it?" he asked. "Some of us may not be so young as some of you. Isn't it eight miles?"

"No, four," people cried out.

He asked for a vote. They were overwhelmingly in favor. "So be it," he said, and sighed, and grinned.

Then they began to discuss singing all the way with Theo Bikel, one of the N.Y. delegates. But Bikel pointed out that he had sung sufficiently these few days, that his voice was not up to it—besides, they would be marching through streets where people were sleeping—that could only cause needless trouble. "Besides," said Bikel, "a silent vigil of men and women marching with lit candles is most impressive. Let us sing our way out of here, and through the blocks immediately about the stockyards, but once we pass the barrier, let us be silent." They agreed. He struck up a song immediately on his guitar, and they moved out.

The reporter did not join them. He had felt an unmistakable pang of fear at the thought of marching with these people through the Black Belt of Chicago or even the Polish neighborhoods in the immediate surroundings. He could see them attacked by gangs, and the thought of taking a terrible beating in this company of non-violent McCarthyites and McGovernites, shoulder to shoulder with Arthur Miller, Jules Feiffer, Theo Bikel and Jeremy Larner, no, if he was going to take a beating, it was best to take it alone or with people he felt close to, people who were not so comparatively innocent of how to fight.

In consequence, as they left the Amphitheatre, he went off by a different route to his car, agitated, ashamed, overcome with the curiosity that these liberals whom he had always scorned had the simple dedication tonight to walk through strange streets, unarmed, and with candles. Was it remotely possible that they possessed more courage than himself?

He drove from the stockyards in a hurry, went up to Lincoln Park to look it over, but the area was dead. Here the war had ended. So he drove back to the Hilton, found a bar in a little hotel called the Essex on Michigan Avenue and had a couple of drinks. He did not know that the march was already finished. The leaders accompanied by a most respectful group of police——he should have anticipated that! ——had decided it was too long a walk after all, so they had been driven in buses to a rallying point not far from the Hilton, and then had walked up Michigan Avenue with their lighted candles, joined soon by the Hippies and the young McCarthy workers in Grant Park, and were now almost directly across the street in the park listening to speeches. He did not know that. He was drinking and contemplating his fear. It seemed to him that he had been afraid all his life, but in recent years, or so it seemed, he had learned how to take a step into his fear, how to take the action which frightened him most (and so could free him the most). He did not do it always, who could? but he had come to think that the secret to growth was to be brave a little more than one was cowardly, simple as that, indeed why should life not be just so simple that the unlettered and untrained might also have their natural chance? It was a working philosophy and he had tried to follow it, but it seemed to him that he was deserting his own knowledge in these hours. Had his courage eroded more than his knowledge of fear the last few days? He continued to drink.

20

The focus of his fear had begun for him on Tuesday, no, put it back to Monday night in Lincoln Park when he had left as Ginsberg and Burroughs and Genet and Terry Southern were going in—up to the front. Of course, he could even put the fear back to Sunday afternoon, when he had heard the music, seen the children on the grass and the police on the walks and felt a sensation in his stomach not different from the dread in the bottom of the lungs one knows after hours of driving on ice. But then he had been afraid of Chicago ever since he had word in December of a Youth Festival which might attempt to make the Democrats nominate Lyndon Johnson under armed guard. So, in fact, this had been a fear he had been living with for a long time—like many another. It was as if different fears found different abodes in the body and dwelled in their place for years.

But yesterday, Tuesday, the fear had grown dimensions, forced consciousness to surface. Usually he did whatever he would do—be it courageous or evasive—without living too intimately with his anxiety. But, this time, it revealed itself. He had a particular reluctance to go to the meeting at the bandshell in Grant Park on Wednesday afternoon, then on the march to the Amphitheatre which would follow. This march would never be allowed to approach the Amphitheatre—one had not felt Mayor Daley's presence in Chicago these days for nothing!

There was much structure to the fear, much reasoned argument in its support. He had an enormous amount of work before him if he was going to describe this convention, and only two weeks in which to do it if his article were to appear before election. A bad beating might lose him days, or a week; each day of writing would be irreplaceable to him. Besides, a variety of militant choices would now be present for years. One simply could not accept the dangerous alternative every time; he would never do any other work. And then with another fear, conservative was this fear, he looked into his reluctance to lose even the America he had had, that insane warmongering technology land with its smog, its superhighways, its experts and

its profound dishonesty. Yet, it had allowed him to write—
it had even not deprived him entirely of honors, certainly
not of an income. He had lived well enough to have six
children, a house on the water, a good apartment, good
meals, good booze, he had even come to enjoy wine. A
revolutionary with taste in wine has come already half the
distance from Marx to Burke; he belonged in England
where one's radicalism might never be tested; no, truth,
he was still enough of a novelist to have the roots of future
work in every vein and stratum he had encountered, and a
profound part of him (exactly that enormous literary
bottom of the mature novelist's property!) detested the
thought of seeing his American society—evil, absurd,
touching, pathetic, sickening, comic, full of novelistic marrow—disappear now in the nihilistic maw of a national disorder. The Yippies might yet disrupt the land—or worse,
since they would not really have the power to do that,
might serve as a pretext to bring in totalitarian phalanxes
of law and order. Of course that was why he was getting
tired of hearing of Negro rights and Black Power—every
Black riot was washing him loose with the rest, pushing him
to that point where he would have to throw his vote in
with revolution—what a tedious perspective of prisons and
law courts and worse; or stand by and watch as the best
Americans white and Black would be picked off, expended,
busted, burned and finally lost. No, exile would be better.
Yet he loathed the thought of living anywhere but in
America—he was too American by now: he did not wish
to walk down foreign streets and think with imperfect nos-
talgia of dirty grease on groovy hamburgers, not when he
didn't even eat them here. And then there might not be any
foreign lands, not for long. The plague he had written
about for years seemed to be coming in—he would understand its social phenomena more quickly than the rest. Or
would, if he did not lose his detachment and have to purchase cheap hope. Drinking across the street from Grant
Park, the possibility of succumbing to fears larger than himself appeared, if no more than a spot on the horizon, still
possible to him. No more than a spot on the horizon had
seemed Humphrey's candidacy when first it was bruited.
Was that why delegates were marching now with candles?
So that they would not succumb to fears larger than themselves?

It was as if the historical temperature in America went up every month. At different heats, the oils of separate psyches were loosened—different good Americans began to fry. Of course their first impulse was to hope the temperature would be quickly reduced. Perhaps they could go back to the larder again. But if it continued, then the particular solution which had provided him with a modicum at least of worldly happiness—the fine balance he might have achieved between the satisfaction of idealism and the satisfaction of need (call it greed) would be disrupted altogether, and then his life could not go on as it had. In the size of his fear, he was discovering how large a loss that would be. He liked his life. He wanted it to go on, which meant that he wanted America to go on—not as it was going, not Vietnam—but what price was he really willing to pay? Was he ready to give up the pleasures of making his movies, writing his books? They were pleasures finally he did not want to lose.

Yet if he indulged his fear, found all the ways to avoid the oncoming ugly encounters, then his life was equally spoiled, and on the poorer side. He was simply not accustomed to living with a conscience as impure as the one with which he had watched from the nineteenth floor. Or had it really been impure? Where was his true engagement? To be forty-five years old, and have lost a sense of where his loyalties belonged—to the revolution or to the stability of the country (at some painful personal price it could be suggested) was to bring upon himself the anguish of the European intellectual in the Thirties. And the most powerful irony for himself is that he had lived for a dozen empty hopeless years after the second world war with the bitterness, rage, and potential militancy of a real revolutionary, he had had some influence perhaps upon this generation of Yippies now in the street, but no revolution had arisen in the years when he was ready—the timing of his soul was apocalyptically maladroit.

These are large thoughts for a reporter to have. Reporters live happily removed from themselves. They have eyes to see, ears to hear, and fingers for the note in their report. It was as if the drink he took in now moved him millimeter by millimeter out from one hat into another. He would be driven yet to participate or keep the shame in his liver—the last place to store such emotion! Liver disease is the warehousing of daily shame—they will trace the chemistry yet!

He had spoken this afternoon at the meeting. He had not wanted to; he had told David Dellinger on Tuesday afternoon that he would not speak—he did not wish to expose prematurely the ideas being stored for his piece. Dellinger nodded. He would not argue. He was a man of sturdy appearance with a simplicity and solidity of manner that was comfortable. He gave the impression of a man who told the truth, but as decently as possible. The reporter had called him to say he wished to visit Mobilization Headquarters to talk to him but since Dellinger was going to be in the Hilton, he came up in fact to the reporter's room on Tuesday afternoon with his son and Rennie Davis. The reporter told him he would not go on the march because he did not wish to get arrested—he could not afford even a few days in jail at this point if they chose to make him an example. So he would not appear at the bandshell either. He simply did not wish to stand there and watch others march off. Dellinger did not argue, nor did he object. He was a man of obvious patience and seemed of the conclusion that everybody brought his own schedule of militancy to each occasion. So he merely sipped his drink and watched the convention on television for a few minutes. It had been his first opportunity to watch it, his first opportunity doubtless to relax in a week. As he got up to go he grinned at the set, and said, "You know, this is kind of interesting."

Wednesday afternoon, the reporter had been at the same set in the same room, watching the debate on the peace plank. After awhile, he knew that he would not be able to stay away from the meeting. Yet when he got there, past the police, the marshals, and stood in the crowd, he knew nothing of what had happened already, he did not know Rennie Davis had been beaten unconscious, nor of Tom Hayden's angry speech and others—there was just Allen Ginsberg giving his address on the calming value of OM. Then Burroughs spoke and Genet. He had to go up himself—it was now impossible not to. So he highstepped his way forward in the crowd, awkwardly, over people seated in the grass, came to the shell, climbed up—there were a dozen people sitting on various chairs back of the podium —then went up to Dellinger and asked if he could speak. Dellinger gave a smile. He was welcome.

So he had spoken at the bandshell. Standing there, seeing the crowd before him, feeling the predictable warmth of this power, all his courage was back, or so it felt—he was finally enough of an actor to face perils on a stage he would not meet as quickly other ways. And felt a surprising respect, even admiration, for the people on the benches and in the grass who had been tear-gassed day after day and were here now ready to march. He had even begun by saying to them, "You're beautiful," a show-biz vulgarity he detested to the root of his nerve, but he said it, and then made jokes about the smell of Mace on the microphone—the odor of stink bombs or Mace pervaded the charcoal-colored sponge over the microphone. Next, he went on to say that they were all at the beginning of a war which would continue for twenty years and this march today would be one battle in it. Then he explained that he would not be on this march because he had a deadline and could not take the chance, "but you will all know what I am full of, if you don't see me on other marches," he had added, and they cheered him, cheered him enthusiastically even before he said that he had come there merely to pay his respects and salute them. It affected him that they cheered him for even this relatively quietistic speech, and when he was done, they cried out, "Write good, baby," and some young Negro from the Panthers or the Rangers or from where he did not know, serving as some kind of pro tem master of ceremonies now held his arm up high with his own, Black and white arms together in the air, he had been given a blessing by this Black, and felt rueful at unkind thoughts of late. And kept his word, and left soon after, and had a good early dinner with friends in order not to get to the convention too late. And had happened to be in his room washing up when the massacre on the march, three hours later, had come. Now, he was drinking in this bar across the street from Grant Park with a pleasant Californian who worked for McGovern. The reporter enjoyed his drinks. The bar was closing and he would go to bed. But the memory of his speech that afternoon was bothering him. It had been too easy. He knew it would have been better if he had been on the march, been in the massacre, even been on the vigil marching up from the Amphitheatre. Through the drinks, shame was warehousing in his liver.

So it was that when he got up to go, and said good night

to his new-found friend, he did not then enter and cross the lobby but stepped outside the hotel and went across Michigan Avenue.

21

The National Guard was out in force. On the side streets of the hotel, two-and-a-half-ton Army trucks were parked, jamming every space. Traffic was cut off. The Daley-dozers, named yesterday by a newspaper man, those Jeeps with barbed-wire grids in front of their bumpers, were lined in file across Michigan Avenue just south of the Hilton, and he crossed over to Grant Park with the sound of Army vehicles revving up, the low coughing urgency of carburetors flooded and goosed and jabbed and choked by nervous drivers, feet riding the accelerator and clutch while their truck waited in place. The huge searchlights near the Hilton were shining from a height of ten or fifteen feet, from a balcony or a truck, he could not see in the glare, but they lit up the debris and clangor of Michigan Avenue, the line of soldiers on the sidewalk of Michigan Avenue just off the edge of Grant Park, the huge pent crowd, thousands here, facing the line of troops. For some reason or other, a hydrant had been opened on Michigan Avenue in the hollow square formed by lines of National Guard and police barriers before the Hilton, and the lights of the searchlight reflecting from the wet street gave that dazzle of light and urgency and *glamour* unique to a movie company shooting in a city late at night, crowds dazzled themselves by their own good luck in being present.

At that moment, he had a sign of what to do, which is to say, he had an impulse. His impulses, perhaps in compensation for his general regime of caution were usually sufficiently sensational to need four drinks for gasoline before they could even be felt. Now without questioning the impulse, he strode down the line of troops walking under their raised guns, not a foot away from their faces, looking (he supposed—perhaps he even did) like an inspecting officer, for he stared severely or thoughtfully or condescendingly into each separate soldier's face with that official scrutiny of character which inspecting officers had once drilled into him. He was in fact fulfilling an old military dream. Since some of the soldiers did not like what he was doing, not altogether! and shifted their rifles abruptly with loud claps of their hand like stallions now nervous and therefore kicking the boards of their stall with abrupt and warning displeasure, he had the obverse pleasure of finding his nerve was firm again, he was sublimely indifferent to the possibility that any of these soldiers might give him a crack on the head with their rifle.

In the middle of examining this line—it must have been two hundred soldiers long, some weary, some bored, some nervous, some curious or friendly, some charged with animosity; nearly all sloppy in their uniforms which he noticed with displeasure—he was indeed an inspecting officer—he passed by the speaker's stand, a park table, or something of the sort, on which a dozen men were standing, one with a microphone attached by a wire to a big portable bullhorn held by another demonstrator. The speeches were going on, and a couple of guitarists appeared ready to perform next.

A woman he knew, who worked on the McCarthy staff, approached him. "Will you speak?" she asked.

He nodded. He felt more or less ready to speak and would have answered, "Yes, just as soon as I conclude this inspection," if some saving wit in a corner of his brain had not recognized how absurd this would seem to her.

So he concluded his inspection, taking the time to regard each soldier in that long line, and felt as if he had joined some private victory between one part of himself and another—just what, would have been tedious to consider at the moment, for he felt charged, ready, full of orator's muscle.

A Yippie wearing a dirty torn sweater, his hair long, curly, knotted, knuckled with coils and thrusting vertically into the air, hair quite the match of Bob Dylan's, was running the program and whispered hello cordially, worked him to the center of this ridiculously small platform, perhaps the area of two large bathtubs put side by side, and told him he would speak as soon as the electric guitarists were done.

He stood then in the center between two guitars who were singing a loud wild banging folk rock, somewhat corny, a patriotic song of the Left whose title eluded him. He did not like the song usually, but up on the platform, flanked by the singers, the bullhorn being held just back of his head turned out to the crowd, he felt insulated by the sound, blasted with it completely and so somehow safe with it, womb-safe with it, womb-cushioned—did the embryo live in such a waterfall of uproar each time the mother's digestion turned over? His mind was agreeably empty as he waited, good sign generally that he was ready to deliver a real speech.

When the song ended and he was given the mike after a generous introduction and a sweet surge of applause beefed up to its good point precisely by the introduction of the youth in the dirty sweater and the hair like Bob Dylan, he spoke out to the crowd just long enough to tell them he wanted to speak first to the soldiers. Then he turned his back, and the loudspeaker turned with him, and he talked to the line of troops he had not long ago passed, introducing himself as a novelist whose war novel some of them might possibly have read since it was famous in many barracks for its filthy passages and four-letter words, although not nearly so famous as another work, *From Here to Eternity*, with whose author he was often confused. He did not wish to disappoint the soldiers, he said, but he was not that fine author, Mr. James Jones, but the other, the one who had written the other book.

These remarks given and enjoyed by him, he then talked to the soldiers as a man who had been a soldier once. "As I walked down your line, inspecting you, I realized that you are all about the kind of soldier I was nearly twenty-five years ago, that is to say, not a very good soldier, somewhat unhappy with the Army I found myself in." But, he went on, the war in which he himself had fought had not bothered his sense of what might be right the way this war in Vietnam must bother them. And he went on to talk about how American soldiers could take little pride in a war where they had the superiority and yet could not win, and he thought that was because they were ashamed of the war. Americans were conceivably the best fighting soldiers in the world if they could ever find a war which was the most honorable war in the world for them, but the war in Vietnam was the worst war for them, and so they could not fight with enthusiasm. At their best, Americans were honest; so they needed an honest war.

It would have been a first rate talk to give to fighting troops. In the general excitement of this occasion he did not necessarily arrive at the central point—the soldiers before him had no wish to serve in Vietnam. That was why they were in the National Guard. Still, his speech to the troops pleased him, it warmed him for his next address which he was able to begin by turning around in place 180°, the loudspeaker doing the same, and now addressing his remarks to the crowd in the park. They were seated in a semicircle perhaps two hundred feet in diameter, a crowd of several thousand at least, with an attention he knew immediately was superb, for it was tender as the fatigue of shared experience and electric as the ringing of pain from a new bruise.

He began once again by paying his respects, explaining how he had missed one fray and then another, not certain if for the best or worst of motives. They were polite even to this, as if a manifest of honesty in a speaker was all they had come to hear. But he had seen them, he explained, over these few days, taking beatings and going back, taking beatings, going back; so he now found himself in this park talking to them (although he had had no such intention earlier). They were fine troops, he declared, they were the sort of troops any general would be proud to have. They had had the courage to live at war for four days in a city which was run by a beast.

A roar of delight came back from them. He felt the heights of the Hilton behind him, the searchlights, and the soldiers. Before him, these revolutionary youth—they were no longer the same young people who had gone to the Pentagon at all. They were soldiers.

"Yes, this is a city run by a beast, and yet we may take no pleasure in it," he said, "because the man is a giant who ended as a beast. And that is another part of the horror. For we have a President who was a giant and ended also as a beast. All over the world are leaders who have ended as beasts; there is a beastliness in the marrow of the century," he said, or words like that and went on, "Let us even have a moment of sorrow for Mayor Daley for he is a fallen giant and that is tragic," and they cheered Daley out of good spirit and some crazy good temper as if Mayor Daley was beautiful, he had given them all this—what a great king of the pigs! and somebody yelled, "Give us some of that good grass, Norman," and he bellowed back, "I haven't had pot in a month." They all roared. "Four good bourbons is all you need," said the demagogue, and the troops were in heaven.

The exchange fired him into his next thought. He repeated again that he had not been ready to march, repeated his desire to avoid arrest or a blow on the head, and "Write! Write!" they yelled back, "You're right, baby, do the writing!" But now, he went on, the time had come for Democratic delegates to march. He had not gone, he said, on the vigil and march from the stockyards to the hotel, because "that was in the wrong direction." Demagogue's metaphor, demagogue's profit. They cheered him richly. No, tomorrow, he told them (the idea coming to his mind at just this instant) he was going to try to get three hundred delegates to march with them to the Amphitheatre. He would march along then! But he would not if there were less than three hundred delegates! Because if little more than a tenth of the Democratic Party was not ready to go out with their bodies as a warrant of safekeeping for all of them, then there was no sense in walking into still one more mauling. They had taken enough. If there was not real outrage in the Democratic Party, then it was time they knew that as well; they could then prepare to go underground. A roar came back again from the new soldiers seated on the grass.

Were there delegates here, he asked? Candles waved in the dark—he was aware of them for the first time. "Spread the word," he called out, "I'll be here tomorrow."

Then he went on to speak of that underground. He would try to explain it. The other side had all the force, all the guns, all the power. They had everything but creative wit. So the underground would have to function on its wit, its creative sense of each new step. They must never repeat a tactic they had used before, no matter how successful. "Once a philosopher, twice a pervert," he bawled out. And in the middle of the happy laughter which came back, he said, "Voltaire!" and they were happy again. It was as good a speech as he had ever made.

For example, he continued, the march tomorrow with three hundred delegates would be a new tactic, and might offer a real chance of reaching the police barriers outside the Amphitheatre, where they could have a rally and quietly disband. That could make the point, for the Mayor had refused to let them even get near until now. Of course if the police chose to attack again tomorrow, well, three hundred Democratic delegates would also be in the crowd —so the nation would know that the authority was even determined to mop up its own. So he would march, he repeated, if the delegates would go, but he was damned, he told the crowd, if he was about to give cops the chance to maul him for nothing after he had made a point of here insulting the Mayor; no, he would not take that chance unless a tenth of the Democratic delegates were also willing to take a chance. On that note, he stepped down, and took a walk forward through the crowd, stopping to shake hands every step with the young men and women on the grass. Some were well-dressed, some were near to wearing rags, some looked as dusty and war-like as Roger's Rangers, others were small and angelic. Everything from ghosts of Robin Hood's band to the worst of the descendants of the worst Bolshevik clerks were here in the Grant Park grass at five in the morning and McCarthyites and McGovernites, and attractive girls, and college boys, and a number of Negroes, more now than any day or night before, and they were shaking hands with him, Black Power was revolving a hint in its profound emplacements. There were kooks and plainclothesmen and security and petty thieves and provocateurs with calculating faces and mouths just out of balance, eyes that glinted with a tell-tale flick; but there were also more attractive adolescents and under-twenties in this crowd than in any like crowd of New Left and Yippies he had seen before, as if the war had indeed been good for them. And he was modest in the warmth of their greeting, and not honored with himself, for they were giving him credit he did not possess—they were ready to forgive all manner of defection on the pleasure of a good speech.

So he circulated, talking, came back to the platform to make one quick amendment. Delegates in the crowd had told him three hundred was too great a number to seek in so short a time. It would not be possible to reach them all. Two hundred was a better expectation. So he relayed that information to the crowd, and added that he would be back in this Park at noon.

He returned to the hotel, pleased with his project, and aware of one whole new notion of himself. All courage was his and all determination, provided he could lead. There seemed no rank in any Army suitable for him below the level of General—extraordinary events deliver exceptional intuitions of oneself. No wonder he had spent so many years being General of an army of one. It was something to discover the secret source of the river of one's own good guts or lack of them. And booze was no bad canoe. He went to bed prepared for heroic events on the morrow.

22

He was to receive instead a lesson in the alphabet of all good politick: which is, that a passion is nothing without a good horse to carry you in visit over your neighbor's lands. He went to sleep at six A.M. prepared to visit different leaders as soon as he had finished his next speech at noon; by six in the evening he hoped they would be ready for the march, all delegates assembled.

Be prepared for total failure.

If this were essentially an account of the reporter's actions, it would be interesting to follow him through the chutes on Thursday, but we are concerned with his actions only as they illumine the event of the Republican Convention in Miami, the Democratic Convention in Chicago, and the war of the near streets. So his speech to the Yippies and children assembled was of value, since he learned for the record of his report that they were a generation with an appetite for the heroic, and an air not without beauty had arisen from their presence; they had been better than he thought, young, devoted, and actually ready to die—they were not like their counterparts ten years ago. Something had happened in America, some forging of the steel. He had

known while speaking that if it came to civil war, there was
a side he could join. At what a cost! At what a cost!

But such discoveries are unsettling. He lay in bed not
able to sleep; he lay in fact on the edge of a twilight slumber
rich as Oriental harems in the happiness of their color,
but he was thus celebrating too soon, because by nine
o'clock in the morning, the last of his liquor now beautifully
metabolized, he was in that kind of unhappy shape on
which comedy is built. Quick calisthenics, a shower, a
shave, and the urgency of his mission, did not quite give
him a brain the equal of three hours in slumber. He would
begin to think well for a minute, then lapse into himself
like a mind become too weak for the concentration of con-
secutive thoughts.

We can spare the day, and report the lesson. He made
his speech in Grant Park at noon, talked then to reporters,
then to delegates (who had been in the Park) at the Hilton,
discussed problems, arranged to meet them again, and
never was able to keep the meetings. He could never get to
see McCarthy quite alone, nor McGovern, lost hours on
the hope he might talk to the New York delegation, did not
know how to reach Peterson of Wisconsin, could have wept
at the absence of a secretary, or a walkie-talkie, since
phones refused to function, or beginning to work, could
reach no soul. He ran back and forth over Chicago, sent
messages—by whomever he could find, to the Park; he
would be back at three, he would be back at four, he saw
Murray Kempton who was ready to march all alone if only
to interpose himself between the police and the body of one
demonstrator (Kempton was indeed to be arrested later
in the day) he saw others, lost connection with delegates
who had volunteered to help, was helpless himself in his
lack of sleep, was too early or too late for each political
figure he wished to find, he was always rushing or waiting
in hallways—he learned the first lesson of a convention:
nothing could be accomplished without the ability to communicate faster than your opponent. If politics was property, a convention was a massive auction, and your bid
had to reach the floor in time.

So he was defeated. He could put nothing together at
all. Hung-over, drained, ashen within, and doubtless looking
as awful as Rockefeller at Opa Locka or McCarthy in
Cambridge, he went back to Grant Park in the late after-

noon to make a speech in which he would declare his failure, and discovered the Park instead was near empty. Whoever had wanted to march had gone off already with
Peterson of Wisconsin, or later with Dick Gregory. (Perhaps a total of fifty Democratic delegates were in those
walks.) Now the Park was all but deserted except for the
National Guard. Perhaps a hundred or two hundred onlookers, malcontents, hoodlums, and odd petty thieves
sauntered about. A mean-looking mulatto passed by the
line of National Guard with his penknife out, blade up, and
whispered, "Here's my bayonet." Yes, Grant Park was now
near to Times Square in Manhattan or Main Street in L.A.
The Yippies were gone; another kind of presence was in.
And the grass looked littered and yellow, a holocaust of
newspapers upon it. Now, a dry wind, dusty and cold,
gave every sentiment of the end of summer. The reporter
went back to his room. He had political lessons to absorb
for a year from all the details of his absolute failure to
deliver the vote.

23

Let us look at the convention on the last night. Two
hours before the final evening session the Progress Printing
Company near the stockyards finished a rush order of
small posters perhaps two feet high which said: CHICAGO
LOVES MAYOR DALEY. They were ready to be handed
out when the crowds arrived tonight; thousands of workers
for the city administration were packed into the spectators'
gallery, then the sections reserved for radio, TV and
periodicals. The crowd fortified with plastic tickets cut to
the size of Diner's Club cards, and therefore cut to the size
of the admission pass one had to insert in the signal box
to enter, had flooded all available seats with their posters
and their good Chicago lungs-for-Daley. The radio, television and periodical men wandered about the outer en-

virons of the Amphitheatre and were forced to watch most of the convention this night from the halls, the ends of the tunnels, the television studios.

Daley had known how to do it. If he had been booed and jeered the first two nights and openly insulted from the podium on Wednesday, despite a gallery already packed in his favor, he was not going to tolerate anything less than a built-in majesty for tonight. Power is addicted to more power. So troughs of pigs were sweet to him as honey to a mouse, and he made certain of the seats.

Shortly after convening, the convention showed a movie thirty-two minutes long, entitled "Robert Kennedy Remembered," and while it went on, through the hall, over the floor, and out across the country on television, a kind of unity came over everyone who was watching, at least for a little while. Idealism rarely moved politicians—it had too little to do with property. But emotion did. It was closer to the land. Somewhere between sorrow and the blind sword of patriotism was the fulcrum of reasonable politics, and as the film progressed, and one saw scene after scene of Bobby Kennedy growing older, a kind of happiness came back from the image, for something in his face grew young over the years—he looked more like a boy on the day of his death, a nice boy, nicer than the kid with the sharp rocky glint in his eye who had gone to work for Joe McCarthy in his early twenties, and had then known everything there was to know about getting ahead in politics. He had grown modest as he grew older, and his wit had grown with him—he had become a funny man as the picture took care to show, wry, simple for one instant, shy and off to the side on the next, but with a sort of marvelous boy's wisdom, as if he knew the world was very bad and knew the intimate style of how it was bad, as only boys can sometimes know (for they feel it in their parents and their schoolteachers and their friends). Yet he had confidence he was going to fix it—the picture had this sweet simple view of him which no one could resent for somehow it was not untrue. Since his brother's death, a subtle sadness had come to live in his tone of confidence, as though he were confident he would win—if he did not lose. That could also happen, and that could happen quickly. He had come into that world where people live with the recognition of tragedy, and so are often afraid of happiness, for they know that one is never in so much danger as when victorious and/or happy—that is when the devils seem to have their hour, and hawks seize something living from the gambol on the field.

The reporter met Bobby Kennedy just once. It was on an afternoon in May in New York just after his victory in the Indiana primary and it had not been a famous meeting, even if it began well. The Senator came in from a conference (for the reporter was being granted an audience) and said quickly with a grin, "Mr. Mailer, you're a mean man with a word." He had answered, "On the contrary, Senator, I like to think of myself as a gracious writer."

"Oh," said Senator Kennedy, with a wave of his hand, "that too, that too!"

So it had begun well enough, and the reporter had been taken with Kennedy's appearance. He was slimmer even than one would have thought, not strong, not weak, somewhere between a blade of grass and a blade of steel, fine, finely drawn, finely honed, a fine flush of color in his cheeks, two very white front teeth, prominent as the two upper teeth of a rabbit, so his mouth had no hint of the cruelty or calculation of a politician who weighs counties, cities, and states, but was rather a mouth ready to nip at anything which attracted its contempt or endangered its ideas. Then there were his eyes. They were most unusual. His brother Teddy Kennedy spoke of those who "followed him, honored him, lived in his mild and magnificent eye," and that was fair description for he had very large blue eyes, the iris wide in diameter, near to twice the width of the average eye, and the blue was a milky blue like a marble so that his eyes, while prominent, did not show the separate steps and slopes of light some bright eyes show, but rather were gentle, indeed beautiful—one was tempted to speak of velvety eyes—their surface seemed made of velvet as if one could touch them, and the surface would not be repelled.

He was as attractive as a movie star. Not attractive like his brother had been, for Jack Kennedy had looked like the sort of vital leading man who would steal the girl from Ronald Reagan every time, no, Bobby Kennedy had looked more like a phenomenon of a movie star—he could have filled some magical empty space between Mickey

Rooney and James Dean, they would have cast him sooner
or later in some remake of *Mr. Smith Goes to Washington,*
and everyone would have said, "Impossible casting! He's
too young." And he was too young. Too young for Senator,
too young for President, it felt strange in his presence
thinking of him as President, as if the country would be
giddy, like the whirl of one's stomach in the drop of an
elevator or jokes about an adolescent falling in love, it
was incredible to think of him as President, and yet marvelous, as if only a marvelous country would finally dare
to have him.

That was the best of the meeting—meeting him! The
reporter spent the rest of his valuable thirty minutes arguing
with the Senator about Senator McCarthy. He begged him
to arrange some sort of truce or liaison, but made a large
mistake from the outset. He went on in a fatuous voice,
sensing error too late to pull back, about how effective two
Irish Catholics would be on the same ticket for if there
were conservative Irishmen who could vote against one of
them, where was the Irish Catholic in America who could
vote against two? and Kennedy had looked at him with
disgust, as if offended by the presumption in this calculation, his upper lip had come down severely over his two
front white teeth, and he had snapped, "I don't want those
votes." How indeed did the reporter presume to tell him
stories about the benightedness of such people when he
knew them only too well. So the joke had been a lame
joke and worse, and they got into a dull argument about
McCarthy, Kennedy having little which was good to say,
and the reporter arguing doggedly in the face of such remarks as: "He doesn't even begin to campaign until
twelve."

They got nowhere. Kennedy's mind was altogether political on this afternoon. It did not deal with ideas except
insofar as ideas were attached to the name of bills, or
speeches, or platforms, or specific debates in specific
places, and the reporter, always hard put to remember
such details, was forced therefore to hammer harder and
harder on the virtues of McCarthy's gamble in entering the
New Hampshire primary until Kennedy said, "I wonder
why you don't support Senator McCarthy. He seems more
like your sort of guy, Mr. Mailer," and in answer, oddly
moved, he had said in a husky voice, "No, I'm supporting

you. I know it wasn't easy for you to go in." And even began to mutter a few remarks about how he understood that powerful politicians would not have trusted Kennedy if he had moved too quickly, for his holding was large, and men with large holdings were not supportable if they leaped too soon. "I know that," he said looking into the Senator's mild and magnificent eye, and Kennedy nodded, and in return a little later Kennedy sighed, and exhaled his breath, looked sad for an instant, and said, "Who knows? Who knows? Perhaps I should have gone in earlier." A few minutes later they said goodbye, not unpleasantly. That was the last he saw of him.

The closest he was to come again was to stand in vigil for fifteen minutes as a member of the honor guard about his coffin in St. Patrick's. Lines filed by. People had waited in line for hours, five hours, six hours, more, inching forward through the day and through the police lines on the street in order to take one last look at the closed coffin.

The poorest part of the working-class of New York had turned out, poor Negro men and women, Puerto Ricans, Irish washerwomen, old Jewish ladies who looked like they ran grubby little newsstands, children, adolescents, families, men with hands thick and lined and horny as oyster shells, calluses like barnacles, came filing by to bob a look at that coffin covered by a flag. Some women walked by praying, and knelt and touched the coffin with their fingertips as they passed, and after a time the flag would slip from the pressure of their fingers and an usher detailed for the purpose would readjust it. The straightest line between two points is the truth of an event, no matter how long it takes or far it winds, and if it had taken these poor people six hours of waiting in line to reach that coffin, then the truth was in the hours. A river of working-class people came down to march past Kennedy's coffin, and this endless line of people had really loved him, loved Bobby Kennedy like no political figure in years had been loved.

The organ played somewhere in the nave and the line moved forward under the vast—this day—tragic vaults of the cathedral so high overhead and he felt love for the figure in the coffin and tragedy for the nation in the years ahead, the future of the nation seemed as dark and tortured, as wrenched out of shape, as the contorted blood-spattered painted sculpture of that garish Christ one could find in every dark little Mexican church. The horror of dried blood was now part of the air, and became part of the air of the funeral next day. That funeral was not nearly so beautiful; the poor people who had waited on line on Friday were now gone, and the mighty were in their place, the President and members of the Congress, and the Establishment, and the Secret Service, and the power of Wall Street; the inside of St. Patrick's for the length of the service was dank with the breath of the over-ambitious offering reverence—there is no gloom so deep unless it is the scent of the upholstery in a mortician's limousine, or the smell of morning in a closed Pullman after executives have talked through the night.

24

The movie came to an end. Even dead, and on film, he was better and more moving than anything which had happened in their convention, and people were crying. An ovation began. Delegates came to their feet, and applauded an empty screen—it was as if the center of American life was now passing the age where it could still look forward; now people looked back into memory, into the past of the nation—was that possible? They applauded the presence of a memory. Bobby Kennedy had now become a beloved property of the party.

Minutes went by and the ovation continued. People stood on their chairs and clapped their hands. Cries broke out. Signs were lifted. Small hand-lettered signs which said, "Bobby, Be With Us," and one enormous sign eight feet high, sorrowful as rue in the throat—"Bobby, We Miss You," it said.

Now the ovation had gone on long enough—for certain people. So signals went back and forth between floor and podium and phone, and Carl Albert stepped forward and banged the gavel for the ovation to end, and asked for order. The party which had come together for five minutes, after five days and five months and five years of festering discord, was now immediately divided again. The New York and California delegations began to sing the "Battle Hymn of the Republic," and the floor heard, and delegations everywhere began to sing, Humphrey delegations as quick as the rest. In every convention there is a steamroller, and a moment when the flattened exhale their steam, and "Mine eyes have seen the glory of the coming of the Lord!" was the cry of the oppressed at this convention, even those unwittingly oppressed in their mind, and not even knowing it in their heart until this instant, now they were defying the Chair, clapping their hands, singing, stamping their feet to mock the chairman's gavel.

Carl Albert brought up Dorothy Bush to read an appreciation the convention would offer for the work of certain delegates. The convention did not wish to hear. Mrs. Bush began to read in a thin mean voice, quivering with the hatreds of an occasion like this, and the crowd sang on, "Glory, Glory, Hallelujah, his truth goes marching on," and they stamped their feet and clapped their hands, and were loose finally and having their day as they sang the song which once, originally, had commemorated a man who preached civil disorder, then mutiny, and attacked a fort in his madness and was executed, John Brown was also being celebrated here, and the Texas and Illinois delegations were now silent, clapping no longer, sitting on their seats, looking bored. Every delegate on the floor who had hated the Kennedys was now looking bored, and the ones who had loved them were now noisier than ever. Once again the party was polarized. Signs waved all over the floor, "Bobby, We'll Remember You," "Bobby, We'll Seek Your Newer World," and the ever-present, "Bobby, We Miss You." Yes they did, missed him as the loving spirit, the tender *germ* in the living plasma of the party. Nothing was going to make them stop: this offering of applause was more valuable to them than any nutrients to be found in the oratorical vitamin pills Hubert would yet be there to offer. The demonstration went on for twenty minutes and gave no sign of stopping at all. Dorothy Bush had long ago given up. Carl Albert, even smaller than Georgie Wallace, was now as furious as only a tiny man can be when his hard-earned authority has turned to wax—he glared across the floor at the New York delegation like a little boy who smells something bad.

However did they stop the demonstration? Well, convention mechanics can be as perfect as the muscle in a good play when professionals have worked their football for a season. Mayor Daley, old lover of the Kennedys, and politically enough of an enigma six months ago for Bobby to have said in his bloodwise political wisdom, "Daley is the ballgame." Mayor Daley, still flirting with the Kennedys these last three days in his desire for Teddy as Vice President, now had come to the end of this political string, and like a good politician he pulled it. He gave the signal. The gallery began to chant, "We love Daley." All his goons and clerks and beef-eaters and healthy parochial school students began to yell and scream and clap, "We love Daley," and the power of their lungs, the power of the freshest and the largest force in this Amphitheatre soon drowned out the Kennedy demonstrators, stuffed their larynxes with larger sound. The Daley demonstration was bona fide too—his people had suffered with their Mayor, so they screamed for him now and clapped their hands, and Mayor Daley clapped his hands too for he also loved Mayor Daley. Simple narcissism gives the power of beasts to politicians, professional wrestlers and female movie stars.

At the height of the Daley demonstration, it was abruptly cut off. By a signal. "Shut your yaps" was an old button, no matter how the signal came. In the momentary silence, Carl Albert got his tongue in, and put Ralph Metcalfe (Daley's Black Man) who was up on the podium already, into voice on the mike, and Metcalfe announced a minute of silence for the memory of Martin Luther King. So New York and California were naturally obliged to be silent with the rest, the floor was silent, the gallery was silent, and before the minute was up, Carl Albert had slipped Dorothy Bush in again, and she was reading the appreciation of the convention for certain delegates. Business had been resumed. The last night proceeded.

25

Senator Edmund S. Muskie of Maine was nominated for Vice President. He was a pleasant fellow with a craggy face, a craggy smile on top of a big and modest jaw, and he had a gift for putting together phrases which would have stood him well if he had been stacking boxes of breakfast food on a grocery shelf. "Freedom does not work unless we work at it," he said, "and that I believe to be part of the reason for the spirit and determination of so many of the young people." Of course, it took a brave man to mention the young on the floor of this convention —Dump the Hump!—but Muskie's rhetoric owed more to supermarket than any Maine country store. Washington, D.C., is a national town!

The balloting for Muskie's candidacy had been void of incident but for the nomination of Julian Bond who was also put up for Vice President as a symbolic gesture to protest police brutality in Chicago. Bond was extraordinarily —no other adjective—popular in this convention, his name alone possessed an instant charisma for the rear of the floor—people cheered hysterically whenever it was mentioned on the podium, and the sound, "Julian Bond," became a chant. He was, of course, at twenty-eight, already an oncoming legend for his skill in gaining and then regaining a seat in the Georgia legislature, for his courage on discovering himself the only man in that legislature to speak out openly against the war in Vietnam, a Negro! and he was adored for his magically good looks. He was handsome not like a movie star, but like a highly touted juvenile, good looking as actors like John Derek, even Freddie Bartholomew, had been when they came along. Bond stood up when his state delegation was called, and gracefully withdrew himself from the nomination because—his direct legal explanation—he was too young (the required age was 35) but he had done this, as he did everything else at the convention, with the sort of fine-humored presence which speaks of future victories of no mean stature. Talking to a few people about his race for Congress, he assured them it was secure. "I don't have any opposition," he said, "just like Daley," and he winked, looked wicked, and was off.

At length, the moment came for Humphrey's acceptance speech. Tonight, he looked good—which is to say he looked good for Humphrey. Indeed if a man could not look good on the night he accepted the nomination of his party for President, then his prospects of longevity must certainly be odd. Humphrey, of course, had been looking terrible for years. His defeat in West Virginia in 1960 by Jack Kennedy seemed to have done something of a permanent nature, perhaps had dissolved some last core of idealism—it was a cruel campaign: if one would dislike the Kennedys, West Virginia was the place to look. Since then, Humphrey had had a face which was as dependent upon cosmetics as the protagonist of a coffin. The results were about as dynamic. Make-up on Hubert's face somehow suggested that the flesh beneath was the color of putty—it gave him the shaky put-together look of a sales manager in a small corporation who takes a drink to get up in the morning, and another drink after he has made his intercom calls: the sort of man who is not proud of drinking; and so in the coffee break, he goes to the john and throws a sen-sen down his throat. All day he exudes odors all over; sen-sen, limewater, pomade, bay rum, deodorant, talcum, garlic, a whiff of the medicinal, the odor of Scotch on a nervous tum, rubbing alcohol! This resemblance Hubert had to a sales manager probably appeared most on those average days when he was making political commercials to be run as spots all over the land—in such hours he must have felt like a pure case of the hollows, a disease reserved usually for semi-retired leading men. They have been actors so long they must be filled with something—lines of a script, a surprise bouquet of attention, a recitation of Shakespeare, a bottle of booze, an interview. Something! Don't leave them alone. They're hollow. That was how Humphrey must have looked on average days, if his commercials were evidence.

Tonight, however, he was not hollow but full. He had a large audience, and his actor's gifts for believing a role. Tonight he was the bachelor uncle who would take over a family (left him by Great-Uncle Baines) and through kindness, simple courtesy, funds of true emotional compassion, and stimulating sternness upon occasion of the sort only a bachelor uncle could comprehend—". . . rioting, burning, sniping, mugging, traffic in narcotics, and disre-

gard for law are the advance guard of anarchy, and they
must and they will be stopped . . ." he would bring back
that old-fashioned harmony to his ravaged folks. Since he
was now up on the podium, the crowd was cheering, and
the gallery on signal from Daley roared like a touchdown
just scored. Hubert Humphrey was warm; he could believe
in victory in the fall. He smiled and waved his hands and
beamed, and the delegates, loosened by the film on Bobby
Kennedy (their treachery spent in revolt against the Chair)
demonstrated for Humphrey. The twenty years in Washington had become this night property to harvest; politicians
who didn't even like him, could think fondly of Hubert at
this instant, he was part of their memory of genteel
glamour at Washington parties, part of the dividend of
having done their exercise in politics with him for twenty
years, for having talked to him ten times, shaken his hand
forty, corresponded personally twice, got drunk with him
once—small property glows in memory, our burning glass!
These Humphrey politicians and delegates, two-thirds of all
this convention, had lived their lives in the shadow of
Washington's Establishment, that eminence of Perle Mesta
parties and Democratic high science, they had lived with
nibbles of society, and gossip about it, clumps of grass from
Hubert's own grounds; but it was their life, or a big part
of it, and it was leaving now—they all sensed that. The
grand Establishment of the Democratic Party and its society life in Washington would soon be shattered—the
world was shattering it. So they rose to cheer Humphrey.
He was the end of the line, a sweet guy in personal relations so far as he was able—and besides the acceptance
speech at a convention was pure rite. In such ceremonies
you were required to feel love even if you didn't like him.
Politicians, being property holders, could feel requisite
emotions at proper ceremonies. Now they gave proper love
to Humphrey, two-thirds of them did. They would only
have to give it for an hour. Everybody knew he would lose.
The poor abstract bugger.

He gave his speech out of that bolt of cloth he had
been weaving for all his life, that springless rhetoric so
suited to the organ pipes of his sweet voice, for it enabled
him to hold any note on any word, and he could cut from
the sorrows of a sigh to the injunctions of a wheeze. He
was a holy Harry Truman. Let us not quote him except

where we must, for the ideas in his speech have already
entered the boundless deep of yesterday's Fourth of July,
and ". . . once again we give our testament to America
. . . each and every one of us in our own way should
once again reaffirm to ourselves and our posterity that we
love this nation, we love America!" If sentiment made the
voter vote, and it did! and sentiment was a button one could
still prick by a word, then Humphrey was still in property
business because he had pushed "Testament" for button,
"America" for button, "each and every one of us in our
own way"—*in our own way*—what a sweet button is that!
and "reaffirm"—pure compost for any man's rhetoric,
"our posterity," speaks to old emotion from the land of
the covered loins, "we love this nation"—pure constipation
is now relieved—"we love America." The last was not
exactly property but rather a reminder to pay the dues.
Not every last bit of politics was property—some portion
consisted of dunning the ghost-haunted property of others.
Nobody had to tell HHH. One could deduce the emotional
holdings and debts of the most mediocre Americans by
studying HHH in the art of political speaking—he showed
you how to catalogue your possessions: Franklin Roosevelt,
Harry Truman, winner! John F. Kennedy, Lyndon Johnson
—there were sudden boos. Lyndon Johnson, he repeated,
and got the cheers from the medicine balls and gallery
ding-dongs for Daley. "And tonight to you, Mr. President,
I say thank you. Thank you, Mr. President." His presumption was that Lyndon Johnson was necessarily listening.

Humphrey went on to speak of the new day. That would
be his real-estate development for the campaign—New Day
Homes. The doors would stick, the dishwashers would
break down, the vinyl floor would crack with the extra sand
in the concrete foundation, but the signs might be all right.

Then he called for Peace in Vietnam, and the crowd
roared and the band played *Dianas* as if he had made a
glorious pass. Peace in Vietnam was now the property
of all politicians; Peace in Vietnam was the girl who had
gone to bed with a thousand different guys, but always took
a bath, and so was virgin. Hubert felt like a virgin every
time he talked of Peace in Vietnam. He spoke with the
innocent satisfaction of a drop of oil sliding down a scallion.

Of course, Hubert was no vegetable. He was the drug-
store liberal. You had better believe it. He knew who had

asthma and who had crabs. It is important to locate him in the pharmacopoeia. Back of that drop of oil, he was an emollifacient, a fifty-gallon drum of lanolin——"We are and we must be one nation, united by liberty and justice for all, one nation, under God, indivisible, with liberty and justice for all. This is our America." He was like honey from which the sugar had been removed and the saccharine added, he was a bar of margarine the color of make-up. He had the voice of a weeper, a sob in every arch corner and cavern of his sweet, his oversweet heart; he was pious with a crooning invocation of all the property of sentiment, he was all the bad faith of twenty years of the Democratic Party's promises and gravy and evasion and empty hollers. He was the hog caller of the mountain and the pigs had put him in——he would promise pig pie in the sky. ". . . With the help of that vast, unfrightened, dedicated, faithful majority of Americans, I say to this great convention tonight, and to this great nation of ours, I am ready to lead our country!" And he ended, and the rite of love went up to its conclusion, and the band played, and the simple common people, and the villainous faces, and the whores with beehive head-dresses in on passes, and the boys and the Southern pols stomped around and were happy, because their man was in, which meant they had won this game, this game, anyway, and happiness consisted of thinking of no future. And Hubert looked shining up on the stage, and made jokes with photographers, and jumped in the air to be tall as Edmund Muskie for one still shot—— Humphrey would be a sport at a party——and McGovern came up to the podium and Hubert took him in, and his eyes were bright with light and love and tears. It is not every man who can run for President after four long years as towel boy in Unca Baines' old haw-house with Madame Rusk. He turned to greet others, and from the back had the look of a squat little Mafioso of middle rank, a guy who might run a bookie shop and be scared of many things, but big with his barber, and the manicurist would have Miami hots for him. Let us give the day to Hubert. He had always seen himself as such a long shot and out.

26

"Have a Whopping Double Burger,
             "Fingerlicking good!"

This sign had been glimpsed on a hash-house past the
stockyards along the road to Midway for the McCarthy
rally back so long ago as Sunday. The sign spoke of a mil-
lennium when every hash-house owner would be poet to
his own promotion, and the stardust of this thought made
the reporter sad enough to smile. He was drinking again
in the bar where he had had four bourbons last night; but
tonight was different. At 3 A.M. the cocktail lounge was
full; some of the boys were on the town to celebrate that
HHH oratory!

Our reporter was not a bigot about the Mafia; or maybe
he was—some of his best friends were in the Mafia.
(Mafia stands for Mothers-and-Friends-in-America.) A
nice joke for a quiet drink; in fact, if one had to choose
between the Maf running America and the military-industrial complex, where was one to choose? The corporation
might build the airports, but they could never conceive of
Las Vegas. On the other hand, a reasonably intelligent
President working for the corporation was not to be altogether despised, not at least when the Mafia was receiving
its blessing from the little bishop now installed—our reporter's thoughts were flavorless to him this night.

Punches did not often hurt in a fight, but there came a
point in following hours when you descended into your
punishment. Pain would begin; a slow exploration of the
damage done. His ineffective effort to get two hundred
delegates had left him with no good view of his own
size; as news had come of two marches on the Amphitheatre turned back, and one group tear-gassed, he knew he
was buried once again in those endless ledgers he kept of
the balance between honor and shame, yes, on the way to
the Amphitheatre tonight, driving south on a street parallel
to Michigan Avenue, he had passed a gas station where
many National Guard were standing about, and the odor
of tear gas was prevalent. There had been a suggestion to
stop and investigate, but he had refused. Perhaps it had
been his fatigue, but he had been feeling undeniably

timorous. He spent time reassuring himself that he had made an honest effort, and by an honest effort had he lost. There had been no need to go out on these last marches. By the terms of his speech, it made no sense to scuffle along with a token number of delegates who could be easily arrested and as easily look foolish—of that, he was still convinced he was correct. No sense therefore to poke one's nose into a scene of tear-gassing a block away. These arguments were no good: all the while he drank he knew he was floundering in bad conscience. He had an early plane in the morning, he was done, the job was done but for the writing. The reporter knew he had much to write about, but could he now enjoy writing it?

Sometimes he thought that the rate of one's ability to do good writing day after day was a function of good conscience. A professional could always push a work by an exercise of will, yet was writing himself right out of his liver if the work was obliged to protect the man. Sipping a drink he consulted his liver, and drank some more. The night was spiritless. Depression hung over his friends.

They tried to talk of the future, of how the party system might finally be dead. For by brute fact there were six or seven parties in America now; the Right, or the party of Wallace and Reagan—they were essentially the same, but for class, the lower and upper classes of the Wild Wasp—and then there was the party of hard-core Republicans—Nixon, we know, was doubtless perfect; next some huge government trough of the Caesarian center where the liberal spenders ought to have a home—Rockefeller and Humphrey might run with Teddy Kennedy here. (They could even use the same speeches.) That made a total of three parties, and Gene McCarthy ought to compose a fourth, a very pure party since his followers would be virtually a sect, although numerous as Volkswagens with their understated sell. Then on the Left was another party, or two or three. The Peace and Freedom Party with Eldridge Cleaver, the talented Black writer and convicted rapist, was one; the Yippies might yet be another. It did not seem so bad an idea for America to have many parties. Everyone would at least be present, and politics could function through coalitions; they would shift from issue to issue. One would learn the shape of the time by the shift. And the parties would be obliged to stay alert. It was an interesting future to discuss. It was actually the sort of thing reporters could talk about late at night. Of course, the reporters also gossiped; they considered the fact Eugene McCarthy had gone over to Grant Park on Thursday at three in the after-noon to speak to the demonstrators—Get-Clean-with-Gene had gone over to talk to America's dirtiest—the Yippies. And the reporters argued mildly whether McCarthy indeed was hitherto not too clean—how much better it might have been if the peace candidate had been willing to get his hands dirty just a little. "It isn't getting your hands dirty that hurts," said one of the journalists, "It's the asses you have to kiss." They laughed. They were unwinding. The job was done.

From time to time, the reporter thought again of matters which did not balance him. He thought of the fear Bobby Kennedy must have known. This was a thought he had been trying to avoid all night—it gave eyes to the darkness of his own fear—that fear which came from knowing some of *them* were implacable, *Them!* All the bad cops, U.S. marshals, generals, corporation executives, high govern-ment bureaucrats, rednecks, insane Black militants, half-crazy provocateurs, Right-wing faggots, Right-wing high-strung geniuses, J. Edgar Hoover, and the worst of the rich surrounding every seat of Establishment in America.

Yet his own side—his own side as of last night—made jokes about putting LSD in drinking water. They believed in drugs and he did not. They talked of burning money— he thought money was the last sanity for a Romantic (and part of the game). They believed in taking the pill and going bare-ass in the park—he had decided by now that the best things in life were most difficult to reach, for they protected themselves, so beware of finding your true love in a night. (For it could be true love, or the disaster of your life.) Or perhaps he was too old for orgies on the green. Still, these white children were his troops. (And all the Left-wing Blacks would be his polemical associates—the Lord pro-tect him!) The children were crazy, but they developed honor every year, they had a vision not void of beauty; the other side had no vision, only a nightmare of smashing a brain with a brick. The fear came back again. His own brain would not be reserved necessarily for the last brick. Of course, a lot of people were going to be living with some such fear over the next few years.

Now it was after four, and the last drinks were on the table, were being consumed. The waitresses were closing up. So they talked of going to the Playboy mansion. A party had been going on there all week. While they debated, the reporter was having psychic artillery battles with the Mafia at the next table. (One might take a look at *An American Dream*, Chap. IV.)

Mafia, of course, was a generic word to him. A crooked politician with a tell-tale jowl was Mafia; so was a guy with a bad cigar, so a crooked judge. They were not real Mafia—real Mafia was subtle and had its own kind of class. (The reporter was sentimental about real Mafia, he gave dispensation the way Lenin in secret preferred Hapsburgs to Romanoffs.) The conservative in his nature admired the wisdom of real Maf! But *petty* Mafia (which is what he generally meant when he used the word) were half of what was wrong with America. (The other half was obviously The Corporation.) Petty Mafia would not know how to get into a fight if the odds for them were less than two to one. So he entered a psychic artillery battle with a nearby foe—a short fat evil-looking type who had a confidence about the blank space he carried between his eyes, a glistening confidence sufficient to suggest he carried a gun. Petty Mafia gun sent curses their way. The reporter received them, sent them back. If the thoughts you sent back were sadistic enough, you could see the other man move. Now the other man moved, looked up, uneasily gathered his curse and took a drink. Here came the return. The reporter felt something unpleasant enter his system—a bona fide and very tricky curse. But he was careful to look unconcerned. That was part of this game: to keep the other from knowing he had had any perceptible effect. Done well, the opponent would worry he had gone into the brink. Now his opponent was leaving. It had been a successful war.

Now they were paid up and on the street—ready to go to Hefner's.

There was an excess of good feeling in him, however, when they reached the street. (The artillery battle had been his first premium victory of the week.) Outside, the Jeeps and trucks were still gunning to be parked, the police barricades were up, the line of National Guard still stood on the far side of Michigan Boulevard. The crowd was small in Grant Park at this hour, the battle was coming to an end. But speakers were still talking, rock groups still played, sound still rose to Humphrey Headquarters on the twenty-fifth floor, and the searchlights from the Hilton still put high illumination on the scene.

He had to take one last look. So the reporter and his two friends took a walk down the line of National Guard. "Once a philosopher, twice a pervert." Still, he was conducting an inspection again. Perhaps it was due to the reduction in the crowd, but the Guard looked meaner tonight.

That was all right. He was now feeling mean himself. He came to a stop before a Jeep with a rectangle of barbed wire on its front. In the exhibition-hall glamour of the searchlight, it glistened like a hard-shell insect eight feet long with an unforgettable radar-like conception of a mouth. He thought it was the most degrading instrument of war he had ever seen; it spoke of a gulf between the people who would administer the law and the people who would be on the wrong side at the wrong minute. They would not necessarily have the rights accorded to cattle behind a fence. The reporter took out his notebook and stood in front of one of these Jeeps and took notes of the dimensions. On a grid by his estimate sixty inches wide and forty-eight inches high, there were thirty-two vertical strands of barbed wire. He made a point of counting each strand with his extended finger before the eyes of the soldiers by each side of the Jeep; he was careful however not to touch this altered Jeep, just to count with his finger a clear inch or two away. After the count, he took out his pencil, made an entry, put his pencil back, made a new estimate of specification. (The reporter had, after all, studied engineering at Harvard.) All the while, the Jeep's motor was running, and the driver, now nervous, gunned it once or twice.

A National Guard officer said, "You'll have to step back."

"Why?"

"Just step back."

"I'm a reporter for *Harper's Magazine,* and I wish to be able to describe the barbed wire on this Jeep."

"I'm asking you to step back." The officer had his name stenciled on a piece of one-inch tape across the breast pocket of his fatigues. HORWITZ, it said. If a Horwitz was an officer in the National Guard, as quickly ask for a Rasmussen! But the Jeep was—*force majeure!*—too offensive. "On days when you take it out," the reporter asked, "what do you do to get the old flesh off?"

"Don't be wise-apple around me," said the officer. "Step back."

"I'm doing a story."

"Step back."

Well, he could not step back. He really had no desire to be taken in, but the officer—he could hardly blame him—had forced the issue. Now one of them would have to lose face; or else Horwitz would have to arrest him.

"It's not quite possible to step back yet," he said in his best Harvard voice.

"All right, take him in!"

"For what? Describing your Jeep?"

He was seized. Three or four soldiers seized him. A complicated little scuffle on the arrest. No one wanted to get marked for life, or even for tomorrow.

Then, victim secure, they all walked across Michigan Avenue in a stiff-armed body-locked routine, the soldiers on each arm trying to bend his arm, and his arms now turned as catatonic as he could make them—in this general grab and rush across the road, their collective limbs must have looked like some odd peripatetic unit of twelve or sixteen compressed sticks of absolute catatonic dynamite. If they had ever struck him, he was ready to go amok; if he struck them! they were equally ready. Stiff and tense and jostling like jockstrap mystics on a collective web of isometric exercises, they went in separate springing steps and yaws across the street, where he was promptly turned over to the cops, and as promptly felt the violence in the cops' arms, more personal, less green, it was like a barroom brawl for maniacs but for the suspended fact that nobody was swinging—everybody holding everybody—and forthwith into the downstairs entrance of the Hilton where the cops delivered him to an officer, while all the while in his ear, he could hear his drinking companions following behind, loyal enough to stay near. He could hear them saying to the soldiers, then the cops, "Have you guys gone crazy? He's a journalist."

At the terminus, in the low lobby of the Hilton, his police officer looked to be a man in his middle fifties, doubtless Irish, with a freckled face, light eyes, and a head of orange-red hair now turning yellow and gray. By the emoluments of his braid, he was obviously a high officer, and as obviously by his smile, he had a sense of humor! A sense of humor!

"Well, what have you been doing?" he asked with a grin.

The reporter had an inkling of how to talk to this officer; this was one officer who knew how to handle gentry—an old-fashioned cop with a wink—so the reporter looked for tag-ends of gentry in himself.

"That's an excellent question," he said, "just ask what I was doing. I was making a report"—into his voice went a hint of genteel Irish "r"—"I'm a reporter for *Harper's Magazine* and I was trying to describe . . ."

"He wouldn't move back," said Horwitz who had just come in.

"I was not touching the equipment. I have a right to describe what I see. It's generally considered the right of a journalist, whether Lieutenant Horwitz is aware of that or not."

"Well, there's been so much trouble in the air," said the police officer. He smiled at the disputants, then cooled them with a sigh. "He was just taking notes," the friends of the reporter made a point of getting in rapidly.

"He wouldn't move back," said Horwitz.

"Are you ready to prefer charges?" the police officer asked the National Guard officer with deliberate sadness.

"It's up to you," Horwitz answered stiffly.

"You see you'll have to bring in charges. . . ."

Horwitz nodded. In the pause, he deliberated, gave a look, went off.

"What is your rank, Officer Lyons?" the reporter asked, for he had now had time to notice the nameplate.

"Oh, I'm a Commander. Commander Tom Lyons."

"Commander, you ought to get more of your family on the force," said one of his friends, also an Irishman.

Lyons winked. "You fellows have given us a hell of a time. You don't know what we been through." But he was interested in the hero he had freed. "You write for *Harper's*. Ohh! What sort of material do you write . . . ?"

"Officer," said his friend, "this man wrote *The Naked and the Dead*."

"Brother, does *that* have bad language in it," stated

Commander Lyons with a happy face. In the pause, he inquired deftly, "Gentlemen, there won't be any more trouble, will there?"

"Remember that the trouble came because I was taking notes for a factual description of the Jeep!"

"Say, we don't have to go around and get into that again," said Lyons with a hint of woe in his look: God save us from honest men, was the expression in his eye.

So they left the lobby the way they had come in, through the front entrance.

"Let's go to Grant Park again," said the reporter. The speaker in Grant Park had just made a telling point, and the crowd had cheered.

"Norman, let's get out of here," said one of his friends.

"I want to go over there for just a minute," and then as if to make his point, he took a few quick steps, and was stopped by a man about his own height, an Italian with pop-eyes. He was wearing a delegate's badge, and looked to be Petty Mafia. But there was something wrong about him. His credentials were false, or he was a police provocateur, or both—who knew what? Maybe he was even a delegate. The man said, "I'd like to kill those cocksuckers across the street."

"Don't call them cocksuckers," the reporter said. "They're my troops, and they're great." It was precisely that kind of conversation.

"They're no good," said the man with pop-eyes. "They're cocksuckers."

"What are you? A musician?" He meant by that: what are you: the kind of guy who plays saxophone at a cheap wedding? and the delegate, bona fide or false, immediately socked him in the eye. It was not much of a punch, but the reporter was just as immediately grabbed from behind by one or two cops—he never knew, because the guy with the pop-eyes hit him again fast enough for him to think the man had once worked in the ring, although not for long because the punches while fast had little enough back of them.

His good friends—in lieu of the cops—now pulled the other guy off, more cops came running up, then the same gripping and grabbing, stiff-armed lurching, isometric dance of the limbs, it all started up once more, but the cops were bad, this time there was murder in their arms,

murder with clubs and bats, he felt, as he was forced along
between them like a traveller in the center of that universe
the screech of a subway car will make in sounding around
a rail—that electric sentiment of electric hatred, virile in
its rage, it was madness, what in hell was going on? They
went flying down some stairs in the hotel, past the men's
room in the basement lobby, now through strange doors
into a large room, a squad room where a dozen police were
standing about. His friends were now barred, he could
hear them protesting outside—here there was nobody but
cops, the man who had hit him, and Commander Lyons
who looked significantly less friendly now.

The delegate, real or false, surrounded by cops, was
telling his story. He had to be a cop himself—his story
was a point-by-point lie: "Then after the guy finishes using
his foul language, he stands off, and for no reason at all,
hits me," he heard the pop-eyed saxophone say with passion.

Meanwhile, they had left the reporter standing all alone.
There were five cops eyeing him. He felt a complete program of violence in their cat walk, these athletic cops, with
crew cuts like Marines. He had the idea that in about a
minute they were going to come over and beat him up. He
had been without sleep for almost two nights, he had half
a bottle in him now, he had been hit and arrested, and the
hatred of the cops' hands on his arms had been a quiver of
murderous starts, he had seen everything he had seen in
this city, thought everything he had thought, and now it
seemed probable to him the police had finally gone privately as well as publicly amok, and soon were going to
gang him on this floor right out of the violent creativity of
their paranoia—there was so much television for them to
absorb in the long winters. And as he thought this, he
realized suddenly that he was not really afraid, he did not
feel weak—scared, he felt, and very awake, but he was
ready, he was going to try to do his best when they started
to work. He did not feel in a jelly or a bath—he felt as
electric and crazy as the cops. The fact that he had this
sentiment now, that he was ready to fight, made him feel
close to some presence with a beatific grace (for he felt it,
he felt with this readiness to fight as if the air were beautiful where it was near to him) and that left him happy,
happier than he had been at any moment since he had

heard the awful cry of the wounded pig in his throat at the news Bobby Kennedy was shot: so he stood there and glared at the policemen who were glaring at him and knew he could wait like this for an hour and not feel weak.

And now Commander Lyons was talking to him. The Commander's face was taking a wicked delight in the powers of his own cynicism, for the Commander's face had succeeded in repressing the twinkle and was now moderately severe and composed. "It's a serious matter, Mr. Mailer, for you to be hitting people for no reason at all, especially after I just let you go."

He liked Commander Lyons, liked him for the relish this officer took in the absolute wickedness of his occupation—a born actor enjoys his life in any station—and so he replied with a wild if internal merriment, for he liked himself again. Dirty he might be, but they were so much filthier. "You wouldn't care to hear my side of it, would you, Commander?"

"I don't know. Look what happened to me the last time I listened to you."

The delegate was repeating his tale, word for word, and the cops on the prance, ten feet away, were pacing again up and back the floor of the room.

"Everything he's saying is a lie," the reporter said huskily, "and you know it even better than me."

But the Commander's eyes had lost their light. The bouncing little light in his look, like the white ball which used to bounce over the printed words of songs on a movie screen, was not bouncing now. "Why do you always get into trouble?" the Commander asked.

Then the phone rang. Lyons went to answer it. He waited, looking at the cops, the cops looking at him.

Some word must just have come down. When Lyons came back, he was smiling. "Tell me your story again," he said. He was one of the few people in the world who could wink while looking at you with honest Irish orbs. Now it was obvious they were going to let him go.

"Why," asked the Commander, "do you always want to get arrested?"

The reporter thought of his children, and for an instant tears nearly came. Not real tears so much as—the Victorians used to say—his eyes were wet with dew.

"Commander, I don't want to get arrested," he said.

"I'm glad to hear that, Mr. Mailer. But it's your repu-tation that you like to get arrested."

"Newspapers lie all the time. Look what they say about you fellows."

Happiness came again into Lyon's face. "I got," he said, "to read one of your books."

In the next two minutes before they let him out to join his friends, even escorted him to a cab—for the trip was still on to Hefner's—he talked with Lyons and a city official (who had suddenly appeared) about the beauties of architecture in Chicago. It was a great city, he made a point of telling them. They did not know from which direction he was putting them on.

And yes, he thought, Chicago was a great city. Finally, it brought everyone into the sort of ratiocinated confron-tation which could end a novel about a week in this big city. You could not say that of Miami.

Of course, he never did find out if shortly before or shortly after his own curious double-bust, the police had charged the McCarthy Headquarters, arrested every kid in sight, beat up on a few, and generally created such con-sternation that the Senator himself remained in town until Friday afternoon for fear his children would be wasted.

No, Norman Mailer went with his good drinking friends, Pete Hamill and Doug Kiker, to Hugh Hefner's Playboy mansion where they had a few last drinks and talked to friends and cheered the end of the week. On the last trip back to the Hilton, Mailer took a pass through Grant Park. It was all but empty. Fifty communicants sat on the grass, mountaineers, varlets, knaves, Hindu saints, musketeers, tank men, and wanly beautiful Yippie girls, while a priest in a violet satin chasuble recited the Mass over their bloody heads and an acolyte held the cross. The sight, by now, after all the sights, seemed perfectly conventional. Then he crossed the line of National Guard for the last time— Horwitz was not there on this sunny Friday morning, and went into the Hilton. On the steps he met Senator Mc-Carthy's daughter, a lovely and formidable young dark-haired lady, now in a quiet horror over the fury of the bust, and she asked him what he would do about it.

"I'm going to catch a plane and see my family," he told her, smiling into the proud disapproval of her eyes. "Dear

Miss," he could have told her, "we will be fighting for forty years."

27

And had no second thoughts about anything all the while he was writing the piece—except for Spiro Agnew. The Greek was conducting himself like a Turk. There was a day when he accused Hubert Humphrey of being soft on Communism. Everyone knew that Communism was the only belief Hubert Humphrey had ever been hard on. Nixon had obviously gotten himself an ignoramus or a liar.

So while the writer thought that the Republic might survive a little longer with old Tricky Dick and New Nixon than Triple Hips, Norman Mailer would probably not vote—not unless it was for Eldridge Cleaver.

Eldridge at least was there to know that the barricades were building across the street from the camps of barbed wire where the conscience of the world might yet be canned. Poor all of us. The fat is in the fire, and the corn is being popped. Mayor Daley, looking suspiciously like a fat and aged version of tough Truman Capote on ugly pills, decried the shame outsiders visited on Chicago. He was a strong and protective mother of a man, but for his jowl which hung now beneath his neck in that lament of the bull frog which goes:

> I was born to run the world
> And here I am;
> KNEE-DEEP
> KNEE-DEEP

Perhaps good Mayor Daley's jowl was the soft underbelly of the New American axis. Put your fingers in V for victory and give a wink. We yet may win, the others are so stupid. Heaven help us when we do.

ABOUT THE AUTHOR

After serving with the 112th Cavalry out of San Antonio, Texas, in the Second World War, Norman Mailer came back to write *The Naked and the Dead*, which was published in 1948. His reputation has since developed with the publication of *Barbary Shore* (1951), *The Deer Park* (1955), *Advertisements for Myself* (1959), *Deaths for the Ladies and Other Disasters* (1962), *The Presidential Papers* (1963), *An American Dream* (1965), *Cannibals and Christians* (1966), *Why Are We in Viet Nam?* (1967), and *The Armies of the Night* (1968). He has also been a contributor to many periodicals, most particularly *Partisan Review, Dissent, The Village Voice, Commentary,* and *Esquire.* Recently he adapted *The Deer Park* for an off-Broadway production which ran for 127 performances, and has produced, directed, and performed in three films.